EAST-WEST CO-OPERATION IN PUBLIC SECTOR REFORM

International Institute of Administrative Sciences Monographs

Volume 18

ISSN: 1382-4414

East-West Co-operation in Public Sector Reform

Cases and Results in Central and Eastern Europe

Edited by

Frits van den Berg

AO, Adviseurs voor Organisatiewerk, The Netherlands

György Jenei

Budapest University of Economic Sciences, Hungary

and

Lance T. Leloup

Washington State University, USA

IOS
Press

Ohmsha

Amsterdam • Berlin • Oxford • Tokyo • Washington, DC

ISBN 1 58603 235 6 (IOS Press)
ISBN 4 274 90510 1 C3034 (Ohmsha)
Library of Congress Control Number: 2002104874

Publisher
IOS Press
Nieuwe Hemweg 6B
1013 BG Amsterdam
The Netherlands
fax: +31 20 620 3419
e-mail: order@iospress.nl

Co-Publisher
International Institute of Administrative Sciences-IIAS
Rue Defacqz, 1
B-1000 Brussels
Belgium
fax: +32 2 537 9702
e-mail: iias@iiasiisa.be

Distributor in the UK and Ireland
IOS Press/Lavis Marketing
73 Lime Walk
Headington
Oxford OX3 7AD
England
fax: +44 1865 75 0079

Distributor in the USA and Canada
IOS Press, Inc.
5795-G Burke Centre Parkway
Burke, VA 22015
USA
fax: +1 703 323 3668
e-mail: iosbooks@iospress.com

Distributor in Germany, Austria and Switzerland
IOS Press/LSL.de
Gerichtsweg 28
D-04103 Leipzig
Germany
fax: +49 341 995 4255

Distributor in Japan
Ohmsha, Ltd.
3-1 Kanda Nishiki-cho
Chiyoda-ku, Tokyo 101-8460
Japan
fax: +81 3 3233 2426

The International Institute of Administrative Sciences

IIAS: What is it?

The IIAS exists to advance the study and practice of public administration and public management. It operates at a global level and is funded by states world-wide; but is independent of any of them and, through its links with the United Nations, seeks to develop a voice and a vision that is neutral, as objective as possible and grounded in the exigency of the fact.

IIAS: What is it for?

Although it has existed for over seventy years, the Institute's focus is on the present and the future. How governance is done and how it could be done better; how the law of administration applies and how it might be applied more correctly; and how the management of public affairs is conducted and how it might be best done – all of these reflect its activities.

IIAS: What are its values?

Accountability is a core value for the Institute. Those who exercise authority must account for its use to those on whose behalf they use it. *Public Administration* is the key activity that connects between the power-holders and the citizen. We believe it should be effective, efficient and economical in its execution of the duties and rights of the state. We support *modern governance* and *proper public administration* and believe these should be carried out in a way that actively acknowledges *diversity*, that is *respectful* of identity and serious belief and that reflects *balance*.

IIAS: How does it work?

A small dedicated bilingual secretariat in Brussels serves an Executive Committee which is in turn accountable to a fully representative Council of Administration. The President and Director General lead and manage the Institute for its members.

Each year IIAS

- holds three conferences in three different countries around the world;
- is host for six-hundred plus delegates;
- publishes four issues of its prestigious *International Review of Administrative Sciences* (in English, French and Arabic) and
- manages a budget of approximately 1 million Euros.

The Institute has two specialised bodies:

- The International Association of Schools and Institutes of Administration (IASIA)
- The European Group of Public Administration (EGPA)

each of which conducts study, research and networking. The Institute has a distinguished library of 15,500 public administration books to reflect the accumulated wisdom and experience of its members; and a Website which receives many thousand 'hits' per month about what it is doing now and what it will do in the future.

Contact details: Tel: 32/2-536 08 80
Fax: 32/2-537 97 02
Web: http://www.iiasiisa.be
Email: iias@iiasiisa.be

Foreword

Hugo Van Hassel and Ignace Snellen[*]

Throughout its existence, EGPA has served as a broker in the field of public policy and administration between Eastern and Western Europe. As early as in 1981, EGPA transgressed the ideological and systems divide in "Mittel Europa" when it organised with the Hungarian Academy of Sciences in Veszprém an International East-West Conference on Consultative Mechanisms of Central Government[1].

A theme was developed: the role of interest-networks in establishing public policies and their implementation. From that time on, Hungarian colleagues became pillars of EGPA in creating a permanent dialogue between East and West among scholars in public management and public organisations, generating openness and exchange.

Following those initial steps, an intensive exchange of theories, technologies, (best) practices and practicalities in the field of democratic governance and administration emerged all over Europe. European public administration developed in sharing emerging common values in respect of human rights, using markets for more quality on behalf of all citizens. When the idea of an overall European Union emerged and became politically possible, appropriate steps were taken on both sides. In EGPA exchanges where stimulated through the creation of appropriate working groups.

The closer the possibility of joining the Union came, the more eager the candidate members of Central and Eastern Europe (CEE) were to live up to the requirements of the "Acquis Communautaire', and to be instructed about the operational aspects of these requirements. Individual advisors, foundations and organisations such as the OECD and the World Bank supported this by transmitting ideas and experiences from "The West" to "The East". The OECD is an example of this development. Through PUMA, its Public Management and Governance Programme, and especially through SIGMA, which is directed at Central and Eastern Europe, it has tried to translate Western "best practices". Not only practices and practicalities such as strategy formulations, budgeting and human resource management were conveyed, but also principles of good governance and ethical behaviour. The European Union is also one of the important actors in this field, notably through its TACIS, Phare and Socrates programmes.

Members of the European Group of Public Administration (EGPA) have participated through all kinds of programmes and settings in those endeavours. Coming from Western, Central and Eastern Europe and even the U.S., they found in a Permanent Study Group of EGPA a common ground for exchange of ideas and experiences. In addition, they were able to reflect on the criteria and value orientations on which an evaluation of the attempts to transpose the achievements between the European countries – not only from West to East or vice-versa but also between countries of the East – may be based.

This process of approach between Western, Central and Eastern Europe is a crucial test for the intentions of the participating countries on both sides. Are they really interested in

---

[*] Hugo Van Hassel, President of EGPA 1991-1998 and Ignace Snellen, President of EGPA 1998-2001.
[1] Van Hassel, H., Varga, J., Consultative Mechanisms for Central Government, Brussels, IIAS, 1985

the improvement of governmental practices, as far as the citizens are concerned? Or is their only concern to smooth their future mutual relationships at state level? The question that must be raised about advisors and supporters of change is this: What kind of public administration discipline are they farming out? In this sense the process is also an acid test for public administration as a discipline itself. Are considerations of efficiency, effectiveness and economy dominating the transfer process? Or is it recognised and accepted that democracy, equality before the law and due administrative process may be at odds with financial/economic aspirations? What are the basic democratic public administration concepts that constitute the discourse in the co-operation between East and West in Europe? What historical and cultural differences have to be bridged?

In this short introduction we should like to point the reader's attention to the discipline of Public Administration that tends to be forgotten in actual practice. However, in co-operation between Eastern and Western Europe the whole breadth of public administration is at stake: from the administrative act and the personal encounter between officials and citizens at local level to the meta-policies and policy strategies at central government level. Our consideration is that public administration is more than a set of recipes for a functional rational government. Public administration is also:

1. **The concept of a citizen**. Citizenship has to be seen as a quality, i.e. more than just a set of rights and obligations. But it has an innate orientation towards state and society. In the co-operation with CEE countries, the discipline of public administration has to balance its focus on the development of citizenship and the involvement of citizens in the making of governmental policies, with attention directed to the improvement of the structure and functioning of state apparatuses and the quality of democracy. A distinction has to be made between roles. As a client, a person is dependent on any kind of social service provided by a public institution. As a customer, a person has some rights and obligations towards a public authority and also relates to public administration as a market party, and as a citizen who participates fully in public life and who, accordingly, feels co-responsible for the common interests, votes and is electable. There is a danger that the development of citizenship is neglected not only in East-West co-operation, but also within the European Union.

2. **The concept of a street level bureaucrat**. According to Lipsky, the founder of the concept of the street-level bureaucrat, street-level bureaucracies reinforce the relationships between citizens and the state. The reform attempts with respect to those relationships in CEE countries might therefore preferably start with interrelationships at the street level. If one realises that street-level bureaucrats, and not their superiors, primarily determine policy implementation, a balanced focus on "appropriate, equitable and respectful encounters" is of utmost importance to improve relationships between citizens and their state. Lipsky has proposed three major lines of analysis: encouraging client autonomy and influence over policy; improving street-level practice; helping street-level bureaucrats become more effective proponents of change. These lines might become the basic ingredients of a programme to develop street-level bureaucracies within CEE countries. They can also be seen in the context of subsidiarity as they relate to local government.

3. **The concept of local governance**. The real world of the citizens is situated at the local level and must be distinguished from the world as perceived by the officials: the system world. Through governance, local authorities acknowledge that the effectiveness of their policies depends on the resources and participation of citizens. As Luc Rouban remarks in the EGPA Yearbook of 1998: "Totalitarian regimes have given us the example of

false effectiveness, just as ultra-liberal governments have given the example of another type of false ineffectiveness, that of a market rationale applied blindly to a variety of human groupings in search of legal or moral norms that, precisely, help create citizenship, meaning a capacity for reciprocal exchange"[2]. Recognition of the dependency of local authorities on the efforts of citizens may lead to stimulation of initiatives by the population to improve the quality of life in their neighbourhood. Allocation of a neighbourhood budget by the municipality to the population, is an excellent way to involve the local population and to make them responsible for the situation in their own direct environment. Building up social capital at the level of local government is at least as important as the building up of financial and marketable capital.

4. **The concept of democratic decentralisation and the subsidiarity principle**. The practical viability of the concepts mentioned above depends on a reframing of the centralistic structure of government. A certain degree of local autonomy is a prerequisite for a sensible involvement of the citizenry in local affairs and for good government. As the Preamble of the European Charter of Local Self-Government rightly states: "local authorities are one of the main foundations of any democratic regime" and "it is at the local level that the right of citizens to participate in the conduct of public affairs, can be most directly exercised". At the local level of government the Civic Society can be mobilised. Moreover, if the conditions of democratic decentralisation are fulfilled, service-delivery responsiveness has a better chance of being attained.

5. **The concept of welfare**. The essential element in the welfare concept, adhered to by the public administration discipline, is that the content as well as the quality of services be determined by needs and preferences, notably as they are defined by the clients working together in solidarity. The situation in the clients' world, and not the situation in the system-world at the desks of officials, has to be decisive with regard to the kind of provisions to be offered. For many public servants, not only in Central and Eastern but also in Western European countries, such a welfare concept requires a cultural switch that is difficult to make.

We believe that the realisation of these concepts all over Europe, and also as a foundation of future co-operation in the extended European Union, is of major importance to the development of Europe. May EGPA persist in playing its role in this matter.

This book aims to contribute to a process of common understanding concerning the basic requirements of a democratic Europe in the future. It is a study of the experience of members of the EGPA permanent study group related to European co-operation across the former divide of political systems and bureaucratic cultures. The case studies of public sector reform and other programmes look back on past performances and suggest future opportunities. The experiences documented in the following pages reflect a practical as well as a theoretical co-operation between public administration in Western and Eastern Europe. The examination of the context of this co-operation may contribute to the realisation of core concepts of public administration, as explained above, and lead perhaps to a genuine individual European citizenship for all of us.

---

[2] Rouban, L. (Ed.), Citizens and the New Governance, Amsterdam, IOS Press, 1999

Contents

East-West Co-operation in Public Sector Reform
F. van den Berg et al. (Eds.)
IOS Press, 2002

1

East-West Co-operation in Public Administration: a Framework for Assessment

György Jenei, Lance T. LeLoup
and Frits van den Berg*

1. Introduction

The fall of the Berlin wall in 1989 helped usher in a period of rapid political and economic change in Central and Eastern Europe (CEE) and the former Soviet Union. With the transitions to market economics and democracy in the region came a legion of advisors, consultants, bankers, economists, and academics from the West. Most were idealistic and highly motivated and they were generally welcomed by their eastern colleagues and political leaders in those nations. What experience has shown in the ensuing years, however, is that there are many different forms of "co-operation" and a number of problems and issues associated with them. This chapter introduces a series of articles which examine East-West co-operation in public administration across a number of countries over the past decade. Our objective in this chapter is to provide a context and a framework for analyzing and comparing collaborative programmes, to better understand what makes programs effective or ineffective, and the factors that would increase the likelihood for appropriate, sustainable, institutionalized partnerships in the long run.

We begin by examining the historical and cultural context for co-operation in terms of the problems and needs of the eastern countries in the post-communist area. We also consider the importance of co-operation given the historical context. Next, we look at the key elements of cooperation and develop a hierarchy of East-West collaborative relationships in order to compare and analyze various efforts to date. The next section examines a number of issues, problems, and pitfalls associated with co-operation. Finally, we pose a series of questions about co-operation that will be explored in depth in the articles that follow in the volume. Our goal is to create a framework for assessment that will allow us in the concluding chapter to analyze the successes, failures, and unintended consequences of various projects and develop a set of tentative conclusions about the main determinants of programme effectiveness. Ultimately, we will also explore in that chapter the question of whether co-operation can survive in the future, and what directions it should take to make programmatic improvements self sustaining.

* György Jenei, Professor and Head of Department of Public Policy and Management, Budapest University of Economic Sciences and Public Administration (Hungary), Lance T. LeLoup, Professor of Political Science, Washington State University (United States), Frits van den Berg, Management Consultant, AO Management Consultants (Driebergen, Netherlands).

2. The Historical and Cultural Context

Forty-five years of command economies dominated by one-party socialist states limited economic growth, grass-roots democratic participation, and political liberty. It resulted in a serious economic, social, and political crisis and led to the inescapable conclusion that socialism was not the appropriate system for modernisation in the region. However, Central and Eastern Europe and the states of the former USSR are far from a monolithic region. Each nation has its own particular historical and cultural context, economic strengths and weaknesses, and political traditions.

The relationship between citizens and public administration varies from country to country. It depends on the essential features of the political systems including basic organisational settings, institutional structures, and political traditions. Political culture and the social organisation - including groups in society - are also crucial variables. In this context, there are patterns of differences across Europe as one moves from West to East.

In the countries of Western Europe, different forms of the welfare state have been developed. Today, all are constitutional states based on the rule of law. Citizenship is a basic, accepted concept within those political systems. In the 1990s, the renewal of public management resulted in reforms to empower ordinary citizens and increase citizen involvement in the policy-making process. Citizen's charters have been established and citizen input and participation have become an official requirement in many instances. Even among the United States and the nations of Western Europe, however, there are significant differences in terms of "citizenship" in terms of the provision of social services. In nations like Sweden, for example, the notion of "social citizenship" has meaning compared to the United States and Great Britain where such ideas are clearly not accepted.

Differences in fundamental notions of citizenship are even greater among the former socialist nations of Central and Eastern Europe. Some of these differences are centuries-old, and have emerged from their histories. The role of the Renaissance, the Reformation, the Enlightenment, and the influence of Orthodox religions in these countries is still relevant to inquiries into citizenship and public administration today. It can be argued that as one goes from west to east, a dividing line occurs when one passes the last Gothic church. West of this one finds nations such as Estonia, Latvia, Lithuania, Poland, the Czech Republic, Slovakia, Hungary, Slovenia, Croatia and certain parts of Belarus and Ukraine. In this group of Central European countries, there has historically been a stronger public expectation for the elements of a constitutional state and pluralist democracy. There are stronger notions of citizenship and historical experience with a civil society. In this sense, they share some elements with the nations of Western Europe although group interests are not as well articulated or organized.

East of this line one finds Eastern European countries dominated by the secularized form of the Orthodox denominations including Romania, Albania, Russia, Bulgaria, Serbia, and the former Yugoslav Republic of Macedonia. In these countries, there is less history and experience with citizenship or civil society because of the oppressive nature of regimes. Revolutions often resulted in a change in ruling elites rather than changes in the fundamental nature of the state.

Although indirect and diffuse, these historical and cultural forces are nonetheless still important for determining the effect of modernisation and reform of public administration. Western influences emerging from co-operation have more potential for impact in the central region than the eastern region where even the concept of public administration itself has been alien. Administration in these countries can more accurately be thought of as state administration rather than public administration. Social groups have nothing to do with public affairs. Often the leaders of these countries today have greater power than the official Communist Parties had in the former regimes. The fundamental notion of citizenship is different as well, more along the lines of client rather than customer which has become more prevalent in public administration reform today.

Reform of public administration is difficult in Central Europe after decades of Soviet domination, but it is even more difficult in nations of Eastern Europe. Many of the reforms of the public sector that are based on the citizen as customer run into the cultural tradition of the citizen as client. The client in this tradition is dependent, unable to articulate his or her own interest, and therefore needs patronage from the state. Although it is difficult to measure with precision exactly how these historical and cultural traditions vary among the nations of this region, we believe that it is still useful to keep these factors in mind when examining the possible impact of East-West co-operation.

3. The Importance of Co-operation

Contacts between scholars from East and West existed before 1989, although they were often limited and concentrated in certain disciplines. After the political changes, which came more slowly to nations farther to the east, political, economic, and educational elites looked to the West for assistance and desired to use western experience and knowledge to help in the transition. Yet from the start, there were concerns about the transferability of knowledge and practices to the situation in a particular nation. Much of the initial activity focused first, on market reforms and the economy, and second, on restructuring political institutions and processes. Yet there were many other areas in need of assistance in the transition, particularly modernizing the public sector.

Unlike economics, the study of government and the bureaucracy had been dominated by socialist theory rather than more western behavioural and empirical approaches, although there were a few early efforts to develop professional expertise among civil servants despite the views of the party leaders. Public administration was dominated by legalistic approaches, and in many nations there was not even an expression for "public policy". In the early 1990s, public spending constituted a huge percentage of GDP in the eastern nations and a large percentage of the work force still worked for the government, (World Bank, 1995). As a result, the need for the development of new educational programmes with a multidimensional view of public administration and accompanying public sector reforms was great.

There was a need to have access to western social science and practical experience, to develop new programmes and curricula, and in-service training programmes for public employees. East-West exchanges in the area of public administration and management had begun before 1989 with conference participation, personal contacts, and exchanges but generally was limited to top executives and academics because of travel restrictions and language barriers. The result was a deficit in information both in terms of scholarly literature and practical experiences. Although some legitimate system reformers participated, pre-1990 contacts were often limited by the orientation of the eastern participants, some of whom were seeking ways to rationalize socialism, others who were seeking greater technical knowledge to help socialist systems compete with the west. This changed in the 1990s as the motivation became more singularly oriented to system reform and the reduction of the information gap that existed. The question was how to do it most effectively.

CEE scholars perceived a need to develop public administration as well as policy analysis and policy studies, a field of inquiry that did not even exist before the era of Soviet domination began after 1945. The latter was attractive because of its interdisciplinary nature, its emphasis on linking the policy process to changes in society, and its applied and evaluative components. Closely related to public administration and political science, it offered the promise of not only helping understand how policies are adopted, but how to help make policies more effective. Because of its potential for helping with practical problems of rapid transition, political leaders were generally supportive of co-operation programmes in public administration and public policy. What would they offer to potential western partners?

Co-operation implies a reciprocal relationship. While the needs remain greater on the eastern side, East-West co-operation has offered benefits to the western partners as well:

- It can broaden narrow perspectives that can be found in Europe and the United States.
- It can expand western understanding by increasing awareness and experience with the consequence of rapid change in political and economic systems and bureaucratic reform.
- It can allow western scholars to test the scope of generalisation concerning concepts and theories developed in the U.S. or Europe.
- It can help scholars and practitioners clarify the role of domestic institutions and processes versus external environmental factors in determining outcomes.
- It can expand the sensitivity of western partners to cultural values and historical factors in policy making and bureaucratic reform.

East-West co-operation, then, has been a promising avenue for both sets of partners, but not without many potential pitfalls. In addition, there are many different degrees of collaboration and models of co-operation.

4. Key Elements of Co-operation and a Hierarchy of Collaborative Relationships

Co-operation in public administration can obviously take many forms:

- Developing new public administration, public policy or public management programmes at universities based on various models at western institutions.
- Making available and accessible to eastern partners, the western public administration literature, including research methods ranging from highly theoretical to highly applied.
- Creating curricula and teaching materials to provide the content of the programmes based on European and American models.
- Fostering collaborative research programmes, including joint conference papers, articles, edited volumes, and research grants.
- Organizing and sponsoring domestic and overseas internship programmes.
- Developing educational resources and technologies, particularly in libraries and computers.
- Assistance in developing in-service training programmes, seminars, and courses for public sector employees.
- Faculty development activities including language skills, research methods, course development, and research activities.
- Faculty and student exchanges between eastern and western partners.

We can identify three main types of participants in East-West co-operation: *the sponsors, the consultants, and the beneficiaries.* Sponsors are the governmental, quasi-governmental, non-profit, or other organisations that desire to provide assistance during the

Figure 1:
A Hierarchy of Collaborative Relationships

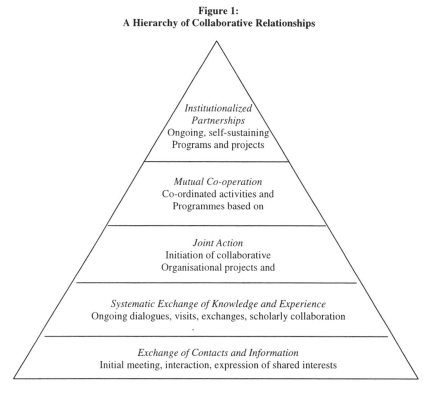

economic and political transition. Consultants are the private or public agencies and individuals including faculty members who are brought in as advisors and to implement programmes. The beneficiaries are the countries or other governmental units, university, agency or other organizations - or even groups who are selected (including self-selected) to participate in co-operation.

Clearly, co-operation can encompass a range of activities and degrees of commitment and collaboration between eastern and western partners. It can range from casual, ad hoc contacts all the way to sustained, institutionalised programes. Figure 1 suggests a hierarchy of collaborative relationships that can exist between organisational units and individuals from the East and West. As collaboration becomes more extensive, serves mutual interests, and becomes more systematic, relationships can begin to move up in the hierarchy. We should note that co-operation and collaboration can be effective at any level and need not necessarily become institutionalized. In the long run, however, institutionalizing programmes created through collaboration is most likely to serve the needs of post-communist nations as well as their western partners.

Exchange of Contacts and Information: Collaboration often begins with meetings, contacts, and the mutual exchange of information. This can be useful since partners may not be well informed about the needs and interests of one another.

Systematic Exchange of Knowledge and Experience: As partners get to know each other better, the relationship can expand to meaningful dialogues, visits, initial exchanges, and the exploration of scholarly collaboration.

Joint Action: The third level of collaborative relationships is marked by the beginning of identifiable projects and activities. The product can be a library, a teaching programme, internships, formalizing exchange relationships, and developing research activities.

Mutual Co-operation: As the collaboration becomes more extensive and regular, a truly mutually co-operative relationship can exist. It is characterized by co-ordinated activities and programmes based on strategies that are agreed upon and meet the needs and interests of both partners.

Institutionalised Partnerships: Finally, the highest level of collaboration is institutionalised partnerships where the relationships are on-going and continuing, not dependent on particular individuals at either end. Perhaps the most important characteristic of these relationships is that they are self-sustaining in terms of funding and organisation on both ends.

Of the many East-West collaborations since 1989, relatively few have reached the highest stage. A large number are still in the initial stages, for gaining sufficient experience and cultural awareness often takes time and sustained commitment. We believe that several factors are important in moving to higher levels of collaboration which we will discuss in more detail below.

5. Mixed Motives and the Problem of Pseudo Co-operation

The word co-operation suggests the idea of "working together on goals on which all participants agree (the common goals) in such a way that each partner contributes activities which must produce the common goals." Of course in each project there are activities which are not related to the common goal but related to individual goals. Pseudo co-operation can occur if the importance of the common goal is less than the importance of the individual goals. This can be the attitude of one side or both sides. A characteristic of pseudo-co-operation is that lip-service is paid to the common goals, but that most activities do not contribute to the common goal. Pseudo co-operation is not necessarily dishonest, but it usually leads to little progress in reaching the common goal. Why do cases of pseudo co-operation occur?

Needs and motives on the eastern side

Most subsidized projects of East-West co-operation take place in a context in which a struggle of survival in daily life on the Eastern side is a matter of fact. This may be individual family needs. In such a context the goals of international co-operation can be too abstract. For example, in one international project, a small amount of money was made available to improve communication capabilities. The money was handed over to the Russian secretary of the common task-force to buy a fax-machine and to use the rest of the money for supplies and telephone costs. For several months the Western members of the task-force tried to reach this fax. Then one of the Russian members (not the secretary involved) explained that (suddenly) the fax-machine was transformed into a chicken and that the chicken was eaten by the family of the secretary.

The western partners were angry, not about the transformation of a fax-machine into a chicken, but because of the time lost by trying to reach a nonexistent fax-machine.

Sometimes newly elected eastern officials want to show their importance and their modern approach by having western visitors in their waiting room. For example, the mayor of a middle-sized city considered it very important to show that he had western consultants. So he invited consultants to his office, arranged meetings with local press and gave interviews. The consultants, who did not realize what was going on, spent their time in these shadow-meetings, hoping that real work would soon start.

Needs and motives on the western side

Although the context is different, there can also be a strong need to survive from the western side, particularly because of financial incentives. In one case, a vacancy occurred because a French consultant could not fulfil his obligations. The French partner of the international consortium sent a German consultant as a replacement. This consultant collected an enormous amount of information but was unable to analyze the information and to formulate recommendations. Later it became clear that the French partner needed the overhead fee but was unable to find a qualified person in the short term; the German consultant was without any assignment for a certain period and needed income. The two western parties found each other, but the beneficiary suffered from it.

Especially in the beginning of East-West co-operation it was important for western consultants "to have projects in Eastern Europe" because of their reputation. So it was more important to have such a project "on your record", than to work for results. For example, one project was offered to an association of Western companies. They decided to participate because "our name can not be missing on the list of participants because this project is too prestigious".

"Rescuers" from the western side

When western partners believe that western knowledge is far superior to eastern knowledge and experience and that western consultants should rescue their eastern colleagues, real co-operation is not possible. For example, a Dutch consultancy firm was interested in participating in an international project, although the fee was far below their standard fee. The firm explained in private and in public that their motivation was to help "our poor colleagues" and explain to them how to train businessmen. So, instead of a consultant, the company sent a team of three "rescuers." Any suggestion from the eastern side was declared to be irrelevant. The result was that the consultants returned with negative feelings because the beneficiary did not want to listen. The beneficiary blamed "all foreign consultants" who were unable to solve their problems because the consultants were not willing to involve local factors in their approach. The consultancy firm decided not to work in Eastern Europe anymore.

Consultants and beneficiaries cannot always reach one another

A dominant approach with a long history in eastern Europe is influenced by the slavophile attitude, which is based on the assumption that the situation in Eastern Europe is unique in history and space. From this point of view co-operation with western partners is useless or even contra-productive. Ignoring differences in national cultures might result in a complete misunderstanding but, on the other hand, stressing the differences too much might result in a breaking off of communication. Sustainability means looking for a balance between accepting and ignoring such cultural differences as discussed above. For example, a management consultant tried to co-operate with a Russian regional administration financed by an international assistance programme. The Eastern partner refused to discuss the co-operation because "you will never understand the Russian soul. Even the fact that you come here to discuss co-operation shows that you don't understand anything of our situation. Give us the money, we know how to spend it in a useful way". When he found interest in co-operation at lower levels of his organisation, he forbade the Western consultant from entering the building again.

Fostering co-operation over pseudo co-operation

Co-operation and pseudo co-operation can be found between national and supra-national institutions, between organisations, and between individuals. Some situations can be described as co-operation at one level (e.g. national level) but pseudo co-operation on another level (e.g. organisations). Wedel cites the example of a group of Russian politicians and representatives of a Western academic institute for international development that participated for several years in projects which had the official goal of economic reform. However, each group had another agenda of money, power and influence. As both group agendas matched and as the groups needed one another to achieve their goals, pseudo co-operation at the level of economic reform was created, but at there was co-operation at a personal level. Although there is a general acceptance that cultural differences between East and West exist, often there is not much attention to the fact that the concept of co-operation itself is strongly, cultural influenced. Questions about "how to co-operate?" do not have a self-evident answer. Ignoring a discussion about this point can result in pseudo co-operation There are several interesting questions about pseudo co-operation. Why does it continue in certain circumstances. One answer is that stopping the project might require more energy than is needed for continuing the project in a formal sense. Pseudo co-operation does not exist solely in Eastern-Western contacts, but it can be particularly damaging to sustainability. In the chapters that follow in the book, we will see more detailed examples of co-operation and pseudo co-operation. They will help us draw some lessons from experience in the conclusion. Another potential obstacle to co-operation is the question of the transferability of knowledge.

6. Issues Concerning the Transferability of Knowledge

Since 1989, East-West co-operation has played an important role in the transition, not only in the area of education and training programmes in public administration, but in a host of other areas. Cooperation can speed the process of adaptation and change, and can simultaneously serve the interests of partners from each side. But co-operation is not an unmitigated good or an end in itself. Poorly planned with ill-chosen partners, it can divert time and resources from other more productive activities and directions. This can be avoided if certain issues and potential problems are addressed.

Perhaps the greatest potential problem is the question of the transferability of knowledge and experience from west to east and the broader question of cultural relativism. It may seem obvious from section II above that the application of existing knowledge to eastern nations must take into account their particular economic, political, social, and cultural factors, but that has not always been the case. Perhaps the least effective orientation is what might be called the "paratrooper" approach: well-meaning western experts landing with all the problems diagnosed and solutions at hand. Examples of co-operation in which western partners tried to act directly rather than through their eastern partners failed to produce positive long-term results, and often alienated both sides.

On the other hand, some eastern partners held the naive view that it would simply be possible to copy the west. In Hungary, for instance, political parties spoke about following the German "soziale marktwirtschaft," unaware of the extent to which it was rooted in very special economic and political circumstances. Participants on both sides must have an understanding of the uniqueness of their own situation and strive to distinguish between areas of knowledge and experiences that are more applicable or less applicable to Central and Eastern Europe and the nations of the former Soviet Union (see Sartori, 1970). Successful co-operation at all levels must be built on a recognition of some limits of transferability and the importance of adapting theory and practice to new situations. Dror (1994:2) has written that policy analysis needs to think in history without being bound to the past. Co-operation should recognize cultural and historical differences, but not to the extent that it stifles innovation or ignores instances where western experiences and knowledge can be adapted.

The issue of the transferability of knowledge is crucial in developing curricula and teaching materials and in developing collaborative research projects. Which approaches and studies are most valuable and applicable? The answer depends on a number of factors: the degree to which studies are basic or applied, comparative and general or country-specific, the degree to which research focuses on methods versus substance, and the degree it focuses on the process versus measuring the outcomes and effects (LeLoup, 1995). With so much western public administration literature to choose from, the questions are difficult to resolve. While the theoretical, general studies may be more applicable, they may be too abstract to address more practical policy questions. On the other hand, more country-specific, substantive studies may simply be too unique to be useful other than as examples of policy research. One of the problems, then, is selecting western studies that balance generalized theory and concepts with more specific substantive studies that can be used as models. The goal of collaborative research projects could be to selectively apply western approaches to particular issues with the additional goal of developing a public administration and public policy literature specific to the region.

The cultural environment can be important in determining the effectiveness of co-operation programmes, particularly when they are designed to modify accepted knowledge and values. Balducci (1995) argues that there are several important cultural characteristics in CEE that can be "dysfunctional" in western-based training programmes for civil servants. He notes the difficulty for CEE participants to distinguish between private and public sector spheres. This creates a host of misunderstandings and may negate the effects of such programmes. Training programs that are to have a lasting impact, according to Balducci, must "teach fishing rather than provide fish" (1995: 67). In training civil servants, he suggests that this entails teaching (1) how to manage information, (2) how to analyze training requirements, (3) how to develop training plans, and (4) how to train trainers.

7. Other Issues and Potential Problems with Co-operation

While it is important for western partners to recognize the value system and cultural differences in CEE nations, host sponsors must have the backing and support of the top echelons of leadership who acknowledge the benefits. It must be clear that they are in support of reform and the transition, otherwise, programmes may be little more than going-through-the-motions. Negative experiences with joint training programmes should be put to use in identifying the kinds of factors that contribute to success or failure.

Ethics is an integral part in all stages of co-operation from sporadic personal contacts to institutional partnerships. Different ethical issues emerge depending on the level: individual, organisational, national and international. Different forms of co-operation on ethical issues are evolving including the relations among scholars as well as civil servants and service providers.

Another issue with co-operation concerns the number and nature of partnerships. There may be a danger of getting involved in too many relationships, with the outcome being that time and resources are stretched thin and the results are less effective than with fewer relationships. On the other hand, it is often pragmatic to take advantage of all opportunities that are available to maximize external resources available. In terms of choosing partners, multidimensional co-operation may have advantages over unidimensional co-operation because much of the time in getting to know the partners is reduced. Working with individuals and institutions on a number of activities can strengthen the partnership as well as make efforts more effective. Similarly, questions surround the issue of bilateral versus multilateral partnerships. Bilateral co-operation may be more straightforward and unambiguous and facilitate communication. On the other hand, true multilateral co-operation, whether involving the U.S. and Europe, or other CEE nations, can add a richness of comparative perspectives that may not be achievable in partnerships between institutions in just two nations.

Finally, one of the critical issues confronting East-West co-operation in the late 1990s is one of continued financial support. The CEE nations face severe budget constraints and reforms in higher education funding. Despite record budget surpluses, the United States and Western Europe are facing self-imposed budget discipline and a public increasingly sceptical about foreign aid programmes. As the transition enters its second phase, will the need for co-operation programmes with CEE be as compelling? If public and nonprofit funding is reduced, will it be possible to maintain co-operation that has worked even if it has not yet been institutionalized? One solution is to seek sustainable sources of funding and have students and training participants pay for a larger share of service costs. This is very controversial, however, and with the severe economic difficulties that still exist in the east, problematic.

8. Conclusion: key questions for assessment

In this chapter, we have looked at the context and reasons for East-West co-operation and suggested a framework for comparing various experiences and approaches to co-operation that will be examined in the subsequent chapters. In the conclusion, we attempt to develop some questions and hypotheses about drawing lessons from recent co-operation experiences. Our ultimate goal is to increase our understanding of the experiences of the past decade in order to increase the chances that future co-operation programmes work.

How do both sides select their partners, how do they choose from among appropriate institutions, with appropriate backgrounds? What are the participants' motivations? Are they involved for the right reasons or are they motivated primarily by personal gain, the desire for travel, or other personal interests? Do certain kinds of funding incentives, such as when resources were available to western partners only if they paired with an eastern partner, produce less successful programmes in the long-term? How can both sides assure that mutual interests are being served?

How carefully have co-operation programmes been planned in advance? Have needs been determined systematically and explicitly? How do programmes compare on organisational criteria and how does this correlate with success? When the transition began, there was a general idea of needs, but they were not well formulated. We expect the record of the first decade to show that poorly conceived and executed efforts usually fail to achieve much of anything. The desire on both sides to move quickly has often produced inadequate time to identify needs, search for appropriate partners, seek funding, and implement programmes.

In both educational and training programmes, how closely are the needs of practitioners in the field assessed? How is this balanced with the academic side? The effectiveness of curricula in public administration will be judged by how well students are prepared when they enter the workforce. Training programmes should also be evaluated to see if they are having any impact in the desired direction. We would hypothesize that programmes that maintain closer contact with practitioners in the field are more likely to be successful and to maintain political support for the programmes.

What were the goals of the cooperation endeavour and how realistic were they? As we will see, there were many different levels of collaboration in the 1990s, most of them not reaching the higher levels of co-operation and institutionalisation suggested in Figure 1. We hypothesize that moving in this direction depends on being realistic about goals and ambitions: overly ambitious plans can founder, leading to disappointment and disenchantment. Although programmes should have clear goals and objectives, we expect the evidence to show that the flexible programmes were also more successful: feedback from experience helped in adapting programmes.

To what extent is research involved in the relationship, and how closely is it linked to teaching? We expect to find that public administration research will be more relevant if it is also applied to the development of appropriate country-specific teaching materials.

In both education and training, what balance between knowledge and practice was maintained in the various programmes? We believe that programmes that exclusively emphasize the development of knowledge in a scientific sense while ignoring practical needs and solving real problems will be less successful. Likewise, programmes that ignore research will promote uniform practices based on abstract knowledge.

Will East-West co-operation in public administration continue to grow in the next decade? We believe that it can if participants learn carefully from experience - and that is the major objective of this book. We will look at a range of programmes and outcomes that have been creative in developing organisations, permanent relationships, and finding new funding sources, and some that have not. Ultimately, the most important purpose of co-operation is to provide programmes that can continue to perform effectively and be adapted to new needs as they arise. That means engaging in ongoing activities on both sides that can contribute to the development of knowledge and understanding of policy issues and solutions, with a more comparative perspective appropriate for the increasingly global environment in which we live.

References

[1]   Balducci, Massimo, "Training Civil Servants in the Administrations of Central and Eastern Europe: A Missed Opportunity?" International Review of Administrative Sciences (London: SAGE, vol. 61, 1995): 61-72.

[2]   Dror, Yehezkel, "Basic Concepts in Advanced Policy Sciences," in Nagel, Stuart, The Encyclopedia of Policy Studies (New York: Marcel Decker, 1994).

[3]   LeLoup, Lance T. "Public Policy Analysis in Hungary: Problems, Prospects, and Strategies in an International Context,: paper for EGPA Conference, Rotterdam, Netherlands (September, 1995).

[4]   Lindblom, Charles, "The Science of Muddling Through," Bobbs-Merrill Reprint Series (1959)

[5]   Sartori, Giovani, "Concept Misformation in Comparative Politics," American Political Science Review (December, 1970): 1033-53.

[6]   Wedel, Janine R., "Collision and collusion, the strange case of western aid to eastern Europe 1989-1998".

[7]   World Bank, Hungary: Structural Reforms for Sustainable Growth (Washington D.C.: 1995).

East-West Co-operation in Public Sector Reform
F. van den Berg et al. (Eds.)
IOS Press, 2002

13

Transformation and Transition: An Introduction

Markku Temmes and Ari Salminen*

1. Transformation and transition – an introduction

Transition is a scientific term which has been used during the last few years to describe the transformation of post-communist states into liberal democracies with a market economy. The number of these countries in Central and Eastern Europe and in Central Asia is about 30. Most of these have been independent or semi-independent republics in the former Soviet Union. The problems of transition are connected to the complicated processes of changing from a communist society towards a society built on liberal democracy, a market economy and the rule of law (Temmes, 2000, p. 258).

Theoretically transition is a complicated pattern consisting of many different elements. Unlike revolution, peaceful transition seeks to achieve change by means of controlled development. On the other hand, transition as a dramatic and fast change differs, from normal evolution typical to most developed countries. The transition of the post-communist countries is basically a case of turning or returning to the development path of countries in Western Europe (Temmes, 2000, p. 258). There are plenty of theories concerning societal change and reforms. The crucial question is which of these theories are useful in a transition environment. Together, we have recently written a monograph in which we try to map theoretical viewpoints and blocks connected to transition experiences and processes (Salminen and Temmes, 2000).

This analysis includes a framework consideration in the form of a comprehensive chart (see an English version of this chart in Temmes, 2000, p.264 and an appendix of this article). In that chart the key factors of administrative transition have been identified. Firstly, the administrative process towards transition development has a core which follows the model of the Weberian ideal-type bureaucracy. For successful transition it is essential that the administrative machinery create a profile of a reliable and objective partner in the society. Another part of the core of transition institutions consists of the most relevant governmental organisations of a market economy which have key roles in regulating and activating state-market relations. The role of these institutions is also to protect the national economic interests of the newly organised societies. Such organisations include central banks, ministries of finance, taxation officials, custom officials etc. The wide political framework of transition is connected to the general principles of liberal democracy, the market economy, and the rule of law and its institutions.

Our comprehensive model also includes four potential threats which can destroy or seriously delay the transition processes. These are the dysfunctional heritage of

---

* Markku Temmes, Professor of Public Administration and Research Director in the Department of Political Science in Helsinki University (Finland), Ari Salminen, Professor of Public Administration and Head of Department of Public Management, University of Vaasa (Finland).

communism, the confusing tension between old and new elements of societal change (this threat is based on Riggs' theory of the prismatic society, see Riggs, 1964), procedural failures and co-ordination problems in reform programmes, and the dangers of either under- or over- organising the political-administrative systems of transition countries. These treats emphasize the dysfunctional elements of transition activities. This also means high social and economic costs for transition countries and their citizens.

This article is based on many dialogues. We both have given lectures and presentations considering transition theories and practices both in Finland and in some transition countries such as Estonia, Lithuania, Russia, Kirghiz, Slovenia etc. We have also been involved in some development projects in the transition countries, and of course we have had numerous discussions with the experts who have more practical development experience in transition countries. We have also directed young students and researchers specialized in Eastern-European and Russian studies, as we call this research area in Finland. Much is going on in this important new forum of political-administrative research. The feedback concerning the main ideas of our approach has been positive (see Larjavaara, 2001). The need for theoretical discussions about transition and transition development experiences seems to be quite positive. On the other hand, there is also much need for finding bridges between theoretical and practical issues of transition.

Our presentation is built on selected main questions which have been raised in these dialogues. The questions are not selected using any theoretical framework or theory. The only reason to present them is to show what kind of themes are relevant when the transition experts are analysing transition processes in the administrative machinery. The questions mainly tackle the administrative reform activities in the transition countries, but many of them have a wider impact on societal development as a part of transition. We do not try to give any comprehensive answers to our questions, but at the same time we emphasize the role of the comprehensive view when analysing transition. What we try to do is to raise a debate and dialogues on those themes which both theoretically and practically influence transition processes. What we think is needed to support transition development is dialogue and networks between academics and practitioners, between the donors and the target countries, and between different scientific and professional groups.

Using the above described "Aristotelian" method of questions and answers, we try to give an impression of the theoretical and practical framework in which the development projects are implemented in the transition countries. In fact, one of the most difficult problems of the comprehensive transition analysis is the practice of analysing separately the questions of political and administrative transformation. In the last two chapters, we try summarize some findings both in comparatively and procedurally. In the last chapter, we collect some experiences, recommendations and aspects of the foreseeable future of transition development.

2. Basic questions concerning state transformation

2.1. What has been – and can be – the role of the European Union?

The development in the former communist countries of Central and Eastern Europe is a great challenge for the European Union. An integrated Europe has good reasons for supporting and taking responsibility for the future of those countries. A great many activities to support development in transition countries have already been on the EU agenda. Aid was first organised by the TACIS and PHARE programmes. In recent years, there has also been a more intimate and flexible aid programme of TWINNING in which the administrations of the member countries directly support the transition countries by sending their civil servant experts to the administrative units of the transition countries. The TWINNING programme is, however, limited to the transition countries which already have submitted their applications for EU membership. All these activities show a very positive EU attitude and development policy towards supporting transition. At the same time, the problems of EU development activities are monumental at the practical level.

In spite of the very positive general policy of the EU, the theory and practice of the role of EU activities in transition countries to achieve positive transition development are far from being based on a clear plan and strategy. What is lacking is a clear vision of the targets which the EU sees as a ideal model of a future member country coming from the former communist countries. The general framework seems to follow our model (Salminen and Temmes, 2000), but practical solutions are full of alternatives which can be confusing both to scientific experts and practitioners. Many times the strategies of aid programmes include competition between different European models and interests rather than genuine and clear advice relative to best practices suitable for transition countries.

At the general level and at the level of principles, the role of the EU has been quite strong, but at the grass-roots level, there are many confusing experiences. There are difficult tensions between EU experts and experts of the target countries; there also tensions between experts coming from different EU countries. There are tensions concerning administrative cultures and languages used in aid programmes. All these can hinder and complicate transition development. In a situation in which transition reforms are the most important issues on the political agenda in transition countries, these kinds of practical problems in implementing EU support are dangerous for development, and are often unnecessary.

2.2. What is a reasonable timetable for transition processes?

One of the most difficult themes in transition discussions is the duration of transition timetables. There are many reasons which make it terribly difficult to foresee the transition timetable. There are differences in economic potentials; the duration of the communist system differed; the attitudes and involvement in the new system and mental connections to the old system vary, etc. In fact, this theme seems to be one of those everlasting questions among transition experts. It is clear that over optimistic estimations of 500 days or a few years as a transition period are unrealistic. We are now speaking of generations, but on the other hand, transition cannot be built solely on a shift from the old to the young generation.

In the planning of transition activities perhaps we must use normal planning procedures, using as a planning unit the normal five-year period (middle range). How many of these periods we shall need to implement a proper transition is very difficult to foresee and certainly estimates vary in the different countries. One approach is to use the comparative GNP of the EU in which the "poorest" member countries reach a level that is 50 percent of the average level in the EU. This means that the transition will also last several decades among most of the new potential member countries of the EU. A more specific and faster way to reach the post-transition phase, or normal evolution phase, is to concentrate on the basics of the political-administrative system, namely its compatibility with the preconditions of liberal democracy, market economy, and the rule of law (see Temmes, 2000, p.267). It is, however, clear that although fulfilling EU requirements concerning development of national legislation (Acquis Communautaire) may be a good start towards good governance, it may not be enough to reach a post- transition phase of development.

2.3. How uniform can development be in the transition countries?

In our book concerning transition theories, we estimated that the group of about 30 transition countries should be roughly divided into three groups because of their different transition processes (Salminen and Temmes, 2000, p. 11). Some of these countries, especially those which have submitted EU membership application, will follow the framework and directions given by the EU; this means development towards the European welfare state. The second group seriously risks being directed towards totalitarian regimes, ethnic conflicts and in many cases, chaos. The third group of transition countries are theoretically interesting because of their long and unclear development; these societies are using both the new models of modern society and the old models. This phenomenon is due to the communistic era and their own historical heritage. This prismatic model (Riggs, 1964) seems to be very much present in many transition countries, also among many EU applicants.

It seems to be quite clear that we cannot see any uniform development in the transition countries. On the contrary, they are developing different ways and taking different directions. This does not mean that we cannot compare the development of transition countries with one another. The diversity of development paths taken by the transition countries may produce a comparative analysis more valuable for benchmarking the best practices in transition.

3. Basic questions concerning theoretical approaches to transition

3.1 Which is more important, neutral bureaucracy or effective management?

The Weberian ideal model of neutral bureaucracy is one of the cornerstones of the modern western state and society. This is perhaps more relevant in the transition countries which are seeking a way out of the communist system in which the administration and civil servants were subordinate to the communist party.

On the other hand, bureaucratic dysfunctions are common in both western and post-communist countries (see the Marxist discussion on bureaucracy, Lenin 1975). It is easy to see reasons to try develop the administration of the transition countries following the guidelines of effective management. In fact, the main part of reform projects organised by the donors who then use the consultant firms, are following management doctrines. The problem can be the undervaluation of the core of the administration which must be built on the model of the neutral bureaucracy. This is especially important when reorganising those units of the central administration and agencies which are responsible for economic policy and regulation, for instance, taxation authorities, custom officials, the central bank, the ministries responsible for economic policy, and state finances, etc. Balance between these two viewpoints is important but difficult to reach. This balance seems to be different in the core administration, in the public services and in the public business sector (Valtioneuvoston periaatepäätös, 1998).

3.2 Where can we find competent theories; among the old ones or the new ones?

The example of the theory of neutral bureaucracy shows how much the basic themes are a part of transition analysis. There are also some other examples of the traditional theories which are of utmost importance to know and follow in transition processes. The theories concerning decentralisation and local administration are good examples (see Hollis and Plokker, 1995).

The problem seems to be to find a comprehensive mix of new and old theories. This mix must be based on the needs of the transition society, not the preferences of the donor organisations. Old theories are needed due to the nature of transition reforms. These reforms mean reorganising the structure and procedures of the politico-administrative system as a whole, including its institutions. Planning and analysing these reforms with the basic theories of state formation and functions is the necessary foundation for transition analysis.

Modern management theories, for example, theories around the so-called New Public Management doctrine, are interesting and often a useful arsenal in transition reforms. The problem with these theories is the great need for selectiveness when using them in the transition environment. There is a relevant threat that when using modern management theories in the transition countries without careful consideration, they may generate new, serious problems. A good example is the privatising of governmental functions without a deeper analysis of the role of these functions from the a rule of law perspective. A privatised office for regulatory licences or permissions can cause real problems according to the reliability or neutrality of the administration. The use of modern management theories in the transition environment seems to require the highest possible carefulness. On the other hand, modern management theories can help the transition countries to speed up development, to create an effective and well-organised administrative machinery. Especially modern information and communication technology can assist in speeding up management development in the administrations of the transition countries.

3.3 Can we use a strictly regulated civil service model or should we use more open models? – What about the training of key civil servants – can we use the ENA-model or should we use more open recruiting models?

The civil service model is one of the key questions in reorganising the administrative machinery in transition countries. The Weberian ideal-model of neutral bureaucracy sets a clear solution concerning the status and position of the civil service (Ridley, 1995 and Aarrevaara, 2000). On the other hand, there are many functions in the public administration in which there is a need for wider flexibility than can be guaranteed by an absolute bureaucratic model of civil service. One possibility is to analyse more thoroughly and carefully what kinds of functions we can find in public administration. In Finland in the 1990's, to describe these main functions we set up categories of core administration, public service sector, and public business sector. In the core administration which includes, for example, the central administration, the need to use the bureaucratic civil service model is clear; in the public business sector, for example in state-owned companies, the personnel has moved totally or partially towards private labour market models (Valtioneuvoston periaatepäätös, 1998).

The so called ENA-model is an alternative which may be of interest to transition countries. It is true that in those countries there is an urgent need to rapidly create a new cadre of key civil servants. On the other hand, this choice means a civil service system in which there are some built-in problems, such as elitism, problems between different civil servant categories etc. It would be wise to evaluate and foresee these problems before choosing this model.

3.4 The heritage of Communism – shall we wipe it out totally or try to modify it to meet the needs of a new society?

This is one of the crucial questions of transition. It is both a theoretically and practically difficult question. Experiences from different transition countries for almost ten years seem to show that optimistic plans to use the structures and systems of the communistic era is tremendously difficult. The main reason is due to the differences between the dominant ideology and societal theories in market economies and the communist doctrine based on a planned economy. These differences have generated many needed reforms in transition countries. The nature of these reforms, such as privatisation or new common rules and the regulation of the economy, has meant a crucial change from the old to the new. We cannot speak solely of a modification of communist society. On the other hand, the governments of transition countries are very much trying to keep the positive achievements of communist society, such as the high level of education, infrastructure in transport and their own industries, etc.

4. Basic questions concerning transition models

4.1 Can the welfare state ideal be a real target for transition?

At the level of principles the development target of the welfare state seems almost too clear. But what are the preconditions and how can the transition countries reach them in practice? Politically, it is not clear that all political movements in transition countries are seeking reforms which, in practice, follow the European or Nordic welfare state models. In fact, the same problems can also be indirectly found in the strategies of some of the donor organisations. What principles are included in the welfare state model, and are there variations. What are the main differences between these potential variations? The term and the welfare state model seem to be quite flexible and partly problematic as a target of transition.

On the other hand, welfare state development has many connections to the basic EU model to strengthen liberal democracy, the market economy and rule of law in transition countries. In fact, these three modalities are the main preconditions to changes that support welfare state development. The supplementary claim is that to manage transition reforms supporting welfare state development, governance and regulation needs must be included in the transition discussion. This raises the question, for example, of the taxation level, the share of education expenditure, and the level of social security. An unregulated market economy cannot guarantee the development of a welfare state.

4.2 What about the legal system? – How to choose between the Anglo-Saxon common law system and the Continental European legalistic tradition?

In Europe and in Central Asia the answer to this question cannot be anything other than a clear direction towards the European model of positive, written legislation and legal tradition. The Anglo-Saxon common law system has its role in international trade and relationships, but there are good reasons which support the European model as the legal system for the transition countries. Firstly, most of these countries have been a part of the European tradition and, in many cases they have an older European legal tradition. Secondly, they are applicants or co-operation partners of the EU. This is a strong plus for the European legal tradition.

4.3 What will the role of the civic society be in transition processes?

This is one of the most difficult questions in transition development. The civic society is, in modern society, a basis of political and economic activities. There is an urgent need to strengthen the civic society to create grass-root development in a transition society. The problem is how to support the strengthening of the civil society without forgetting the main principles of civic activities. The initiatives must come from civic activities, from the bottom up, and that is why the organised development projects in that field are not easy to approve and implement.

Strengthening the national cultural features of the transition society is a natural part of developing the civil society. There is also the need to strengthen the basis of liberal democracy, for instance, the party system and all civil society organisations that support economic development. For historical reasons, in some transition countries, these aspects of civil society may be rare or quite unfamiliar to the national culture. Maybe the best way to strengthen civil society is to create bilateral connections from country to country, notably between civil society organisations in donor countries and those in transition countries.

5. Basic questions concerning the administration and the process of transition

5.1 What is the impact of the country-size scale? Which is better in transition development, large or small?

There are about 30 transition countries. Most of them are relatively small countries. The transition experiences from the 1990s seem to show that the best development has often been achieved in the small transition countries. In the large ones, such as Russia or Ukraine, the results have not been as positive. In spite of this kind of evidence, we cannot assert that transition development is easier in the small countries, like the Baltic countries or Slovenia, but we know that their examples are interesting, especially for their bigger transition colleagues, as they set up relevant models to solve transition problems.

5.2 How can we manage tensions between new and old impacts?

This question has not been given any particular consideration with regard to transition countries. Theoretically, Riggs' prismatic model of the transition society in which the new and old impacts struggle to balance one another seems to be one of the most relevant theoretical views to explain transition development and its problems (Riggs, 1964). But we are almost totally lacking empirical data and evidence relating to these relationships. The transition processes and reform programmes are planned and implemented as though old structures, procedures, or values cannot impact transition. Maybe this has also been one reason for unsuccessful transition reforms and failures in international aid programmes.

5.3 What are the principles for organising local administration in the transition countries?

Self-governance problems related to local administration are most difficult when reorganising the administrative structure in transition countries. There has been an urgent and very relevant need to create local self governance in the transition countries because of the former soviet system. In that system the local administration was almost totally subordinate to the central political and administrative regime (Hollis and Plokker, 1995).

The problems involved in these projects are due to several factors. First, there seem to be exaggerated targets and many actors influencing the principles of these reforms. The European Council, The European Union, and the many donor organisations seem to recommend different kinds of self-governance models. At the same time, quite different solutions for organising the local administration and municipalities give the transition countries models that are difficult to analyse. The Nordic model of strong municipalities with civil servant management is, in fact, in competion with the Central and Southern European small municipality model with an elected mayor.

5.4 What are the principles for organising regional administration in the transition countries and what is the role of regional development policies?

The structural problems to find benchmarking models for transition countries at the local level are also relevant at regional level. In Europe there is no single model of regional administration. Owing to major differences between the member countries of the European Union, the new potential member countries from transition countries have trouble in trying to find good models on which to reorganise their regional administrations.

There is an urgent need for regional development policies in almost every transition country. Those countries which are applicants for EU membership are also potential target countries in EU cohesion policies and structural funds. In practice, however, regional development policies have not been very active in most transition countries, mainly because of poor financial means. Nonetheless in some transition countries, especially in Russia, decisions to support regional units have followed the model in which rich and powerful regions with good negotiation positions have attained better conditions than the poor ones.

5.5 What about the agencies - what are the principles for organising central level agencies?

The question of agencies has been one of the key questions in the dominant New Public Management doctrine among most developed countries in the 1990's. One the of the key ideas in this doctrine has been to move the functional client responsibilities from the ministerial level to the agency level. In the transition environment, this solution and direction is very tempting. On the other hand, in transition development, the moving of responsibilities can generate a different impact than in most developed countries. This kind of decentralisation can cause gaps in the responsibility chain when a ministry loses control, for instance, of authorisation activities or some economic or social activities that are crucial to achieving political targets. There are both genuine threats and great options concerning the agency model, the public enterprise model or the company model in transition environments, provided that the modification is implemented separately and without a proper and comprehensive analysis.

5.6 What is the role and the right number of ministries?

This is a classic question among experts of central administrations. The changes in transition processes to modernise ministries is an urgent and important task in launching transition development. The irrelevant discussions around "strong or power" ministries typical to the disintegrating communist regimes and some transition countries, illustrate the serious problems which are linked to the difficulties in changing the roles and behaviour of former soviet ministries into modern ministries based on a liberal democracy, the market economy and the welfare state.

The number of ministries in the transition countries has been reduced from the high number during the communist regime and are based on western models in which the number of ministries is 15-20 units (see Blondel, 1982, 1995). The bigger problem seems to be the role, decision-making and planning capacity of those reorganised ministries. Moving from the central planning systems of the communist government towards modern planning, budgeting and steering systems does not seem to be easy.

5.7 How do we understand the role of presidential administrations as vanguards of transition reforms?

This is also an interesting question which concerns many transition countries. In many of these countries, the presidential administration has incorporated the former coordination role of the communist party. In many transition countries there are good reasons to approve a strong presidential role for guaranteeing the direction and activity of transition. On the other hand, unbalanced presidential administration can be a threat to the development of liberal democracy.

5.8 What are the principles concerning the political appointment of civil servants?

The political appointments of civil servants have been a common problem in many transition countries. The rapid shift of key civil servants has created an uncertain climate in central administration and has adversely affected progress in reform processes (Ridley, 1995 and Aarrevaara, 2000).

The division between politicians and civil servants is also a difficult question in most developed countries. Because of the urgent need to promote continuation and responsibility within a neutral administration in transition countries, would it be better to use models built on a neutral civil service, including the highest posts of central administration? Political steering could then be increased in the future when the political-administrative system was more stable.

5.9 How can we create systems that forecast future development and provide visions and scenarios in the planning systems of transition countries? What about steering and evaluation systems?

These aspects of modern strategic planning and steering at national level are difficult functions when reorganising the central administration of transition countries. In these activities, there is an urgent need to make modern management knowledge available for the use of transition governments. The TWINNIG programme which uses ministry experts might be one effective way to carry out the transformation from a central planning system of the communist regime to modern governance. In that area the use of most modern managerial innovations is possible and recommended because of their limited and controlled use strictly at the top of the machinery and because of the importance of these tools to direct the economic core of the transition state and society.

5.10 What would be the right processing order? Which reforms first, and which after the first phase?

The practice of developing processes in transition countries has already partly provided answers to this question. First, the momentum of revolutionary changes in the beginning of the 1990s, raised questions relative to structural reorganisation and constitutional principles. After that, transition countries moved to implement administrative, managerial and economic reforms. It is very difficult to write any common reform agenda for transition countries, but after a decade of development, we have much more comparative knowledge of transition procedures and the order of reforms. The need for comparative analysis to develop and direct transition procedures is urgent and obvious (see Corkery, Oud Daddah, O'Nuallain and Land, 1998).

It seems clear that after political momentum there was a phase of rapid reorganisation:

the main structure of administration, the civil service and the state finance system. After this phase, many alternatives have emerged and choices are difficult to make. Making good choices requires relevant information. This we can obtain from comparative analysis between transition countries.

6. Some conclusions

The Aristotelian analysis presented in the previous chapters shows that there are different types and levels of the questions concerning the content and procedures of transition development. Also, the actors involved in transition procedures are numerous and have different roles. Because of this complexity, we must use general frameworks to analyse transition procedures. The need for a comprehensive view increases when transition spreads to all sectors of society.

There are both cohesive trends and differentiation among the transition countries. After a decade, the post-communist countries have developed in their own directions at their own speed. Although the political-administrative system of the communist regime was a model that was meant to create similar political and administrative frameworks in all those countries, already there were differences from country to country. These differences have increased significantly since the beginning of the 1990s.

On the other hand, the cohesive impact of international models, benchmarking and development co-operation is also present in transition countries. The impact of the EU can especially increase cohesion among applicant countries. At same time, this same impact can mean differentiation between EU applicants and those which are outside the EU. This cohesive impact is so relevant in Central European countries that European Union Commission units involved in developing aid for new member candidates, must be aware of their responsibility in development trends.

6.1 Comparative analysis concerning the premises and development among transition countries

We can use a comparative analysis in making use of transition experiences (comparative method in a broader sense, see Salminen 1999). There are some issues that are especially relevant in comparing transition experiences because of comparative information. These are: models and ideas in targeting transition, the development of a civic society, the development of a political system and climate, the development of the division of tasks at different levels of the administrative machinery, the development of ministerial sectors and the role of the presidential or semi-presidential function. All these issues are also important because of their institutional relevance. These issues can create preconditions for the better development of a transition society. In chapters 4 and 5 we tackle these questions.

It is obvious that a transition country needs a comprehensive plan for analysing and directing its general development of the political-administrative system. At same time, it is clear that this kind of plan is very difficult to formulate. In fact, a realistic level concerning the programming of institutional-level administrative reforms can be prepared by the unit specialised in administrative reform policies. The role of this kind of development agency (see Corkery, Oud Daddah, O'Nuallain and Land, 1998) is indeed crucial to guarantee the planning of the architecture of the future machinery and reforms, to create the necessary international networks and comparative knowledge, and to keep the reforms under political steering. This unit (which also can be organised partly or wholly as a part of the ministry or the presidential administration) also has a crucial role ino coordinating the activities of the various donor organisations. This unit's task is important and complex. The training and consultancy units supporting the implementation of the reforms also belong to the national administrative reform organisation; the latter can direct reforms in the complex environment of the transition with its many actors and competing development trends.

6.2 Comparative analysis concerning procedural aspects of transition

The procedural aspects are also important in transition processes because of the enormous task of directing the transition society from a very specific system (the communist regime) to a liberal democracy, the market economy, and the legal state. In these development processes, timetables, the order of reforms, and the co-operation and tensions between development actors have crucial relevance. In chapter 5 we tackle these questions.

After a decade of development experiences, there are astonishingly few analyses of the underlying reasons of successful or failed transition processes. The lack of this kind of information seems to be due to the limited activity in carrying out comparative research in this field. The normal evaluation reports of the development projects are prepared separately and in such a way as to make a wider comparative analysis difficult. There is an urgent need to increase comparative research concerning the procedural aspects of transition, notably because of the urgent practical needs of development programmes in all transition countries.

6.3 Theoretical aspects

It is not at all clear what the theoretical bases of transition processes are. In fact, there is more tension than concensus among experts concerning the theoretical aspects of transition. The theoretical discussions tackle the tension between basic and traditional theories and modern theories. They also tackle the nature and future of the core transition. The tension between bureaucracy and management is also crucial because of the importance in setting up an impartial and reliable bureaucracy to support economic and social development in transition countries. The modern management theories, which are the main tools of western experts, are also important but in the framework of basic development of the administrative machinery. Because of this tension, the civil service models have a crucial importance in development in transition countries. In chapters 2 and 3 we tackle these questions.

7. Experiences in transition development

This huge transition task envelopes numerous issues, of which only some are political or administrative. Nonetheless these issues have much relevance with regard to stable development. The institutions and structures of the political-administrative system steer the development towards a liberal democracy and a legal state and create preconditions for development. Also, the principles of the market economy rely on political and administrative institutions, the most important of which is a neutral and reliable bureaucracy. Many of the problems in transition countries, such as Russia, Ukraine etc., are due to the non-existence of a reliable administration. The co-operation between the political regime and administration is also relevant in bad governance; if political life is unstable and includes corruption, we can almost certainly find the same features in the administration.

The main systems, like budgeting and public sector planning systems are the skeleton of effective societal machinery in welfare states. The political-administrative culture of the country is also one of those rapidly changing aspects of the transition process. All of these aspects impact the sectoral policies implemented in the country. Good governance can produce good economic or social policy. On the contrary, if there are major problems in organising good governance, public sector results are also poor because of corruption and ineffective public activities, etc.

The major challenges of transition development are connected to the main targets of the transition countries in economic policy and in different sectors of welfare state policies. The European Union's ideals have without a doubt, some impact on targeting, but there are also a growing number of critics against EU policies and the whole idea of the union. In a general consideration, however, the EU political-administrative models have direct influence in transition countries. At the same time, this is a great responsibility for the EU and its member countries. Hopes and options abound.

Problems in transition development experiences are more practical. We can divide these problems into categories as follows:
- commitment,
- expertise,
- competition, and
- modelling.

Commitment problems in transition development projects are common and difficult. Good planning and implementation of projects require solid commitment from both sides. In the transition environment, this is often difficult to guarantee. There can be unclear relations among the key organisations of the transition government. Also, there may often be commitment problems among the donor organisations. If these problems cannot be solved, the failure of the development project is almost certain. Examples of some successful development projects clearly show how important the active commitment of local organisations has been; all experts have taken part in all phases of the project. All key actors should be committed and local experts should be very carefully selected and motivated. They should also have direct connections with the real decision-makers (in the ideal case both administrative and political).

The expertise of western experts is often a real problem. A lack of substance knowledge, but mostly the project management, including skills in analysing and evaluating, training, and EU competence, may be too narrow. This very common problem is related to co-operation building, notably using individuals whose connections to their institutions are too weak for continuing co-operation. There are examples in which the wrong counterparts have been chosen and this naturally cannot lead to any productive outcome. Too many times, foreign experts come to transition countries with their ready-made models and are not willing to see and understand the real needs and possibilities . On the other side, too often local counterparts are not strong enough to defend their ideas for greater flexibility and tailor-made solutions to their specific needs. In fact, this means that among the experts, there is a lack of real development and evaluation skills adapted to the difficult transition requirements.

Competition problems between international actors, but also between national partners, may be quite complex and time consuming. A transition country needs a clearly defined development agency (which can also be part of the ministry) to co-ordinate development programmes and channel international aid. International donors are not working in co-ordination, but offer their projects and aid in a wild competition forum in which the transition country has the difficult task to protect national views and coherent programming. There are some areas in which all multi- and bilateral donors want to be active and offer aid. Today in EU candidate countries, training is one of them. It seems, for example, that all donors want to offer general training on EU matters, although needs at the present preparatory phase should be much more specified.

The most crucial point is the hard competition between institutional models from which the transition country must make their choices. Often the proper analysis for these choices are made too difficult. Sometimes, even the results of good development projects cannot be effectively utilised if other parts of the administration or civil service are not prepared for reform. It is not enough, for instance, to develop individual civil service training programmes or institutions if the national training system of civil servants is not functioning well enough. It is absolutely necessary to develop synchronously both the training functions of ministries and agencies and these specific training institutions. Because of this confusing situation, the common international associations of international co-operation, like EGPA, NISPAcee, OECD PUMA etc., are very important to transition countries.

The last threat to and problem with transition processes has to do with unorganised competition among the development partners. This competition is causing transition countries to adopt too readily foreign models which have not been tested and analysed for their use. It is not difficult to find examples in most transition countries of direct American, French, German, and Scandinavian models. Unfortunately, it is also easy to see cases where these very different models inside the same administration cause enormous problems in co-ordinating a comprehensive reform process.

Maybe the most important instruction received from transition experiences is again the leading role of the national development organisation of the transition country. By creating a strong, intensive unit with skilful knowledge to plan and direct political and administrative reforms, a transition country can also gain greater independence in reform policies and better choose models that match their needs and administrative culture.

References:

[1]   Aarrevaara, Timo: Councillors and Civil Servants in the Ukrainian Self-government, Kiev 1998.
[2]   Blonde, Jean: The Organizations and Governments, Sage, London 1982.
[3]   Corkery, Joan, Ould Daddah, Turkia, O'Nuallain, Colm and Land, Tony: Management of Public Service [4] Reform - A Comparative Review of Experiences in the Management of the Reform of the Administrative Arm of Central Government. IOS. Press. Amsterdam 1998.
[5]   Hollis, Guy and Plokker, Karin: Towards democratic Decentralisation: Transforming Regional and Local Government in the New Europe. Tacis services DG !A, Brussels 1995.
[6]   Larjavaara, Ilmo: Byrokratiako ratkaisu Venäjän vaikeuksiin? (Can bureaucracy be a solution of the difficulties of Russia?, Book critics concerning Salminen nad Temmes, 2000, Seeking the transition theory), Idäntukimus, The Finnish Review of East European Studies, 3-4, 2000, p. 80-83
[7]   Ridley, F.,F.: For a Democratic Civil Service, In Public Administration in Transition, published by NISPAcee, ed. Jak Jabes and Mirko Vintar, Hanulova 1995.
[8]   Riggs, Fred W.: Administration in Developing Countries: The Theory of Prismatic Society, Houghton Mifflin Company, Boston 1964.
[9]   Salminen, Ari: Vertailevan metodin tutkimuksellinen perusta (Theoretical grounds of comparative method). University of Vaasa. Research Papers 223. Vaasa 1999.
[10]   Salminen, Ari and Temmes, Markku: Transitioteoriaa etsimässä (Seeking the transition theory), Aleksanteri-insituutti, Kikimora Publications, Series B:10, Helsinki 2000.
[11]   Temmes, Markku: State transformation and transition theory, International Review of Administrative Sciences, Vol. 66(2000), 258-268.
[12]   Valtioneuvoston periaatepäätös, Laadukkaat palvelut, hyvä hallinto ja vastuullinen kansalaisyhteiskunta (High-Quality Services, Good Governance and a Responsible Civic Society, Guidelines of the Policy of Governance, Helsinki 2000.
[13]   Practical experiences is also collected by interviewing and getting comments from following Finnish experts of transition development:
        Reijo Lind (Finnish Institute of Public Management),
        Anneli Temmes (Finnish Institute of Public Management),
        Yrjö Venna (Finnish Institute of Public Management), and
        Pekka Väänänen (Ministry of Trade and Industry)

Appendix: Megatheory of Transition
(Markku Temmes: International Review of Administrative Sciences 66/2)

FIGURE 1
Megatheory of transition

Threat 1:
Prismatic Degeneration:
- cliques
- corruption
- nepotism
- Lack of consensus
(Prismatic theory of Fred W. Riggs)

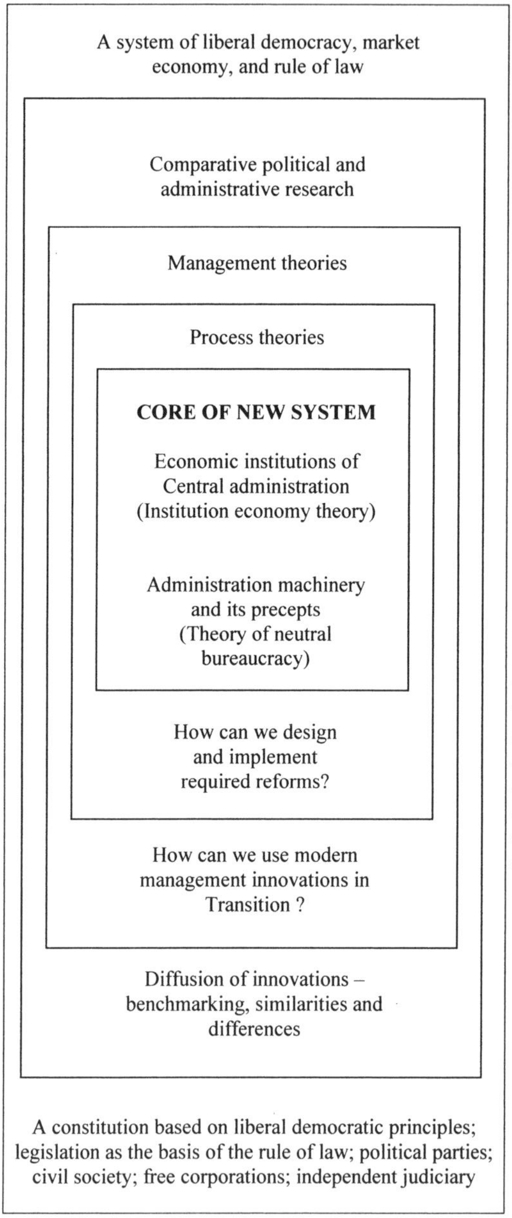

Threat 3:
Bad results of developme
projects:
- Difficulties in coordinating conflicting innovations
- Lack of coordination among donors
- Difficulties in nationa coordination (Manageme and process theories)

A system of liberal democracy, market economy, and rule of law

Comparative political and administrative research

Management theories

Process theories

CORE OF NEW SYSTEM

Economic institutions of Central administration
(Institution economy theory)

Administration machinery and its precepts
(Theory of neutral bureaucracy)

Threat 2:
Resistance and problems originating from the heritage of communism:
- Nomenclature system
- Command economy
- Continuity of Soviet type

How can we design and implement required reforms?

How can we use modern management innovations in Transition ?

Diffusion of innovations – benchmarking, similarities and differences

Threat 4:
Transformation of crisis symptoms of welfare stat development:
- the virus problem
- dysfunctional development of bureaucr.
(Welfare state theory)

A constitution based on liberal democratic principles; legislation as the basis of the rule of law; political parties; civil society; free corporations; independent judiciary

East-West Co-operation in Public Sector Reform
F. van den Berg et al. (Eds.)
IOS Press, 2002

27

Assistance or Co-operation?

Svetlana N. Khapova*

A decade of East-West joint activities was a challenging period for both Eastern and Western Europe. Misunderstandings were created due to different expectations built up on wrong interpretations of the terms commonly used by the assisting agencies. This chapter discusses some of these observations.

The point when the Iron Curtain was opened between the two worlds marked the end of the Cold War. This was not only a political victory of the West, but also a moral and an ideological one. Alongside this victory, the West felt responsible to assist the process of transition to democracy by transferring their "it fits all" expertise and knowledge and uniting Europe by breaking down the isolation between the two worlds. The expectation was to transfer former Soviet states in the twinkle of an eye to countries of democracy and free markets. Many technical assistance programmes were developed by the donor countries to assist this process. Donors aimed to create politically independent and economically prosperous societies in the given countries, which in the future could become adequate partners of the European Community. This always has been an official aim of the West. In reality, experiences of Western assistance after a decade have shown that the help given did not achieve its aims and has been fragmented and insufficient.

In this chapter I discuss some of the reasons for dissatisfaction of both the assistance donors and recipients with regard to their expectations. Misunderstandings were created by a different interpretation of terms commonly used by the assisting agencies.

I discuss this question in the light of my own personal experience in the project of the European Commission on strengthening Public Administration in the Russian Federation, which has been a truly international co-operation involving participants from Russia, the Netherlands, France, Italy, Germany and the UK, and also the international experience that I gained during my participation in the MBA programme in the Netherlands, the UK and the USA. These experiences helped me to understand the meaning of contacts between East and West, as also the consequences of misunderstandings in project terminology.

The original meaning of 'technical assistance' implies giving assistance through training and consultancy. This seems to be a logical thing to offer to countries that are in a transitional period. Many Eastern European citizens got involved in co-operation expecting to receive large financial grants and advanced equipment, but instead were granted foreign advice and training. People felt that Westerners were attaining their own objectives, hiding behind the words "technical assistance." In the beginning the idea of assistance from the Western side sounded very promising to the people of Central and Eastern Europe. Having finally achieved their long-awaited independence, they met their new 'friends' from the West with the hope that they would help them to transform their devastated economies overnight with (a little) monetary help. They hoped that this transition would be simple,

* Svetlana N. Khapova, Faculty of Public Administration and Public Policy, University of Twente (Netherlands).

straightforward and painless. This Eastern attitude was especially prevailing during the first years of Western assistance in the beginning of the 1990s.

This attitude towards Western assistance was built on some communication misunderstandings. Firstly, it was due to a literal interpretation of technical assistance in translations to local languages from the English language - used as one of the key business languages in the technical assistance projects. Secondly, there was a misunderstanding in interpretation of what a Western consultant was and what could be expected from him/her.

Assistance is a term brought from the Western countries. In the preliminary stage of East-West contacts, a decade ago, the term 'assistance' was more common in describing joint activities of countries. This reflected the important divide between East and West due to the Cold War and different historical roots of relations among Eastern European countries. This division was created in terms of cultural differences, languages, available information and closed borders. It was tangibly determined by the Berlin Wall separating the Western-capitalist and the Eastern-socialist ways of thinking. The term 'assistance' conveyed the idea of co-operation between countries, with the West providing assistance and the East receiving.

For the Eastern countries, their contacts with the West have meant either tangible aid or other types of co-operation. The fact that assistance could also take the form of advice or consultation from the West was difficult to understand. Although the original meaning of 'technical assistance' implies assistance to countries through training and education, many Eastern participants in projects expected more material input than just training. A major cause of this confusion comes from the literal translation of the official term 'technical assistance'. According to the Soviet Encyclopedic Dictionary the word *'technica'* in Russian means integral means of human activities, developed for execution of production processes and serving production needs of society (Prokhorov, 1983). This complex definition of the term *'technica'* is easily interpreted by the local population as the means for electronic equipment or machinery.

The word 'assistance' has two meanings in Russian. The first one is support. The traditional meaning of support most often implies one's participation in something that makes the situation easier (Ozhegov, 1996). In simple terms, this means that the party that has been asked for assistance should take over and lead the activity started by the requesting party. The second meaning is help – *'pomostch'*, which means help in any of its meanings: physical, material, emotional, etc. This was exactly the translation adopted in projects of Western assistance. However, in combination with the word 'technical,' or *'technica'*, assistance means to help with different types of equipment and training of how to use it.

However, misunderstandings in the definition of technical assistance do not stop here. When the first consulting projects started in Russia in the late 1980s, few Russian participants could understand what the word 'consultant' meant and what a consultant's job was. Ten years ago the word 'consultancy' and the activity itself did not exist in Russia. This created many misunderstandings and declarations that this kind of profession was not possible in Russia. Local governments blamed Western experts for collecting strategic and industrial information in the regions, for spying, and simply for wasting the money of the European Commission. The fact that the job of a consultant is to observe the problem and raise important questions, gather data and stimulate thinking, identify alternatives and help to assess consequences, etc. was not understood. Over the last decade, the term has become better understood. Now there is Association of Russian Management Consultants and the services they offer are quite popular and well paid (Dementjeva, 1996).

In the Russian translation, the English word 'consultant' also has two meanings. First of all, it is *'sovetnic'* which means someone who can give advice on how to deal with an issue.

Originally this related to a very high position in the government or the justice. Only a few people in the whole country had the honour to be an advisor. They were not masters in the art of consulting, but instead gurus in their field. Another translation for the word consultant ('*consul'tant*') is a specialist who gives advice (Ozhegov, 1996). This term is often used in relation to an academic or juridical advisor who gives advice about existing legislation. In both of the translations, the meaning of the word 'consultant' implies that the advisor gives a solution to the problem, based on either his knowledge and experience or his native talent and intelligence.

These differences made it difficult for Russian participants to understand what the "assistance" was all about, especially if there was neither equipment to be provided nor a solution to their problems. In this respect, Russian participants often felt that their contribution should be perceived as an equal participation in projects. For them, these projects were viewed as co-operation instead of assistance.

However, the Eastern participants involved in technical assistance could never reach an 'equal' position with their Western colleagues. This difference was artificially created by the donor agencies by allocating much more money to pay the Western consultants. This made Eastern participants feel undervalued. Many Eastern Europeans proudly believe that Westerners have little to teach and show them. This problem was exacerbated by the fact that during the early stages of technical assistance, many of the Western consultants had very limited experience and knowledge of business, economics, and the culture of Eastern Europe. Although in theory Western technical assistance parties recognised the distinctiveness of Central and Eastern Europe, the point of reference for many advisors was their Third-World experience. Thus, in some cases they had trouble providing useful advice to their Eastern European counterparts.

On the other hand, the recipients of technical assistance believed that all these programmes were used as a good base for Western companies in expanding their market and new business opportunities. It was often mentioned by the Eastern recipients of technical assistance that the Western consultants were ill-prepared for working in Eastern Europe and had poor knowledge of its economic, legal and psychological realities. There was (and still is), a widely held view in the East that Western Europe was just putting money into the pockets of their own experts and companies. This perception was based on the fact that there were almost no experts who had an in-depth understanding of the political and economical characteristics of the countries of Eastern Europe, let alone the cultural background of those countries.

As explained above, differences in meanings of the same terms may cause major misunderstandings and create problems. Sometimes this is called a "language barrier" (Dementjeva, 1996). Remarkable examples of this barrier occur when co-operating parties discuss issues in one chosen language and later realise that the two sides heard very different things. In these situations, interpreters are blamed for bad interpretation or the other party is blamed for incompetence and poor understanding of simple things.

While many years of East-West joint activities have increased cross-cultural understanding, differences in language, culture and traditions continue to raise conflicting issues. It is often forgotten that not only the languages are different, but also that the same words often have different definitions. Definitions give images about the content of co-operation to the participants, and therefore influence their expectations and actions. A few years ago, several Russian newspapers published articles about foreign intervention in Russia. Foreign projects were criticised for collecting information about industrial infrastructure and production potential of Russia for the benefit of EU countries looking for sales markets in Russia for western products. High-ranking officials in the local governments suspected Western experts sent from Western bodies, ranging from the IMF and the EU to multinational corporations, of spying to assess the competitiveness of Central and Eastern European nations. These officials even intimated that the 'advice' they received could be intended to sabotage their nation's future competitiveness. Situations like this likely would have occurred less frequently if a word such as 'consultant' would have been introduced adequately to the Russian recipients of technical assistance because officials would have understood more fully the purpose and nature of the assistance.

The last ten years have been a difficult period for both Eastern and Western participants. They learned to understand and value each other and to open their borders for an exchange of ideas and developments. There are concerns in the West that all goals have not been achieved and that co-operation with Eastern participants has been difficult. While this might be true, many positive things have been achieved, and I believe that every little seed adds to the attainment of the final goal. The solution is not one of immediate transformation (an unrealistic goal anyway), but instead one of sustainable development.

References:

[1]   Dementjeva Y. (1996). Language adequacy and acceptability as the condition for successful cross-cultural communication. Budapest, EGPA

[2]   Ozhegov S.I., Shvedova N.Y. (1996). Dictionary of Russian Language. Moscow, Az.

[3]   Prokhorov, A.M. (1983). Soviet Encyclopedic Dictionary. Moscow, Soviet Encyclopedia.

[4]   Wedel, J. R. (1998). Collision and collusion : the strange case of Western aid to Eastern Europe, 1989-1998. New York, St. Martin's Press.

East-West Co-operation in Public Sector Reform
F. van den Berg et al. (Eds.)
IOS Press, 2002

31

Cultural Issues – Success and Failure in Finland's Neighbouring Areas Co-operation

Pirkko Vartiainen*

1. Introduction

The aim of this article is to analyse Finland's co-operation with its neighbouring countries mainly from the strategic point of view. The reason for this is that Finland has actively participated in efforts to support the political and economic transition process in neighbouring areas in the 1990s. The strategy for co-operation has been adopted by the Government in the years 1993, 1996, 1999 and 2000, and these strategies have served as a foundation for co-operation. So, the co-operation has become a part of Finland's foreign policy and external economic relations.

Empirically the article will focus on two different cases. The selected cases are co-operation projects with the Republic of Karelia and Estonia. The cases are defined in detail in Chapter Three. The main research problems are:

How is the co-operation in the neighbouring areas organised and implemented, and
How well has the co-operation for the selected cases succeeded?

To be able to answer these questions I first have to discuss the conceptual meaning of co-operation as well as the strategic principles of co-operation between Finland's neighbouring areas. These discussions are presented in Chapters Two and Three. Chapters Fourand Five contain the analysis of the selected cases.

1.1 How to analyse the cases?

This paper is based on the principles of comparative study. Comparative study refers to the research in which the process and results of the study are set in a comparative framework. According to Salminen (2000) the comparative method rests on the idea that political, social and economic systems in society regularly change, and that these changes can be analysed by comparing these systems to each other.

The comparative method is used when the research process has two or several comparable cases available. The analysis aims at finding the similarities and/or dissimilarities of the cases. The crucial part of the comparative process is the selection of the research cases and objectives. There are several possibilities when selecting the object of comparison and the literature does not give an unambiguous answer to it. We can nevertheless mention a few classical examples. According to Argyris (1962), in the context of evaluation processes one has to decide whether to evaluate individual action, behaviour,

---

* Pirkko Vartiainen, Faculty of Social Sciences, University of Vaasa (Finland).

or contentment. Pennings & Goodman (1979) and Manns & March (1978) suggest concentrating on the co-ordination and goal-achievement of different organisational units, and Weiss (1972) speculates whether organisations should be analysed as entities or merely on the programmes they practice.

The definitions of the research object presented above suggest interesting questions. Comparative research connected with the internal structures and functions of organisations or programmes contains elements of individualism, behaviour, and contentment. For example in the sector of public welfare projects the diversity of interaction with customers places requirements both on the professional competence of the employees and the ability of the working community to function properly. Therefore, one has to take into account the project's social environment and its internal structures and systems while doing a comparative study. In practice this means that the comparative process has to deliberate about factors such as resources, behaviour, social norms and implementation. (Vartiainen 2000). This article uses the comparative method by comparing two welfare projects. The selected study objects are similar in their nature; both projects are long-term and versatile welfare projects that aim at developing individual and social well-being.

Theoretically the implementation of the projects is analysed in the framework of recourse dependence perspective and the theory of co-operative behaviour. Empirically the research is a document analysis. The empirical material analysed in the study consists of governmental documents, evaluation reports and other documents concerning the selected cases.

2. The conceptual framework of co-operation

A short definition of the concept of co-operation is somewhat difficult because of the wide amount of overlapping and parallel concepts. The concept of coordination can be briefly classified in two categories. The first category emphasises the levels of co-operation. In this case the co-operation can be defined on the one hand as the interaction between different actors. On the other hand the co-operation can be defined as the acting in concert over the mutual goals. The second category defines co-operation by emphasising the structural and administrative points of view. In these cases the definition focuses on organisational and functional elements concerning for example the structural development of implementation. From the point of view of this article the core definition of the co-operation becomes the first-mentioned category. *Co-operation is mainly seen here as interactive and a goal-based way of acting.*

The definition mentioned above can be compared to Jenei & LeLoup (1999) classification where they divide co-operation into five different categories or hierarchical stages. At the third stage the co-operation is based on *joint action* where collaborative relationship is marked by the beginning of identifiable projects and activities. The fourth stage of collaborative relationship is *mutual co-operation*, which exists when the collaboration becomes more extensive and regular. The mutual co-operation can be characterised by co-ordinated activities and programmes based on agreed strategies that meet the needs and interests of both partners.

Theories concerning co-operation and co-operative behaviour can be viewed from several perspectives. From the point of view of this article the most interesting theories are the resource dependence theory and the co-operative behaviour theory, which both make a different contribution to the understanding of the co-operation strategy. Both theories mentioned are mainly organisational ones, but I assume they are worth discussing here as a starting point for the better understanding of Finland's strategy for co-operation in the neighbouring areas. In the next chapters I will discuss the issues more deeply.

2.1. Resource dependence perspective

Emerson (1962) and Pfeffer & Salancik (1978) are widely known representatives of resource dependence perspective. The theory focuses on the context and environment of the organisation on which they rely for resources. Pfeffer (1982: 192-193) defines the resource dependence theory in relation two elements. The first element is an element of external constraint. It means that "organisationss will respond more to the demands of those organisations or groups in the environment that control critical resources". The second element is an element of control vis-à-vis resources and circumstances. "Managers and administrators attempt to manage their external dependencies both to ensure the survival of the organisation and to acquire, if possible, more autonomy and freedom from external constraints". This means that the organisation has a high level relationship with its environment. Co-operation between organisations exists primarily to provide organisations with financial resources and expertise.

How are these thoughts then applied to the co-operation studied in this article? My assumption is that above-mentioned organisational facts are also relevant to project management and implementation. This proves to be true especially when deliberating the principles of the theory more deeply. In the end the resource dependence theory also includes the questions of power and influence over the partnership and co-operation. As Barnard (1968) puts it: "The efficiency of a co-operative system is its capacity to maintain itself by the individual satisfactions it affords".

2.2. Co-operative behaviour

The most interesting dimension of co-operative theory relevant to this article is the perspective of collaborative behaviour. When discussing the question of co-operation between two different nations many different problems will have to be solved. Although the cost advantages or resource-based synergies of the transaction have often been said to be the reason for successful co-operation, my opinion is that the more important aspect is the collaborative behaviour – how two different countries can actually work successfully together. Faulkner's (1995: 186) ideas give support to my opinion. In his research, trust and commitment prove to be characteristics that are associated with co-operative success. He wrote: "positive attitudes in managing the alliance, and actions to stimulate bonding and organisational learning during the evolution of the alliance, were strongly associated with its effectiveness".

Faulkner & de Rond (2000: 28) classify co-operative behaviour in three categories; culture, trust and commitment. My hypothesis is that these are themes which ought also to be analysed in relation to co-operation in the neighbouring area.

Culture

The literature on culture is wide especially in the field of organisations. In this context we have to focus mostly on the questions of national cultures. The interesting works of Hofstede (1984, 1997) may serve as a starting point for the subject. The national culture relates to the values and norms of society. Faulkner and de Rond (2000: 28) state it as follows: "the co-operation engaged in international strategic collaboration will have to take into account both types in setting realistic expectations and putting into place appropriate operating rules." Differences in national culture cannot be neglected. Hofstede (1997: 12) describes this difference by stating, "within nations that have existed for some time there are strong forces towards further integration". These forces are for example language, common mass media, a national education system, a national army, a national political system and a national market for certain skills, products, and services.

Summarising the discussion above gives you the possibility to believe that sensitivity to culture is a very important factor in predicting co-operation effectiveness. How this has been taken care of in co-operation between Finland and its neighbouring areas is the issue which will be discussed later when analysing the selected cases.

Trust

When identifying co-operative behaviour as a part of theoretical dimensions of international co-operation, trust has been found to play a significant role in the success of alliances of all kinds. The interesting question is how the trust has been defined in organisation literature and if the definitions are applicable to the co-operation between nations.

Faulkner (2000: 341) classifies trust by analysing co-operation in the business world. He found three different types of trust: calculative, predictive and affective. Calculative trust refers to the risk taking, predictive trust to the trust which has been built over the period of successful co-operation, and affective trust to the co-operation that turns into friendship between the partners. The more useful classification of trust in relation to this article however seems to be in Sako´s (1998: 89) analysis. Furthermore, Sako has found three different categories, these are contractual, competence and goodwill trust. Contractual trust means that the partners are expected to fulfil their contractual agreements and it rests on a shared moral norm of honesty and promise-keeping. Competence trust means that the partner is capable and willing to do what it has promised to do. This requires that partners share an understanding of professional conduct and technical and managerial standards. The goodwill trust means that partners make a commitment to take initiatives for mutual benefit while refraining from taking unfair advantage of the other partners. Goodwill trust can exist only when there is consensus on the principles of fairness.

As for the co-operation between nations it seems to me that two of Sako´s definitions could well prove to be important, namely contractual and competence trust. These categories will be analysed later when studying the selected projects.

In addition to previous statements Kanter (1989) stresses that running alliances requires very different attitudes and behaviour from running hierarchies. Building consensus replaces decision-making , and respect in alliances comes not with rank but with knowledge and the ability to get things done. Sako (1998: 90-91) puts this as follows: "trust is a social norm which lessens the need to use hierarchy... whatever the formal governance structure, the higher the level of mutual trust, the better the performance is likely to be". These statements are worthwhile when analysing Finland's co-operation in neighbouring areas in the sense that this co-operation is managed and co-ordinated by the traditionally hierarchical government administration.

Commitment

According to Faulkner and de Rond (2000: 31) commitment differs from trust. It is possible to be very committed to co-operation with partners, but still not trust them. Vice versa it is also possible to trust the partner, but at the same time be committed only to a limited degree. Commitment can be signalled in many different ways. It may be shown by investments in projects, which can be either material (i.e. financing, equipment and technical assistance) or immaterial in their nature (i.e. education, advice and guidance).

Referring to Spekman and Isabella (2000: 48-49) commitment is a virtual cycle. When the partner demonstrates commitment, there is often a similar response from the other. To put it simply we could state that commitment is the partner's willingness to devote time, energy and/or resources to the alliance. Commitment is also a signal which can tell us how well the co-operation is functioning. Committed partners are willing to work together so that the co-operation functions well and the potential problems and risks can be solved. The commitment cycle demands shared information between partners.

3. The strategy of co-operation with neighbouring areas

The starting point of Finland's strategy for co-operation in the neighbouring areas is to develop and maintain good relations between partnering countries and support the political and financial development process of the partners. The Finnish Cabinet Neighbouring Areas Committee prepared the latest strategy of co-operation on 26 May 2000. The main goals of the strategy are:

- Strengthen the interaction between Russia and Europe in general. This goal aims to support the development of democracy, the principle of the rule of law, civil society, and the establishment of the market economy and administration in Finland's neighbouring areas.
- The co-operation strives to help the Baltic countries meet the membership criteria of the European Union.
- The change processes of the partners are supported by means of legislative and administrative reforms and improvement of the infrastructure.
- The networking of the partners is supported with co-operation.
- The implementation of the co-operation follows those forms of activity and procedures that prevent corruption and maintain good administration.
- The co-operation supports the networking of civil organisations in partner countries. (Ulkoministeriö 2000: 6)

3.1. Coordination

The Cabinet Neighbouring Areas Committee chaired by Finland's Prime Minister manages bilateral co-operation. The Cabinet also decides the policy framework of co-operation and provides general guidelines for its implementation. General coordination of co-operation between Finland and Russia is the responsibility of an inter-governmental development committee for neighbouring area co-operation operating under the leadership of the foreign ministries of both countries. Four regional working groups are subordinate to the development committee and represent the Murmansk Region, the Republic of Karelia, the Leningrad Region and the City of St. Petersburg. Co-operation with Estonia is based on an inter-governmental agreement signed in 1993. (Ulkoministeriö 1998). The organisation of neighbouring area co-operation is shown in Figure 1.

The Unit for Co-operation with Neighbouring Areas takes responsibility for the day-to-day administration and coordination of co-operation. The sector ministries and their subordinate administration are closely involved in planning and implementation of the programmes and projects.

3.2. Instruments of co-operation

In the implementation of the bilateral co-operation strategy five different instruments are used: co-operation between authorities, project co-operation, co-operation with international organisations and financial institutions, small-scale purchasing co-operation of

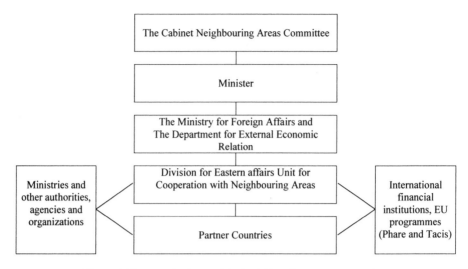

Figure 1. The organization model of neighbouring areas cooperation
(Ministry of Foreign Affairs of Finland 1998: 33)

embassies, and civil organisation networking. The most useful instruments from the point of view of this article are co-operation between authorities and project co-operation. These are now discussed in more detail. (Ulkoministeriö 2000: 10-13).

Co-operation between authorities
Here, the concept of authority co-operation means co-operation between Finnish and sector ministries of the partner country. It includes co-operation processes, authority and expert change, and arranging common training and seminars.

Project co-operation
Project co-operation is here classified as an undertaking which fulfils certain conditions. The project plan has to fulfil the following conditions:
- The objectives are clearly and realistically stated and they reflect, from the point of view of the beneficiaries, the desired improvement the project aims at creating.
- The time-schedule of the project is clear and realistic and covers its whole lifetime.
- The project has a clear and effective organisational model. The model describes the responsibilities of various actors, all partners and key actors and their role and responsibility in the project as well as the management and decision-making processes of the project.
- The resources are specified and sufficient in relation to the objects and expected outcomes of the project.
- Clients and organisations that benefit from the outputs and services provided by the project can be defined.

The planning process tries to form an overall picture of the project. These procedures will ensure that the project is planned as an entity instead of a partial piece of planning. From the point of view of implementation it is important that the project plan is checked and changed if needed, for example if the foundations for the operation so require.

The project cycle
According to the co-operation strategy the co-operation between neighbouring areas has to create clear planning and administrative procedures. The creation of these procedures can be called a project cycle, the aim of which is to make the co-operation as successful as possible. The key elements of the project cycle are the partner country's own programmes, the strategies and objectives of Finnish bilateral co-operation, and the international strategies and programmes. The fusion of these three levels aims to find those projects that best implement the bilateral partners' own strategies and goals. The project cycle of the Finnish bilateral co-operation is shown in Figure 2.

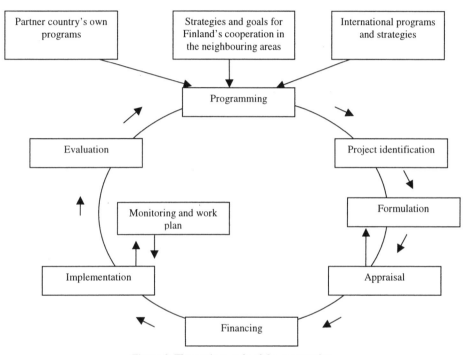

Figure 2. The project cycle of the cooperation
(Ministry of Foreign Affairs of Finland 2000: 43)

As we can see from Figure 2 the bilateral co-operation starts with preparing ministry and/or sector programmes, and ends in the final evaluation. The project cycle comprises a learning process on which plans are focused during the project life cycle. The evaluation and the monitoring are linked to promote project implementation and development. As to the usefulness of the evaluation information, it is important that the evaluation process should contain those indicators and criteria that are essential to the whole project. It is also important that the evaluation method used in the evaluation process is applicable to the project contents.

4. Two cases – Organising and Implementing the Co-operation

During the 1990s, Finland has allocated a total of FIM 5.5 billion to co-operation with the neighbouring areas (of which about 50 per cent in the form of grants) and to activities supporting the process of transition in Central and Eastern Europe and the former Soviet Union. In the year 2000 the number of ongoing projects came to 211. In this article I shall briefly describe and analyse two of these projects. The projects selected for the study are large and long-term development projects, firstly the Ingria Old-Age Welfare Development project and secondly the Social and Health Care Reform project in the Republic of Karelia.

4.1. The Ingria[1] Case

The Ingria old-age welfare development project was implemented in the years 1992-1997 as a part of Finland's neighbouring areas co-operation in north-western Russia and Estonia. The aim of the project was to promote general stability and welfare in the area. The more specific goal of the project was to support the independent and active living of the elderly in the area as well as to improve their living conditions.

The project was at first co-ordinated by the Ministry of Social Affairs and Health, and later on by the Ministry of Labour in Finland. The project implementation was concretised to develop regional and local services for old people by establishing housing facilities and by offering Finnish models and know-how on old-age welfare.

The responsibility of the project coordination was also given to the working group that had representatives from different authority and stakeholder groups. In the working group there was a representative from the building trade but there were no experts representing education or pedagogy.

The Ingria project was financed with a total of 24 million Finnish marks during the years 1992 – 1997. With this amount ten different service houses (seven in Russia and three in Estonia) were built and renovated as well as equipped. The resources were also used for education and consultation for the staff working in these houses. In the project about 90 different training functions were arranged, including in all 386 days of education.

Resource dependence in the project

The evaluation report of the Ingria Project does not explicitly analyse the relationship between partners from the point of view of resource dependence. According to Jämsén et al. (1998) it was very difficult to draw any conclusions concerning the resource allocation and the effectiveness of the project. It was impossible to extract comparative information for example from the costs of the subprojects because the monitoring process was defective.

It is however possible to make some implicit observations on the basis of the evaluation report. The most interesting observation is that in the evaluation report there are no signs of one-sided power effects coming from the financiers or demands concerning the project implementation. Neither do any of the forty participants, interviewed in the evaluation process, signal events of this kind during the project implementation. Also the evidence that the service houses founded through the project are still functioning and serve as established models for old-age care in the regions supports these observations. (A service house is a home for the elderly where they can get all the help they need to manage their lives. The houses are run and financed by the local community but the residents pay for the services provided, depending on their pension and other financial resources.)

Culture, trust and commitment in the project

The evaluation report of the project (Jämsén et al. 1998) did not directly express an opinion

---

[1] The term Ingria refers to the people whose origin is in Finland. Nowadays about 100 000 Ingrian-Finnish people are living in Russia and partly in Estonia.

on the project organisation by analysing how well the project organisation and partners worked together. Neither did the evaluation draw direct conclusions about the culture, trust and commitment of the co-operation in the Ingria project. Implicitly, however, the evaluation allows us to conclude that the cultural factors effect the project implementation. (See also Salminen & Temmes 2000).

The starting point of the service house project and its implementation plan aimed at directing attention to the historical, cultural and economic context of the partner countries. Cultural differences were seen, for example, in the ways the project was put into effect. In Russia the relation between the project and local communities was quite inflexible, which made the project work hierarchically. Also the networking with the project and its environment was insignificant. In Estonia the project relied more heavily on the networks and on support from the surrounding society. The functions of the service houses were also mostly based on the teamwork and client participation in Estonia. (Jämsén 1998: 19).

Within the project a working committee was established for every service house with representatives from different authority and stakeholder groups. The working committee's responsibility was to make plans to project economy, to spell out the contents of the action, take care of personnel management as well as overall project control. In practice, the working committee functioned only in one service house. This leads to the conclusion that participants nominated to the committees were not sufficiently committed to the project.

As for education and training, it can be stated that the application of Finnish old-age care models in the Republic of Karelia ran into many difficulties. One of them was a lack of resources. However, many small-scale pioneer projects and trials were put into practice. People working in the service houses were interested in the different working methods, and the project made them aware of the need to develop the working methods. The most significant effect of the education was however the staff motivation and commitment to the care of old people.

When analysing the project coordination, the evaluation report (Jämsén 1998: 10) shows some problems. Not enough attention was paid to the educational plan as a whole. It seems that education was nobody's special responsibility in the project organisation.

The Ingria project also lacked a specific information plan. The active aspect of communication was mostly via the mass media, although the managers of service houses and the Ingrain Association also partly looked after communication activities. When thinking of the project implementation and the effectiveness of the project work it seems to me that an official information plan for every project would be important.

I have raised here the most critical points in the implementation of the Ingria old-age welfare development project. In fact, however, the project was long-lasting and multidimensional and did have many useful effects. The evaluation report of the project concludes as follows:

"it can be stated that the (project) impact in the region has been significant. The service houses established through the project are now part of the regional and local service system for the aged. All service houses have essentially improved old age welfare. The project has supported and hastened the establishment of the open service centres in the project areas. Because the object of the project was old people, it has improved the appreciation of the aged and humanised their treatment in those areas".

4.2. The Karelia[2] Case

The transition process to market economy has strongly affected the Karelia social and

---

[2] The Republic of Karelia is situated in the north-western corner of the Russian Federation, stretching to Murmansk in the north and to about 150 km from St Petersburg in the south.

health care system. During the 1990s the transition from the earlier central administration and financing system to the regional and local administration and financing has caused crises. Especially the lack of resources makes it difficult to develop and maintain effective social and health care. Differences in regional and local service production are remarkable, and the crisis touches the worst cities that are located in the areas with regressed production and in outlying villages. (STAKES 2000).

At the same time the income difficulties for families and individuals have also increased. This has given rise to new and growing health and social problems in Karelia. The welfare systems are now at the point where services do not respond to the citizen's needs and expectations.

The Karelia social and health care reform project has aimed at responding to the problems mentioned above. The main goal of the project is to improve welfare by developing the social and welfare services that respond to the needs of the population.

The Karelia social and health care reform project started in 1994 and continues to the year 2003. The history of the project began in 1993 when the Finnish authorities launched the idea of working together with the Republic of Karelia in health and social sector. In the spring of 1994 the Finnish Ministry of Social Affairs and Health decided to take the initiative and the planning of the project began. Funding was provided by the Ministry of Social Affairs and Health and later on by the Ministry of Foreign Affairs. (Arsalo – Vesikansa 2000)

Planning started in co-operation with the Karelia authorities in October 1994, and in March 1995 a long-term comprehensive programme was defined. At the first stage the co-operation focused on five different priority areas:

- the development of primary health care,
- the development of types of social security,
- capacity-building through training and advising social services and health care schemes,
- the development of managerial and planning capacity, and
- the coordination of various international social and health projects to improve their effectiveness. (STAKES 1997)

Implementation

Several authorities from Finland and Karelia are responsible for the implementation of the project. The central actors are however the Finnish National Research and Development Centre for Welfare and Health (STAKES) and the ministries of the Republic of Karelia.

The latest project plan includes years 2001-2003 and the total budget for these years is FIM 3.6 million. At this stage the project's goals are indicated in three main components:

- the development of operational systems,
- the development of services, and
- the development of human resources.

The development of the operational systems focuses on development of infrastructures and actions in social and health care so that the focus lies on the authorities' point of view. The service component aims at developing the content and the quality of services focusing on the clients' point of view. Human resources are developed especially by developing professional skills and training and educational possibilities as well as co-operation with different interest groups.

The project organisation

The project organisation consists of four different levels, namely monitoring group, management board, working groups of components and development groups of pilot projects.

The responsibility of the monitoring group is to take care of the strategic planning of the project entity and to approve the co-operation programmes and the project's annual reports. The task of the monitoring board is to co-ordinate the project plan and to follow up project implementation. The management board reports to the monitoring group and implements the decisions made by it. The working groups of the different components are responsible for putting the project plan into action. The development groups of the pilot projects plan and implement the sub-projects decided upon.

Resource dependence of the project
It is difficult to draw conclusions concerning resource dependencies in the Karelia social and health care reform project. The project plans underline the co-operation in every detail, especially in planning and implementation. However, when the project continues as long as this one, some types of resource dependencies can be found. In this case they are mostly concrete ones, which means that the development of the Karelia social and health service production will also depend on project financing in the near future.

According to the project documents it is however possible to conclude, from the experiences of the first five years of the project, that in this project there are no signs of one-sided power effects coming from the financiers nor of demands concerning the project implementation.

Culture, trust and commitment in the project
When analysing the cultural aspects of the implementation of the Karelia social and health care reform project some interesting aspects emerged. One of the biggest problems, caused by the cultural differences, was the lack of common concepts. In the beginning, the partners had difficulty understanding each other in terms of social policy. One reason for this was that at that time there was no university-level education in social care in the Republic of Karelia. According to Arsalo & Vesikansa (2000), for example such concepts as family doctor, social worker, preventive health care or community-based social care were unknown or had a misleading connotation.

The second cultural difference between partners focuses on administrative structures. At the onset of the project the Russian management and administration structures were based on hierarchical and authority principles. The administrative systems lacked horizontal contacts and networking. This was taken into account in the project plan by attempting to create better communication channels between different sectors and authorities. This work is still continuing in the ongoing projects.

During the first years of project implementation, the central planning ideology from the Soviet times was still noticeable in the service structure, training and the educational system as well as in working attitudes. Clients were still learning to be clients and the welfare organisations and workers were learning to be service providers. (Arsalo & Vesikansa 2000). As we noticed earlier, the latest project plan continues to work with the service system by developing the content and quality of services. This is done especially by bearing in mind the needs and expectations of clients.

The mutual co-operation between Finland and Karelia and especially between STAKES and the Karelian ministries during the first two or three years of the project seems to have been important and trust generating. Key policy-makers in the ministries and district administration were committed to the project work and the enthusiasm and belief in the development work has been growing during the project implementation.

The trust building was also greater with participatory approach in the project. For example, all levels of personnel were included in the human resources development plans.

Everyone was encouraged to accept responsibility for achieving progress and goals set for the project. According to Arsalo & Vesikansa (2000), especially the motivation in the local pilot districts was high and led to the situation where the role of the municipalities in the implementation process was further strengthened.

5. Two cases in the comparative setting – some conclusions

When comparing the implementation of the two projects in the light of the theoretical framework of this article it can be stated that there has been lots of success but also some problems in the implementation of both projects (Table 1).

Table 1. Comparative analysis of the cases

Cases / Dimensions	The Ingria Case	The Karelia Case
Resource dependence	*Resource dependence:* No signs from the financiers' one-sided power effects or demands concerning project implementation. Concrete dependencies: The project serves now as established model of the old-age care in the region.	*Resource dependence:* No signs from the financiers' one-sided power effects or demands concerning project implementation. Concrete dependencies: Social and health care development in Karelia needs project financing also in the near future.
Culture	*Cultural differences:* In the project implementation. Difficulties in adapting the "Finnish model" of elderly care.	*Cultural differences:* Lack of common concepts Differences in partners' administrative structures and service, education and training systems as well as in working attitudes.
Trust	The project participants trusted the need for new ideas and attitudes towards old-age care.	The project focuses on generating trust and participatory approaches.
Commitment	Some difficulties in commitment to the project, e.g. failure in commitment of the working committees.	High motivation and commitment to the project especially in the Karelia local districts.
Strategy	The project followed the main principles of Finland's strategy of cooperation.	The project followed the main principles of Finland's strategy of.

As to the resource dependence perspective detailed observations show that in the study of the project implementation there were no unwanted power effects caused by the resource dependencies in the project. Neither did any of the participants interviewed during the implementation process of both projects raise potential power dominances connected to resource possessions. And yet, concrete resource dependencies can quite clearly be seen in the Karelia social and health care reform project. In practice development still depends on the project financing.

In co-operation between two different countries some cultural problems easily occur. This was also the case in the projects analysed in this article. As to the Ingria project, I have stated earlier that it was problematic to apply Finnish old-age care models in the different cultural contexts. Cultural differences were also found in the working attitudes and implementation of the sub-projects. Team working and networking methods were more common in Estonia than in Russian sub-projects. Some problems appeared also in communication in the beginning of the Karelia social and health care project. The partners had difficulty finding common concepts concerning social work.

When analysing the phenomena of trust it can be concluded that in both projects there were signs of an atmosphere of trust. The signs of competence trust were significant and partners were capable and willing to keep their promises. The trust was reached by the participatory approach. Especially in the Karelia social and health care project all levels of personnel were included in the human resources development plans, and it was considered crucial to encourage everyone to accept responsibility for achieving progress. This made it easier for the partners to trust the project and its aims and goals.

As to the commitment to the project implementation there seems to have been more problems in the Ingria than in the Karelia project. However, when analysing the project implementation as a whole it can be stated that the signals of "disengagement" were not strong, and the references to the lack of commitment in the project documents were quite few.

From the strategic point of view the projects studied in this article mainly fulfill the targets and goals set in Finland's strategy for neighbouring area co-operation. The projects have been successful in many ways and lasting outcomes have been reached in both projects. In the Ingria project ten old-age service houses that are still functioning were built, renovated and equipped. Furthermore, the project carried out almost one hundred different educational and training tasks as well as lots of consultation, which the participants found useful. The Karelia social and health care reform has already produced positive effects in the field of politics, administration and practical social and health work. It can even be considered that this large-scale social development project has, at least to some degree, influenced the overall social development of Karelia.

5.1 Some concrete observations on future cooperation

This study analyzed two different cooperation projects and this gives us some possibilities to deliberate the lessons to further East – West cooperation. I shall here bring up four different themes that are important to be taken into account in future development projects. The themes discussed here are: cultural differences, commitment and trust, learning process, and project planning.

Cultural differences. The analysis of the Ingria and the Karelia projects clearly show that the project implementation had some problems that can be based on cultural differences. The differences were seen both in the administrative cultures and in the working cultures and attitudes of the cooperating countries. How could it then be possible to avoid the problems that are based on cultural aspects? The answer is not simple. One possible solution could be the following: the cooperation project is begun with the work that identifies and carries out the conversation on the potential cultural problems in the project implementation. This concerns especially the main concepts used in the project work as well as the overall attitudes to the working ideology. If the project aims at teamwork, three different issues ought to be discussed among the partners: what do we mean by teamwork, where do we aim at it, and how is the responsibility and duties shared in the project based on teamwork?

Commitment and trust. How is commitment and trust reached in the cooperation between different nations? This question could be raised in every cooperation situation, but it is particularly important in the cooperation between two countries. My opinion is that commitment and trust are linked to culture. If the project aims from the beginning at avoiding cultural problems, the ground for good standards of commitment and trust is prepared. Another part of strengthening commitment and trust in the project is project planning. The project participants are entitled to know how the project is planned to be implemented and what is their part in the implementation in every detail.

Learning process. The cooperation project has always educational aspects. The project is planned to develop the functions in selected areas and thus the project has also educational goals. The question is how the learning process of the project is built up. As for the analysis of Ingria and Karelia projects, we can state that if the project aims at education and training, it also needs persons who take care of the educational planning from the very beginning. These persons should preferably be professionals in the fields of education and pedagogy.

Project planning. The successful project planning has some significant characteristics. It seems to me that a project plan that is flexible and practical enough has better possibilities to succeed than a project with solid framework. The flexibility makes it possible to consider the different objects of the projects. The utilization of the project cycle, presented earlier in this article, can be a good aid on the following conditions: the project cycle has to be concrete enough, that is, it must be applied to the particular project in hand. The project planning should also take a stand on the information change between cooperative countries and participants in the project. As to the experiences of the Ingria project it is possible to state that the project organization should have a person who takes the responsibility of information change between different actors.

The above-mentioned suggestions for future cooperation are mostly practical ones. An interesting theme to discuss is the future research. With this analysis it is easy to point out some future research aims. Firstly, the cultural factors of international cooperation are worth to additional analytical discussion in the future. Secondly, it would be motivating to analyze more closely how different administrative and organizational factors affect the project implementation. And thirdly, it seems to me that the particular project monitoring system is not a sufficient method alone, but the East-West cooperation needs also analytical, scientific evaluation concerning the project's effectiveness.

References

[1]   Argyris, C. (1962) Interpersonal Competence and Organizational Effectiveness. Richard D. Irwin, Inc., Homewood, IL.

[2]   Emerson, Richard M. (1962). Power-dependence relations. American Sociological Review 27: 31-41.

[3]   Faulkner, David O. (1995). International Strategic Alliance: Co-operating to Compete. Maidenhead: McGraw-Hill.

[4]   Faulkner, David O. & Mark de Rond (2000). Perspectives on Cooperative Strategy. In D.O. Faulkner and M, de Rond (eds.), Cooperative Strategy. Economic, Business, and Organizational Issues. Oxford University Press, New York.

[5]   Faulkner, David O. (2000). Trust and Control. Opposing or Complementary Functions? In D.O. Faulkner and M, de Rond (eds.), Cooperative Strategy. Economic, Business, and Organizational Issues. Oxford University Press, New York.

[6]   Hofstede, Geert (1984). Culture's Consequences: International Differences in Work-Related Values. Sage, Beverly Hills, California.

[7]   Hofstede, Geert (1997). Culture and Organizations. Software of the mind. McGraw-Hill.

[8]   Jenei, Gyorgy & Lance T. Leloup (1999). East West Cooperation in Public Administration An Agenda for the Second Stage. Paper presented at the EGPA Conference, Cape Sounion, Greece.

[9]   Kanter, R.M (1989). When Giants Learn to Dance. Simon & Schuster, London.

[10]   Manns, C. L. and J.G. March (1978) Financial Adversity, Internal Competition and Curriculum Change in a University. Administrative Science Quarterly 23: December, 541–542.
[11]   Pennings, J.M. and P.S. Goodman (1979) Toward a Workable Framework. In: J.M. Pennings & P. S. Goodman (eds.), New Perspectives on Organizational Effectiveness, Jossey-Bass, San Francisco, CA., 146–184.
[12]   Pfeffer, Jeffrey & Gerald R. Salancik (1978). The External Control of Organizations. A Resource Dependence Perspective. Harper & Row, Publishers, New York.
[13]   Peffer, Jeffrey (1982). Organizations and Organizational Theory. Pitman, London.
[14]   Sako, Mari (1998). Does Trust Improve Business Performance? In C. Lane and R. Bachmann (eds.) Trust Within And Between Organizations. Oxford University Press, Oxford.
[15]   Salminen, Ari (2000) Hallintovertailu ja vertailumenetelmien käyttökelpoisuus. In A. Salminen (ed.) Hallintovertailun metodologia. (The Methodology of Comparative Administration), Vaasan yliopiston julkaisuja, tutkimuksia 234. Vaasa, 11-35.
[16]   Salminen, Ari & Markku Temmes (2000). Transitioteoriaa etsimässä. (Seeking the Transition Theory). Kikimora Publications, Series B:10, Helsinki.
[17]   Spekman, Robert E. & Lynn A. Isabella (2000). Alliance Competence. Maximizing the Value of Your Partnerships. John Wiley & Sons, Inc., New York.
[18]   Vartiainen, Pirkko (2000). Evaluation methods and Comparative Study. Paper presented in European Evaluation Society, EES-Conference 12-14.10.2000 Lausanne.
[19]   Weiss, C. H. (1972) Evaluation Research: Methods for Assessing Program Effectiveness. Prentice Hall, Englewood Cliffs, NJ.

Case documents

Arsalo, Ali & Sanna Vesikansa (2000). Experiences of Finnish cooperation in the health and social sectors in the Republic of Karelia. A case study. Policy Learning Curve Series, Number 3. European Centre for Health Policy, Brussels.
Jämsén, A. & J. Knaappi & S. Leskinen & M. A. Salo & S. Syrjäläinen (1998). Inkerin vanhustenhuollon kehittämishankkeen arviointi. (Evaluation of The Ingria Old-Age Development Project). Joensuun yliopisto, Joensuu.
Ministry of Foreign Affairs of Finland (2000a). Finland's Strategy for Cooperation in the Neighbouring Areas.
Ministry of Foreign Affairs of Finland (2000b). Guidelines for Project Planning, Monitoring and Reporting. FTO International Oy, Finnconsult Oy, Helsinki.
STAKES, the National Research and Development Centre for Welfare and Health (1997). Karjalan tasavallan sosiaali- ja terveydenhuollon reformien tukeminen vuosina 1995-2000. (Support to the implementation of the Social and Health Care Reforms in the Republic of Karelia, years 2001-2003). Sosiaali- ja terveysalan tutkimus- ja kehittämiskeskus. Ulkomaan avun yksikkö, Helsinki.
STAKES, the National Research and Development Centre for Welfare and Health (2000). Ehdotus yhteistyöhankkeeksi 2001-2003. (Proposals for the cooperation projects in 2001-2003). Sosiaali- ja terveysalan tutkimus- ja kehittämiskeskus. Ulkomaanavun yksikkö, Helsinki.
Ulkoministeriö, Ministry of Foreign Affairs of Finland (1998). Lähialue yhteistyön tavoitteet, toteutus ja toimintatavat. (Aims, Implementation and Future Outlook for Cooperation Between Finlanf and her Neigbouring Areas). Toimintakertomus. Helsinki.
Ulkoministeriö, Ministry of Foreign Affairs of Finland (2000). Suomen lähialueyhteistyön hallinnolliset menettelytavat. (The Administration of Finland's Neighbouring area Cooperation). FTP International Oy, Finnconsult Oy, Helsinki.

East-West Co-operation in Public Sector Reform
F. van den Berg et al. (Eds.)
IOS Press, 2002

47

Models of Knowledge Transfer in East-West Collaboration: Organisational Co-Learning or Ships that Pass in the Night?

Tony Bovaird*

Abstract. Participants in cross-cultural projects have learning needs which have not typically been built into East-West interchange projects in the last decade. Specifically, they need to experience a programme in which explicit knowledge and tacit knowledge are carefully intertwined, so that the necessary explicit knowledge is in place before tacit knowledge is explored, and sufficient tacit knowledge is acquired before deeper levels of explicit knowledge are pursued.

The chapter uses illustrations from the experience of the TEMPUS project between BUES and Aston Business School, which was intended to enable both universities to build their capacities for contributing to public sector innovation, and particularly to help BUES to become a focus for public sector improvement in Hungary. It suggests some lessons which could make future co-operation more effective in the future. Specifically, it suggests that in university-based cross-cultural projects, such as the TEMPUS project between BUES in Hungary and Aston Business School in the UK, links between universities should, right from the beginning, be complemented by links between public 'practitioner' institutions, because these links are particularly rich in tacit knowledge at craft and professional levels.

Introduction

This chapter is based on the experience of the TEMPUS project which included the Budapest University of Economic Sciences (BUES) in Hungary and Aston Business School in the UK. The project was intended to enable both university institutions to build their capacities for contributing to public sector innovation. While the primary focus was on helping BUES to become a focus for public sector improvement in Hungary, it was recognised from the outset that Aston Business School should also be able to grow new competences in contributing to the management development of public sector organisations in Central and Eastern European countries.

In order to provide a conceptual framework for the analysis of this link, the paper explores the importance of explicit and implicit knowledge in cross-cultural knowledge transfer. It highlights the importance of links between academics and practitioners in order to ensure that the importance of tacit knowledge is not underestimated in such links. It shows how these academic-practitioner links might have different importance in different learning situations, but, if they are to allow allow access to 'deep knowledge', they are likely to require, at some stage, intensive (usually one-to-one) learning experiences, which are only occasionally built-in to current exchange relationships.

---

* Tony Bovaird, Professor of Strategy and Public Services Management, Bristol Business School, University of the West of England (United Kingdom).

This paper illustrates these points from the Aston-BUES link. It gives a brief outline of the activities which were undertaken under the link and highlights the main successes and failures from the link. It shows that much of what happened was emergent rather than planned (even 'accidental' in some senses), that much of the success came in the consolidation phase rather than in the initiation period. It suggests a number of emerging lessons from the experience, including mechanisms which might be used in future to allow more access to the tacit knowledge of which the partner universities already have and to which they have access through their links to practitioners. It suggests that the implementation of these lessons would make it more likely that the actors in both countries would get satisfactory levels of payoffs from their inputs, and could set a faster pace in collaborative ventures.

Models of cross-cultural learning

In order to construct alternative models of co-operative links, it is necessary to understand the ways in which cross-cultural learning might – and occasionally does – take place. There are two dimensions on which this paper will concentrate:
- The distinction between explicit and tacit knowledge, where explicit knowledge is 'objective' or 'transmissable' (Penrose, 1959), whereas tacit knowledge is that knowledge which is very difficult to communicate simply in words – indeed, we may not even know what we know (Polanyi, 1967) or why we know (Hampden-Turner and Trompenaars, 1993), and we may even have completely wrong mental maps of this 'knowing-in-action' so that we give entirely misleading accounts of this knowledge when asked to describe it (Schön, 1994).
- The number of actors between whom interactions take place.

The distinction between explicit and tacit knowledge is quite fundamental in cross-cultural learning. Since the hypothetico-deductive method finds it difficult to tolerate tacit knowledge, cultures where this form of logic is given especial prominence often underplay the importance of tacit knowledge (Hampden-Turner and Trompenaars, 1993). Yet both are critical in learning. In all learning processes, there is a threshold level of explicit knowledge which is needed before it is possible to mine the deepest areas of tacit knowledge. At the same time, certain levels of tacit knowledge are a prerequisite to gaining access to the confidence of key players in the system, even in the sense of getting access to their explicit knowledge. For example, there is no point in asking key civil servants about the underlying priorities of ministers in respect of privatisation policy if one does not know or understand the main policy acts relevant to privatisation passed by Parliament and the main documents on privatisation published by the government. And it helps to know the system by which policy priorites are formally agreed. Once this level of explicit knowledge – reasonably widely available – has been absorbed, it is more possible to quiz top civil servants about what really lies 'between the lines'. With this tacit knowledge, a researcher has more credibility in approaching a ministry to get access to departmental minutes and working papers (again at the level of explicit knowledge) to assess whether privatisation policy has really been thought through fully and whether its full consequences for all stakeholders have been considered. Therefore, we must expect that gains in explicit and tacit knowledge must go hand-in-hand and cannot be kept wholly separate from each other.

The second dimension which is important to consider is the number of actors and how they inter-relate. There are four possibilities here:

- One to one: learning at the personal level
- One to many: group learning from one person
- Many to one: personal learning from a group
- Many to many: group learning from a group

These different actor relationships are important in both the kind of knowledge which is transferred and the intensity of the learning process. Essentially, the learning process is likely to be especially intense when experienced by one person rather than many (although this may be less the case in cultures which are less individualist and more collectivist). And the kind of knowledge that gets passed on is more likely to be explicit rather than tacit when it comes from a group rather than one person.

This allows us to construct the matrix in Figure 1. As can be seen, Box A is best for conveying of tacit knowledge, but is very expensive. In Box B, tacit knowledge can also be conveyed, but there is less opportunity for the recipients to understand it fully, as they are in a group learning situation where personal interaction with the tutor or mentor is limited. In boxes C and D, it is likely to be extremely difficult to convey tacit knowledge (although focus groups, where they are specifically designed to allow participants to question and challenge each other, can allow a researcher to explore tacit knowledge in a Box C situation).

Figure 1. Inter-relationship of actor numbers and type of learning

PURPOSE		Receiving the knowledge	
	Persons	**One**	**Many**
Transmitting the knowledge	**One**	*A* *Intensive but expensive. Best method for transmitting tacit knowledge*	*B* *Extensive but quite cheap. Can convey tacit knowledge, but may be superficially understood*
	Many	*C* *Intensive and diverse in messages transmitted – but very expensive and can be superficially understood. Must be carefully designed to convey much tacit knowledge*	*D* *Extensive and diverse in messages transmitted – but not very cheap and can be superficial. Limited largely to explicit knowledge*

Of course, the judgements in the cells in Figure 1 are generalised and crude. It is likely that the ideal pathway for cross-cultural learning might be quite elaborate. For example, it might be regarded as desirable that cross-cultural learning projects should start off in Box D, to map out the main bases of explicit knowledge, so that all the recipients can then go away and do some in-depth study of areas which interest them. The next stage might involve either Box B, which would hint at the areas of tacit knowledge which will eventually need to be explored and understood. When visiting overseas, Box C knowledge transfer can bring economies of scale for the recipient and cuts down organising costs. Finally, Box A knowledge transfer can be productive whether it is in the host country or overseas, but it is expensive and it needs to be preceded by the appropriate level transfer of explicit knowledge. After Box A knowledge transfer has taken place then it is possible for a new cycle to begin at a new, higher level of understanding – the tacit knowledge gains allows a reinterpretation of all explicit knowledge so far gained, but also encourages partner organisations to induct the learner(s) into new, higher levels of explicit knowledge.

Role of tacit knowledge in cross-cultural collaborations

There are seven key areas in which tacit knowledge can play a major area in knowledge transfers in a cross-cultural context:

• *Ideological* – tacit knowledge about the role of ideology in decision-making and in rhetoric (for example, when to sense that a privatising solution would not be acceptable in an 'NPM' civil service or that a privatising solution might be acceptable in a socialist country) (see Eagleton, 1991).

• *National culture* – tacit knowledge about behaviour or attitudes important in forming successful relationships in a country (e.g. when to use the familiar second person form of the verb in Germany or France to a person of similar age and standing) (see Hofstede, 1994; Hampden-Turner and Trompenaars, 1993).

• *Industry or sector culture* – the set of beliefs, values and norms of an industry or a sector – what has variously been termed the 'sector recipe' (Spender, 1989) or the 'industrial wisdom' (Hellgren and Melin, 1992).

• *Organisational culture* – tacit knowledge about the underlying norms and assumptions of the organisation (e.g. whether it is advisable strongly to contest organisational policies or strategies with the Chief Executive or Director of a public enterprise in an interview or seminar) (see Trompenaars, 1997; Johnson, 1992)

• *Craft/professional culture* – tacit knowledge about how an activity can and/or should be carried out successfully, according to the accumulated experience of the craft or professional practitioners (e.g. how to write a report on performance measurement in a particular service in such a way as to attract interest from practitioners) (see Mintzberg, 1983).

• *Epistemological* – tacit knowledge about the underlying assumptions in relation to a paradigm or set of scientific procedures, as accepted by the most influential followers of that epistemological approach ((e.g. when to distrust statistically significant findings in relation to voters' stated political preferences, on the basis of qualitative data gathered from focus groups, or certain patterns of autocorrelation in the data set) (see Jameson 1984).

• *Ethical/spiritual* – tacit knowledge about the role of ethical norms and spiritual values in the society or the community in which the knowledge transfer takes place (e.g. knowing the boundary between a challenging and questioning approach to all issues, on the one hand, and an attitude which will appear insulting or disrespectful to deeply-held values, on the other) (see Bovaird and Rubienska, 1999).

The BUES–ABS TEMPUS link

The TEMPUS-funded project brought together a number of institutions to help in the development of the Center for Public Affairs Studies (CPAS) in BUES. The core members throughout the project were:

• The Public Management Centre, Katholieke Universitaet Leuven ('Leuven')
• Department of Political Science, Erasmus University Rotterdam ('Erasmus')
• Athens School of Economics and Business ('Athens')
• Aston Business School, Aston University ('Aston')

At various times from 1992, other European universities were involved, including, briefly, a French university and then, more intensively,

- Mannheim University ('Mannheim')
- Deutsche Hochschule für Verwaltungswissenschaften, Speyer – the German Civil Service College ('Speyer')

In the latter years of the programme, the project widened out to work with the University of Pecs, in addition to BUES. In addition, close links were established by BUES with a number of other public administration and public management centres in universities in other countries in Central and Eastern Europe, and representatives from these centres were sometimes involved in the activities of the link, although they did not benefit from TEMPUS funding.

Furthermore, it is important to recognise that the TEMPUS project always worked together with a variety of projects which were US-funded and which involved a small number of US public administration and management schools in working with BUES towards a very similar set of objectives. The main US partners included:

- Syracuse, New York State ('Syracuse')
- NASPA

The activities undertaken bilaterally with BUES in this multi-national project varied between each of the bilateral links. The main activities in the Aston-BUES link included:

- staff exchange
- student exchange
- courses run by Aston staff in BUES for CPAS students
- workshops for curriculum design
- workshops for the evaluation of progress to date

In addition, a number of other associated activities cemented the link, increased its value to both partners and allowed it to develop more quickly. These included:

- joint research activities
- two summer school study trips by Aston MBA students to Budapest
- post-experience workshops for Hungarian public sector managers, run by Aston staff

The funding from TEMPUS was intended to be for three years in the first instance. The first year of the link was spent in making the application. After the first three years, an evaluation was carried out by a team sent by the EC in Brussels, a further application for 3 years was made successfully, and the link continued until 2000.

The outputs and outcomes of the link

Over the eight years of the programme, there were a number of clear outputs and rather less clear outcomes.

One member of Aston staff attended each of the (nearly) annual TEMPUS workshops at BUES, to contribute to the curriculum development discussions and the project progress assessments.

In total, seven BUES staff spent periods at Aston on exchange visits, in periods varying from several weeks to three months. One Aston member of staff took part in (nearly) annual exchange visits in BUES, for periods of between a week and two weeks – usually timed to coincide with TEMPUS workshops in Budapest. During this time, he ran a number of modules on the CPAS postgraduate programme and ran some workshops for practitioners.

Seven BUES students undertook exchange study visits at Aston during this period, in all but one cases for a full year. (The exception was a student who was only able to come for a term). No Aston students expressed a wish to work in Budapest during the whole period of the programme. However, an innovative exchange relationship was engineered by a different route. In two successive summers, Aston brought a group of MBA students to Budapest for a one-week long study trip. This fitted very well into the Aston MBA programme, offering an unusual and valuable educational opportunity for MBA delegates (and, of course, a very enjoyable break), although it did not lead to credits for the students who participated.

As a result of these activities in the TEMPUS programme, a number of other ancillary activities were sparked off. Several of the CPAS staff were able to develop their research programmes further while in the UK. One in particular was able to write a large section of a book which has since become an important part of the curriculum at CPAS. Another became a member of the editorial board of the journal 'Public Management Review', which is edited by Stephen Osborne at Aston. Another forged research links with other UK universities, including LSE, which resulted in subsequent publications. Through links forged with BUES staff, the main Aston participant in the TEMPUS programme eventually became a resource person in one of the annual summer schools of the Central European University, which is based in Budapest and funded by the Soros Foundation.

Even more indirectly, the links between Aston and the participants from other Western European universities grew over time, particularly with Mannheim and Leuven. However, these links were not initially forged by the TEMPUS project nor were they mainly developed by the project – there were other mechanisms which were more important in sustaining and developing them.

Building of the network – accidents, ingenuity and 'emergence'

The initial TEMPUS network which was put together by BUES was based on some accidental contacts (and 'grapevine' information). Thereafter, accident continued to play a part - for example, the main Aston participant was only brought into the picture because the initial contacts decided to bow out, as they were not very interested in developing contacts in Hungary. However, the various participants showed significant ingenuity in bringing in other partners and making the most of other events and activities to further the interests of the TEMPUS project - for example, one TEMPUS project meeting was held in Leuven after an IIAS workshop meeting. Again, the design of summer school study trips for the Aston MBA students was an ingenious solution to the problem of Aston students being reluctant to spend long periods of study in Budapest.

Furthermore, over time, one can see the network-building strategy as 'emergent', as it became part of the culture of the network to find ways of growing its substantive activities and its resource base by associating itself with other networks. The links mentioned above, both with a network of other Central and Eastern European universities and, on a different front, with US agencies and universities, provide good evidence of this. In the later stages of the project, consolidation was possible and a relatively stable but adaptive network was in place. At this stage, for example, it had become a pattern that meetings of network members would occur, formally or informally, at the annual EGPA and IIAS conferences. At the same time, the network showed its ability to expand when Mannheim came on board.

One might also have expected to find typical network patterns of behaviour such as cartelisation of the network to bolster its position against other networks which were potential rivals. In fact, the opposite happened. The TEMPUS network became a catalyst for catapulting CPAS staff into other networks, in which they became influential. For example, a permanent EGPA Study Group was founded and chaired by a member of the project, one of the CPAS staff became secretary of NIPAcee (the network of National Institutes and Schools of Public Administration in Central and Eastern Europe) and strong links were established with other institutions in Central and Eastern Europe and in countries of the former Soviet Union through the annual summer school co-ordinated on behalf of the Central European University in Budapest. This perhaps suggests that the project was regarded, explicitly or implicitly, as a funding mechanism to catalyse futher activities in other arenas, rather than as an end in itself. Moreover, since it was always understood to have a strictly limited time span, it was always regarded as a short-term springboard to other, more long-lived, activities, rather than a network which should behave defensively to protect its own future. This may have been a key to its success in promoting co-operative rather than competitive behaviour *vis-à-vis* other networks.

Some missing links

The outputs and outcomes listed above were, of course, interesting and useful. However, they represented a very small return from the effort put in by staff on both sides. And more intriguingly, there were a number of links between Aston and BUES and other Hungarian universities which developed during this period which were not initiated by and did not make use of the TEMPUS link. For example, a group of marketing researchers at both Aston and BUES engaged in a long-term multi-country research project on the role of marketing in organisations in Central and Eastern European countries. They made no contact with the TEMPUS project at any time (in spite of several attempts by the project to forge some links).

Again, Stephen Osborne, a member of Aston staff, working in the same Public Services Management group as the main TEMPUS participant from Aston, developed close working links with the Universities of Debrecen and Pecs, on the role of non-profit organisations in civil society in Hungary, with significant research output, but did not work with the TEMPUS project. These 'missing links' raise questions about the extent to which the project was able to mobilise and make best use of all the expertise which might have contributed to its goals in each of the universities (never mind the countries) which participated.

Of course, it can be argued that the project was essentially directed at helping BUES. In this sense, the 'missing links' could be conceived as largely irrelevant. However, this appears to miss the point about 'critical mass' and 'economies of scope'. In designing and running any such projects, it is vital to align as many positive forces as possible behind the initiatives undertaken – thus achieving critical mass – and to make use of all network members, their competences and their contacts to widen the reach of the initiatives and to deepen their impact – achieving economies of scope. Clearly, this did not happen successfully in relation to the Aston contribution to the project.

Lessons emerging from the Aston-BUES link

These lessons will be separated into those relating to the characteristics of interaction between participants, those relating to knowledge transfer and those relating to the role of tacit knowledge in the link.

Lessons on interaction characteristics

A number of lessons are suggested by the eight years of experience of the link:

• It can take a long time – too long – to find out the potential contributions which each member of the link can make to the project's success.

• It can take a very long time – far too much time – for participants to become familiar with the key issues in the host country (in this case, British partners in Hungary and Hungarian partners in Britain).

• It is not realistic to expect exchange staff to make sufficient contacts for themselves when they are making visits to another country – their programmes have to be worked out in advance.

• Ideas are easily generated in such two-way links – but it is especially easy to lose the follow-through into implementation, as both parties tend to lose contact with each other very quickly after they depart for their own countries

• Few people turn down the chance to meet an overseas visitor, but few make contacts off their own bat, few widen initial contacts made to include other relevant colleagues, and few offer extended opportunities for gaining experience (like secondments, 'shadowing' arrangements, etc.).

• There is enormous frustration on both sides at the length of time it takes to make links work in ways which mutually satisfy both parties and which respond to the opportunities which arise during the course of such contacts.

• The links between university institutions were not replicated by links between 'practice' institutions – public sector or public service bodies – and such links proved difficult to forge during the course of the project.

Lessons on knowledge transfer

In terms of the categories in Figure 1, the nature of the TEMPUS project and the limited budgets available meant that much of the activity in Budapest was of the type in boxes B and D. The formal inputs from the Aston participant in Budapest were largely at the level of Box D, other than the courses given to postgraduate students and the workshops of practitioners, which were Box B. This meant that knowledge transfer through most of the project focused primarily on explicit knowledge.

In terms of informing the Aston participant about the situation and issues in Hungary, most situations were at the level of Box C (e.g. discussions with student and practitioner groups) and Box D (e.g. visits by the TEMPUS experts to local authorities or university departments in Hungary). Only at the informal level was there a significant opportunity for one-to-one discussions, at which tacit knowledge (on the part of both actors) could be explored in depth. As the project developed, this limitation, essentially confining the project to the realm of explicit knowledge, became more obvious and frustrating.

On the other hand, the visits of CPAS staff to Britain provided opportunities for largely Box A and Box B type activities, as staff had interviews with one or more staff in universities or public service organisations. This could have ensured that there was a good opportunity for CPAS staff to tap into the tacit knowledge of those they met. However, in the early years of the project, CPAS staff were still building up to the threshold levels of explicit knowledge which we have identified as a prerequisite for understanding the underlying tacit knowledge.

Lessons on the role of tacit knowledge in the link

These different aspects of tacit knowledge have each been important in the experience of the TEMPUS project. Some key dimensions of the role of tacit knowledge in the link include:

• *Ideological* – it was unclear throughout the link how central writers in postmodern management and policy making who write from a Marxist perspective could be introduced into the curriculum of BUES courses and raised in practitioner seminars. This meant, for example, that it was difficult to push for writers such as Harvey on social justice and Jessop on political decision-making as core to the curriculum for CPAS courses. This was a topic which was so slippery that it was very difficult to raise in a serious way even in informal one-to-one discussions, never mind in formal round-table discussions. Only a small number of BUES faculty appeared interested in modern Marxist approaches to their own subject, and they did not raise it in public at any time over the period of the link. Consequently, this tacit knowledge was particularly difficult for 'outsiders' to acquire.

• Another dimension to this issue was the personal political and ideological background of the various faculty and senior government officials with whom we worked in the project. Here, there was some willingness to mention, even in public, if rather *sotto voce*, that certain individuals had particular difficulties because of their affiliation to the Party or governments during the communist era. However, it was difficult for 'outsiders' to divine what exactly these references meant, as we had so little background against which these fragments of history could be judged.

• *National culture* – in distinction to tacit knowledge about ideological background, there was a great willingness to talk about national cultural characteristics. Much play was made of the doggedly pessimistic character of the Magyars, together with their thousand-year record of never having been on the winning side in a war. Sadly, this openness did not seem to help the work of the project greatly – there did not appear to be many areas in which the national cultural characteristics of Hungary led to significant differences in the context or the behaviour of university faculty or public sector officials.

• *Industry or sector culture* – the different cultures of public sector working in Britain and Hungary were very evident from all visits made by faculty from both sides. However, there were very few opportunities to map the distinctive characteristics of 'public service' in the two countries and the extent to which these actually differentiated workplace behaviour or professional behaviour in public sector organisations from private sector organisations in the two countries.

• *Organisational culture* – over the period of the project, the TEMPUS partners came to understand clearly the organisational culture of BUES, and more particularly, of CPAS. The range of formal activities undertaken supported this understanding and the depth of the informal contacts reinforced it. It was never clear whether this strongly cohesive culture was due to the national heritage – a mode of thinking and behaviour engendered by a determination never to go back to the evils of the old communist regime – or due to the shared experience of CPAS faculty – many of whom had known each other for over 20 years and had provided warm and loyal support to each other during very difficult times. Whatever the source, the culture was strong and relatively easy to identify. There was a sense in which the TEMPUS partners slowly became a part of the CPAS culture, even to point at times of being willing to be complicit in the CPAS view of the university and the external public sector 'customer base' – perhaps an example of 'regulatory capture', in the sense that it placed some bounds on our capacity to be critical.

• However, there was never the opportunity to come to grips with the organisational cultures of the public sector organisations which were meant to be the subject of the studies being designed and implemented at CPAS. This would have involved much more opportunity to work in different ways with those organisations, in order to absorb their atmosphere and explore the tacit knowledge within them.

• *Craft/professional culture* – the passing on of tacit knowledge on the craft/professional side worked well in one direction: BUES faculty got the chance to see how a number of the faculty from the TEMPUS partners ran seminars, workshops and classes for student and practitioner groups – both in Budapest and, sometimes, in their own countries. This was probably one of the richest arenas for learning, especially in relation to the tacit knowledge about how to run lively and imaginative sessions for practitioner groups – something we observed was not widely shared in Hungary. However, there was little opportunity for TEMPUS partners to observe BUES staff 'in action', other than in academic seminars, which is, of course, a very different setting, so that we did not get the reciprocal opportunity to acquire the tacit knowledge of how to connect more successfully with Hungarian public officials in seminar and workshop settings.

• More worryingly, there were little opportunities for BUES faculty or TEMPUS partners to work sufficiently closely with the professionals and managers of the public sector during their exchange visits. This meant that even the tacit knowledge about the public sector which was absorbed during the link was second-hand and arms-length – a disappointing and potentially misleading situation.

• *Epistemological* – the set-up of the annual TEMPUS meetings was well designed to encourage debate about pedagogy and, to a lesser extent, scientific method, so that this aspect of tacit knowledge became well aired over the period of the project, and both sides gained significantly from this.

• *Spiritual/ethical* – this aspect of tacit knowledge is perhaps the most difficult to tap, because it is intensely personal and needs to be explored in real-life settings, rather than in the abstract. In the TEMPUS exchange, it was impossible not to be deeply impressed by the ethical stance represented by the BUES faculty. It was a privilege to be associated with a group of people so driven by their value system, while so open and humorous about the conflicts (even hypocrisies) required for survival in Hungarian economy and society. The ability to absorb this aspect of life at BUES was perhaps the most valuable and enriching experience in the whole project, from a personal standpoint. Of course, it took much longer to explore this aspect of tacit knowledge, and to become confident that surface appearances did not deceive. However, this turned out to be a particularly important process, as an understanding of the ethical stance in the department proved an important lens through which to view the other aspects of knowledge absorbed throughout the project. For example, one of the core values in CPAS, which is evidenced by almost all the faculty, is a deep commitment to the understanding of history in general, and public sector behaviour in particular, based on a philosophical stance which is clear and explicit – even though it may be different from the stance of one's colleagues. Postmodern eclecticism is not very welcome in this environment ! Paradoxically, this appears to offer some explanation for the tolerant way in which Hungarian politics and public sector managed the transition from a communist state to a democratic state, with little of the witch-hunting which so disfigured countries such as East Germany. While clearly bitterness existed – and remains – about roles played in the communist era, individuals have been given the benefit of the doubt as people who acted in accordance with their beliefs. When it is thought that an individual's actions are merely self-serving, and all rationales are mere rhetoric, then it is harder to forgive past excesses.

Some tentative principles of cross-cultural knowledge transfer

In this final section, a number of principles of cross-cultural knowledge transfer are suggested which follow from the above analysis. It is not suggested that they are hard-and-fast principles which will apply in every situation, but rather tendencies which should be taken into account in building up cross-cultural knowledge transfer programmes.

First, the knowledge transfer programme must ensure that *all parties have a programme of knowledge transfer which is carefully tailored to their individual needs* as well as the financial realities of the project.

Second, *each participant needs to experience a programme in which explicit knowledge and tacit knowledge are carefully intertwined,* so that the necessary explicit knowledge is in place before tacit knowledge is explored, and sufficient tacit knowledge has been acquired before deeper levels of explicit knowledge are investigated.

Third, *the links between universities should be complemented by links between public 'practitioner' institutions right from the beginning of the project,* because it is in these links that all partners will find particular opportunities to explore tacit knowledge at the craft and professional level.

Fourth, *both the contacts with university departments and the practitioner organisations need to be designed to allow personal one-to-one interactions at an intense level.* There is a need for extended opportunities for gaining 'deep experience' which cannot be transferred by lectures, seminar discussions, documentation, etc. but can only be mediated by individuals in specific jobs, through mechanisms such as secondments, 'shadowing' arrangements, etc.

Fifth, *the project is more likely to succeed if has embedded within it a research design which involves all the partners in action research as a core part of the project.* This has two major advantages:

a) it ensures that the project proceeds by establishing and testing 'evidence-based policies and practices', rather than merely accepting the prejudices and untested assumptions of the dominant partners – this is an especially important insurance policy for the practitioners who get involved, both at the level of university management and in public services; and

b) it gives partners a much greater incentive to participate fully in the project from the beginning, because it offers them research outputs in addition to the core project outputs – something upon which most academics in the partner countries place great value.

Finally, *there is a need to take a stakeholder approach throughout the design and implementation of cross-cultural knowledge transfer projects.* There are no universally valid knowledge bases to be transferred, no universal sets of mechanisms which will work in every case, no universal outputs which can always be achieved. There are simply different groups of stakeholders, on all sides of the cross-cultural divides, who are seeking diverse payoffs from their involvements and who need to be kept on-board throughout. This minimises the problems of non-alignment in the interests of the participating parties. Indeed, it makes it more likely that successful projects will actually seek to include quite diverse partners, as it may be easier to find elements of the project which can provide them with satisficing payoffs than it will for a group of partners which are almost all looking for the same outcomes, in what could become a zero-sum game.

Acknowledgements

The author gratefully acknowledges the help of the faculty of CPAS in coping with all the problems outlined in this chapter, while simultaneously providing a source of enormous wisdom and warm companionship. The pivotal role of Gyorgy Jenei and Laszlo Varadi has been especially important – and their friendship has been inspirational. Pat Murtagh introduced the author to the ideas of Polanyi, which underlie the formulation of Figure 1. Finally, the author has greatly benefited from the comments and suggestions of Frits van den Berg on an earlier version of this paper.

References

[1]   Tony Bovaird and Annie Rubienska (1999), "Performance management and organisational learning: matching processes to cultures in the UK and Chinese civil services", International Review of Administrative Sciences, Vol. 65 No. 2, 1999 (with A. Rubienska), pp. 297-319.

[2]   Terry Eagleton (1991), Ideology. London: Verso.

[3]   Charles Hampden-Turner and Fons Trompenaars (1993), The Seven Cultures of Capitalism. New York: Doubleday.

[4]   Bo Hellgren and Leif Melin (1992), "Business Systems, Industrial Wisdom and Corporate Strategies" in Richard Whitley, European Business Systems: Firms and Markets in their National Contexts. London: Sage.

[5]   Geert Hofstede (1994), Cultures and Organisations: Intercultural Co-operation and its Importance for Survival. London: HarperCollins.

[6]   Frederic Jameson (1984), "The politics of theory: ideological positions in the post-modernism debate" New German Critique. Vol. 33, 53-65

[7]   Gerry Johnson (1992), "Managing strategic change – strategy, culture and action" Long Range Planning. 25 (2), 28-36.

[8]   Henry Mintzberg (1983), Structure in Fives: Designing Organisational Effectiveness. London: Prentice-Hall.

[9]   Edith Penrose (1959), Theory of the Growth of the Firm. Oxford: Oxford University Press.

[10]   Michael Polanyi (1967), The Tacit Dimension. New York: Doubleday.

[11]   Donald Schön (1994), "Teaching artistry through reflexion-in-action" in Haridimos Tsoukas (ed), New Thinking in Organisational Behaviour. Oxford: Butterworth-Heinemann.

[12]   J-C Spender (1989), Industry Recipes – the Nature and Source of Managerial Judgement. Oxford: Blackwell.

[13]   Fons Trompenaars (1997), Riding the Waves of Culture: Understanding Cultural Diversity in Business. 2nd edition. London: Nicholas Brealey.

East-West Co-operation in Public Sector Reform
F. van den Berg et al. (Eds.)
IOS Press, 2002

59

Administrative Convergence in the EU: Some Conclusions for CEECs

Geert Bouckaert*

This article is about converging administrative systems within the EU with reference to the requirements of convergence for candidate member states in Central and Eastern Europe (CEEC). This convergence could be looked at from different points of view.

First, there is a common pressure on public sectors in the Western world in general, and in the EU in particular. Being a civil servant is not an obvious thing anymore. Public performance and pride are not necessarily linked. There is a cultural pressure which could result in a converging strategy because of a common 'Zeitgeist'.

Second, there is a general trend of modernisation and reform. Many scholars observe a commonality of objectives and instruments implemented. However there are also some variations on themes or even diverging trends.

A third level of analysis is an explicit European policy to have a European Administrative Space (EAS) with criteria for convergence. There are several indications that European policies are implemented in national administrations and therefore a guaranteed quality of these national machineries is indispensable. This results in a pressure for a converging focus on the quality of administrations in Europe. There are two dimensions: a legal and a managerial one.

Candidate members for the EU of Central and Eastern European Countries (CEECs) will have to cope with all three of the above levels of pressure for convergence. On top of that there will be a pressure to focus on a systemic approach which should guarantee a simultaneous modernisation of the market, the political system, civil society and the administrative system. In some countries this results in a sequence of strategies of reform and development. In other parts of Central and Eastern Europe there is a sequence of focus from transition to modernisation to integration (Jabès, 2001:10).

Cultural convergence: the civil service as the weakest part of the societal chain ?

The awareness of the importance of the public sector, also as a producer of services, for societal welfare and well-being has been increasing (OECD, 1996). Therefore the public sector should not become the weakest link in a societal chain if a sustainable governance system is to be guaranteed. Hence there is a need for a main focus, not only on the market, the political system and the civil society, but also the functioning of the public sector as such. The quality of the civil service is a key issue in this respect.

According to Bourgault and Gusella (2001) the importance of linking performance in the public sector with pride and recognition is not always perceived as clearly as it should be. "Thus the public service cannot be isolated from society: its performance will be more than

* Geert Bouckaert, Professor, Instituut voor de Overheid - Public Management Institute (Belgium).

ever exposed to the general public and the various levels and expressions of recognition which may follow, all of this will affect more directly than ever the pride of public servants since public service and morale reflect those of the civil society" (Bourgault and Gusella, 2001:44-45). This statement is applicable to the EU and in the CEECs.

According to Jenei and Zupko (2001) it is not easy to harmonise the requirements of political democracy with those of a market economy. The current issue is more complicated in the CEECs which need not the reinterpretation but the creation of an independent and neutral civil service which is based on professional expertise and which is democratically responsible (Jenei and Zupko, 2001:92).

The capacity of a society to attract and to keep a good civil service is at stake in both the EU and the CEECs. In an overview, across Western and other countries, including Hungary, on the links between performance and pride in the public sector Kernaghan concludes "(t)here is also a common realisation that, to overcome the public's traditional animosity toward the public service, public servants must improve their performance. Thus, public servants themselves bear heavy responsibility for enhancing the public's understanding of their contributions to economic and social development and to the health of democratic institutions" (Kernaghan, 2001:14).

There is a common and converging objective between the EU and the CEECs "to have a strong, well-performing, competent, motivated and proud public service. It will be important that the public service be perceived and recognised as such by citizens, customers (individual users and companies), politicians and civil society" (Bouckaert, 2001:16). This, it is assumed, should result in satisfaction, trust and legitimate institutions and hence in loyal participation in the governance system, thereby avoiding extreme voting behaviour (voice) or even exit (migration).

Models of Reform: degrees of converging patterns of modernisation

In an OECD report 'Government of the Future' (2000) the question of 'Why public management reform?' is answered in three ways. First, governments need to keep up with society in terms of responsiveness and better, faster and more services. Second, re-establishment of trust in government. A third reason is that government's role is changing under new pressures including the loss of the government monopoly, greater competition, the opening up of societies and international structures.

These arguments also apply to the governments of the EU and to their administrations. The administrations of the EU Member Countries are not a homogeneous set of organisations, nor are their reform processes. Their reform processes are quite divergent. Recent articles or conferences refer, for example, to Germany's trajectory of public sector modernisation as continuities and discontinuities (Wollmann, 2001) and in France the eleventh colloquium (October 2001) of the *Revue Politiques et Management Public* is about "Reconfigurer l'action publique: big-bang ou réforme?" (Redesigning public action: big bang or reform?).

The European scenery is a medley of systems. As Ridley says: "Of course the countries of Europe, marked by their different histories, not only have different forms of civil service organisations but different philosophies about the values civil servants should express and the roles they should play in a democratic state. There are many ways of regulating public service in a democracy, not just in detail but in fundamental orientations. There is no agreed European model" (Ridley, 1995:13).

The list of common challenges in the Western world seems to result in an equally common list of about six qualities for governments and their administrations in volatile environments (Bouckaert, Ormond, Peters, 2000: 7-16). Administrations need to focus on integration which is about management across governments. Governments need to address issues that respect no organisational boundaries in an effective cross-governmental way. Vision and capacity to develop a balanced strategic view of the public interest is a second quality. This involves putting short-term projects in a longer-term perspective in the context of budget realities, and the views of civil society and individual citizens. A third feature is effectiveness, including economy and efficiency. Today's challenge is to draw on a much wider set of means and networks or relationships in order to implement public programmes successfully, and achieve desired outcomes. Fourth, internationalisation requires adapting domestically, and influencing others to mutual benefit. As frontiers get lower, smaller countries have relatively more to gain by timely organisational and economic adjustment, while external co-ordination impacts on all government activity. Fifth, trust and legitimacy are related to building new relationships. Although some countries are better placed than others, no country is immune to a decline in trust. This requires anticipatory action by governments to bring about the responsible engagement of citizens, and make them confident that their public institutions cater to their needs. Sixth and final feature is responsiveness as a quality of adapting to change. More than ever, an unpredictable environment requires governments to have the capacity to scan ahead, detect trends and think creatively about ways of shaping policies and institutions to respond to new challenges.

This results in about 4 main strategies of maintaining, modernising, marketising and minimising (Pollitt and Bouckaert, 2000) in all fields of management and policy (Bouckaert 2000a; Bouckaert 2000b). It is not obvious so far, neither theoretically , nor empirically, to what extent results have been obtained (Pollitt, Bouckaert, 2002).

The European Administrative Space (EAS): degrees of converging principles of Public Administration

In the EU there is no *de jure acquis communautaire* for systems of governance or for national public administrations. Nevertheless, a general consensus on key components of good governance has emerged among democratic states. These shared principles of public administration among EU Member Countries constitute the so called European Administrative Space (EAS). This EAS is being developed and becomes a *de facto acquis communautaire* which is required to guarantee the principle of *obligatory results.*

The dynamics of EAS is not so obvious as it may seem. There are several subsections which are defined at different levels.

First, there is the level of the relevance of the EAS as a common European space in itself.Is EAS desirable and necessary? Is there such a thing as European criteria, or common criteria in Europe? What could or should these be? What is a minimal common standard? Should these criteria be applicable to all levels of government, from local level to the European Commission? Who is assessing these, who is monitoring these, or even auditing and evaluating these? What is functional variation?

Second, there is an empirical level.In most OECD countries the public sectors have been evolving fundamentally in the last twenty years (Pollitt and Bouckaert, 2000) towards renewal of public administrations which is sometimes labelled as new public management. Is there a converging tendency between these trends and what may evolve on the European scene across such different administrative and political regimes as Westminster, Rechtsstaat, Scandinavian systems or Latin systems?

Third, there is a normative level.What is an optimal administration in the European

Union, including the candidate countries for accession? How should history, culture, and political systems matter?

Within the relevance of these questions and the ambiguity of the answers, the EAS is being developed and recognised and a common managerial setting of the Common Assessment Framework (CAF) is being established.

According to Sigma (1999) "(t)he notion of a European administrative space is taken from the more common notions of European economic and social spaces, widely debated upon in EU constitutional negotiations. (…) A common administrative space, properly speaking, is possible when a set of administrative principles, rules, and regulations are uniformly enforced in a given territory covered by a national constitution. (…) The absence of a formal legal body regulating public administration, its procedural rules, and its institutional arrangements does not mean that European supranational administrative law is meaningless or unknown to EU Member States. There exists a common *acquis* made up of administrative law principles, which could be referred to as a 'non-formalised *acquis communautaire*' in the sense that there is no formal convention. It could, however, represent a common European general administrative law." (Sigma, 1999:15-16).

In general these common principles are reliability and predictability, openness and transparency, accountability, and efficiency and effectiveness.

Reliability and predictability:

The rule of law (Rechtsstaat, Etat de droit) implies administration through law which is considered to be a mechanism for reliability and predictability, eradicating arbitrariness in the conduct of public affairs. Related concepts are 'legal competence', administrative discretion, the legal principle of proportionality, procedural fairness, timeliness, professionalism and professional integrity in the civil service.

Openness and transparency:

Openness and transparency are part of an open society with countervailing powers. "Openness suggests that the administration is available for outside scrutiny, while transparency suggests that, when examined closely, it can be 'seen through' for the purpose of scrutiny and supervision" (Sigma, 1999:11).

Accountability:

In administrative law this means that any administrative body should be answerable for its actions to other administrative, legislative or judicial authorities.

Efficiency and effectiveness:

The requirement of obligatory results means in operational terms efficiency and effectiveness. "The recognition of efficiency as an important value for public administration and civil service is relatively recent. Insofar as the state has become the producer of public services, the notion of productivity has entered the public administration. (…) A related value is effectiveness, which basically consists of ensuring that the performance of public administration is successful in achieving the goals and solving the public problems set for it by law and government" (Sigma, 1999:13-14).

This EAS has one serious bias. With Ridley one could say that "(t)he Rule of Law is often stressed as the essential of civil service democratization by continental European advisers with a legal background. Though respect for the law is important, it is insufficient in the relationship between official and citizen. (…) More important is the 'systemic' effect which the definition of public administration as the application of law is likely to have on the self-image of officials and the way they relate to citizens" (Ridley, 1995:14).

The emerging existence of an EAS is necessary but not sufficient for a converging practice and a comparable and effective guarantee of the "obligatory results" ('obligation de résultat'). It is the difference between a shared law or a principle and its related but divergent implementation.

The EAS has a converging capacity inside the EU between the national administrative legal orders and administrative practices of Member States.

Harmonising public administration standards does not necessarily imply that there will be an equalisation of the administrative institutions across EU Member States.

The implementation issue, which is influenced by all dimensions outside the legal one, will make the difference. It is about administrative culture, political traditions, economic potentials, historical momentum, and psychological possibilities.

The Common Assessment Framework (CAF) is the first important effort to guarantee the reliable and effective implementation across EU Member States of EU policies by national administrations.

In 1997, under the Austrian Presidency, a survey on the use of performance indicators in national administrations was developed. In 1998 a steering group of Directors General of Public Administration was established to improve the co-ordination of improvement processes in the national administrations. Major initiatives of this group were the First European Conference of Quality in the Public Sector in Lisbon (May 2000), the development of a measurement tool, i.e. the CAF, and 'learning labs' about customer-oriented indicators and on knowledge management. In the 'Innovative Public Services Group' (IPSG) each Member Country is represented by two experts.

The CAF Guidelines started from the analytical work under the Austrians and were announced, produced and pilot tested under the Portuguese Presidency (first half of 2000). CAF was further prepared under the French Presidency (second half of 2000), approved under the Swedish Presidency (first half of 2001), and tentatively implemented under the Belgian Presidency (second half of 2001).

According to the CAF website (which is hosted by EIPA), it is offered as an aid to public administrations in the EU to understand and use quality management techniques in public administrations. The purpose of CAF is to provide a simple, easy-to-use framework which is suitable for a self-assessment of public sector organisations. Two main principles are based in the framework:

• Relevance to and suitability for the specific features of organisations in the public administration sector, and

• Compatibility with the main organisational models in use, both in public administration and private organisations in Europe.

CAF wants to serve as an introductory tool for public administrators who want to improve their managerial skills; to act as a 'bridge' across various models and methodologies in use in Quality Management in public administration in various EU countries, to have some measure of comparability between the results produced and the different systems; and to allow the introduction of benchmarking studies between public sector organisations.

The focus is on 9 boxes to identify the main aspects of an organisation which requires consideration in any organisational setting. These nine key elements of focus are:

- Leadership (develop a clear vision, mission and value statement; demonstrate personal commitment to and role model for continuous improvement; motivate and support the people in the organisation; create involvement with customer/ citizens and partners)
- Policy and Strategy (develop, review and update Policy and Strategy based on clear criteria; base Policy and Strategy on information relating to present and future needs of stakeholders; implement Policy and Strategy through process cascading, aligning, prioritising, agreeing and communicating plans, objectives and targets; build capacity with regard to organisational learning and continuous improvement)
- Human Resource Management (plan, manage and improve human resource policies aligned with the policy, strategy, structure and processes of the organisation; manage recruitment, career development in relation to fairness of employment and equal opportunities; develop the skills and new competencies of employees; develop practices which allow employees to become involved in improvement activities and ensure that they are empowered to take action)
- External Partnerships and Resources (external partnerships are managed; the performance of the organisation is benchmarked against leading counterpart organisations; finances are managed; Information resources are managed; Information technology is managed; other resources are managed)
- Process and Change Management (creation of a conceptual and analytical framework to support effective planning; systematic design and management of processes; effective resource allocation; effective project management; planning and management of change; establishment of a suitable reform process; mobilisation/qualification of employees for reform; management of customer/citizen orientation and involvement (improve openness and understanding, improve public access to services, actions taken to empower customer/citizens)
- Customer/Citizen Oriented Results (meet the needs and expectations of customers and citizens through reactions to results of customer/citizen perceptions, results of actions taken to improve access to services, and results of actions taken to empower customer/citizens)
- People (Employee) Results (results achieved in respect of people's perception of the organisation's leadership and management; results achieved in respect of people's satisfaction with the organisation's working conditions; results achieved in relation to competency development; results achieved in relation to active involvement in the organisation; measures indicating levels of motivation/morale)
- Impact on Society (results relating to improved perception by society of the organisation's social performance; results achieved in relation to the prevention of harm and nuisance; results of activities to assist in preservation and sustainability of resources; results of other indicators of societal responsibility)
- Key Performance Results (financial outcomes; non-financial outcomes; measurement of performance)

The components or elements of the cluster enabling the results_are judged on a scale from one ('we have not started or implemented relevant actions') to five ('we have introduced a permanent quality improvement cycle, based on review of previous programmes'); results are assessed on a scale from one ('no results have been measured, or results are in decline') to five ('results are consistently achieved at the highest level of performance in this field (by reference to benchmarking, awards, favourable reviews, audits or other external assessments)).

These key indicators will be measured across EU Member Countries in a context of self-assessment, benchmarking and improvement strategies with learning cycles. All EU Member Country administrations are in fact "a chain of national administrations. That chain

(...) is only as strong as its weakest link. While candidate countries are not under any requirement as to the means they use (noone dictates how they should organise their administration), they do have to satisfy what lawyers call 'performance requirements' or 'obligation of results'" (Sigma, 1998;13). This is where the EAS is emerging as a logical and legal framework.

Lessons for EU Candidate Member Countries

The CEECs and the EU have converging management challenges, capacities and systems.Whether the CEECs are at the stage of transition and transformation, consolidation, modernisation, or adaptation (Hesse, 1998; see also Jabes, 2000:9-10), there is a complex interrelation of three aspects of change, i.e. (i) transitions from command to market economies, (ii) development of international cultural, economic and security relationships, and (iii) efforts to embrace constitutionally democratic politics and administration (Newland, Jenei & Suchorzewski, 1999:217).

This is the reason why, contrary to the usual formula of 'one size fits all', there should be a match between the situation and the required action. This principle of '*situation*' is aimed at ensuring the relevance and validity of the reforms undertaken (Bouckaert & Timsit, 2000:5).

One could distinguish between three situations and combine these with a coherent set of actions in the public and private sector (hierarchies), the market and the networks.

The first situation concerns the formation of an administrative system (institutionalise), the second aims at changing the system (transform), the third concerns change, not of the system but to the system (modernise). This has an operational impact on public and private organisations, on markets and on networks as demonstrated in Table 1.

Table 1. Governance: Situation and tendencies (Bouckaert & Timsit, 2000:22)

	INSTITUTIONALISE	TRANSFORM	MODERNISE
PUBLIC SECTOR ORGANISATIONS	Create public institutions and organisations	Open public institutions	Install transparent new forms of public management
PRIVATE SECTOR ORGANISATIONS	Create private institutions and organisations	Open private institutions	Adapt to ICT and knowledge-based economy
MARKETS	Create markets	Open markets	Generalise market-type mechanisms
NETWORKS	Create civil society	Open civil society	Trigger networked multi-layered ICT societies

EU public sectors are neither perfect nor beyond the need for reform. The need for change varies between misgovernment and more sophisticated fine tuning. Hood (1998) referred to four general categories to remedy misgovernment in Western countries in general, i.e. oversight and review, mutuality, competition and contrived randomness. He suggests the mix among the remedies may even need to be altered with contemporary changes in public management "but it seems unlikely that any of the basic forms can be dispensed with altogether for any length or time" (Hood, 1998:9).

Different models are for different circumstances. Models are contingent on the environment. Jenei (1997) refers to the influence of three West European models on CEECs, i.e. Weberian, managerialism and co-production. Since the rule of law is fragile, "the role of the Weberian model is crucial. Without an existing Weberian model the impact of managerialism and co-production are dysfunctional. But, that does not mean that East-West co-operation should be limited to the Weberian model" (Jenei, 1997:220). He pleads for a combined strategy in which the different components of Weberianism, managerialism and co-production are involved.

Specifically in the Hungarian case Jenei and Zupko (2001) ask themselves: "(t)he problem is whether the new methods of public management can be applied in the CEE directly without having a strong Weberian tradition. It was a great step forward for Hungary to set up a Weberian type of bureaucracy. But on that basis we have to apply new methods and techniques of public management" (Jenei and Zupko, 2001:82).

The degree of compatibility of the modernisation of the public sector and the other segments of society is also crucial for a sustainable system of governance. According to Felts and Jos (2000) the philosophical underpinnings of new public management is to be situated within the evolution of capitalism. This of course is historically more in line and therefore compatible with the EU than with the CEECs even if, as in the Hungarian case, in matters of "governmental modernisation, performance orientation has had an increasing role and the importance of injecting managerialism into the reform process has gradually become more evident" (Jenei and Zupko, 2001:81). According to Jabes "(m)ore and more practice has shown that applying western models into cultural contexts which are either very different or not ready to absorb them leads not only to resistance but often to delays in reform processes" (Jabes, 1995:7).

The question of what are optimal learning conditions depends heavily on the typology of partnerships between the EU and the CEECs. Results and (psychological) effects will be different depending on three types of partnership (Metcalfe, 1998:50-52): principle vs agent; purchaser vs provider; and professional vs client. There are different roles involved which are probably not quite compatible. Of course the decisions made at the Copenhagen (June 1993) and the Madrid (December 1995) European Councils remain very general. The Madrid decision refers only to the adjustment of administrative structures for a harmonious integration of the CEECs into the EU. According to Fournier (1998) the Opinions do not provide a specific model for the organisation and functioning of public administrations. However, they do take more definite positions on certain aspects, and in particular on the civil service. Even if a variable geometry seems to be suggested, the EAS looks less variable. Standards on democracy, on the Rule of Law, and on market economy do have a clear impact on the Member States' civil service (Ziller, 1998:141). This could imply a stronger principle-agent modelling of the partnership.

Five years later Jabes confirms that "(i)n the last ten years, the most important event for ten central and eastern European countries was their formal application to become members of the European Union. (...) To do that, candidate countries not only had to change their national laws to fit with those of Europe, but in the process also had to transform nearly every active institution in their public administration systems. (...) save perhaps for the civil service administrations where and when they existed, as Europe did not have any direct acquis which governed the civil service. But even in this area, some argued that a 'European Administrative Space' had been established, based mostly on common values" (Jabes, 2001:8-9; see also Forgacs, Puntscher-Riekmann, 2001; Haav, 2001).

In any case the current reforms must be based on at least two basic principles (Forgacs and Puntscher-Riekmann, 2001:311; see also Haav, 2001:315), i.e. the Quality Governance and the Europeanisation of Public Administration. Some would argue that there is only a strong, indirect but real link between European integration and the public administration reform (Sigma, 1998:13).

In the order of priorities the "crucial issue in the region is not to redesign, but to *establish* an independent, neutral civil service. This has to be done while democratisation continues, far-reaching changes occur in the role of government, and the market economy establishes itself. So this civil service must be professionally expert and at the same time transparent and democratically accountable" (Jenei, 199X:61). This is almost echoed in the Bulgarian case where the key problem "lies not with the content of the laws, but with the effective implementation of the legislation. It is extremely difficult to apply laws in an environment of underdeveloped administrative capacity and weak institutions, which employ unqualified staff" (Todorova, 2001:399; in general see also Metcalfe, 1998:47).

In summary some lessons emerge from the European practice that could be beneficial to the CEECs.

First, there are several learning cycles involved in shifting from one transformation stage to another. A first-loop level of learning is to conform to existing standards, self-imposed or externally imposed. The purpose is to find techniques for transformation to narrow the gap between reality and standards of operation. A second-loop level of learning is to generate mechanisms to adjust the standards to the needs. Even if standards are reached, these could be unfit for the circumstances. Therefore it is necessary to allow a learning cycle to adjust the standards as such. A third level is to generate mechanisms to learn how to learn. This meta-level of learning is necessary in a dynamic situation where standards are contingent. To be able to have these three levels of learning it is indispensable to have a considerable capacity of know-how inside the administration. In operational terms it could be beneficial to circulate civil servants, for example through internships, across levels of administration (from local to European), across ministries (from line to finance), and across segments of society (private and public, across countries).

A second lesson is to have a mix of learning contexts. These could be a relation between the principle and the agent, between the professional and the client, and between the purchaser and the provider. It is necessary that civil servants have the capacity to combine these different role models (inside each set and among the sets) for relations among domestic civil servants, with politicians, with citizens, with consultants, or with foreign civil servants.

A third lesson is to develop administrative and political leadership to push the coherence of processes of change. Structures, procedures and cultures should match in a consistent way. Local government autonomy does not make sense fully if there is no financial implication and a culture of taking responsibilities and providing accountability. Reform requires a consistent vision, consistent implementation and consistent evaluation.

References

[1]   Bouckaert Geert (2000a) Techniques de modernisation et modernisation des techniques: Evaluer la modernisation de la gestion publique. In Rouban Luc (Réd) Le Service Public en Devenir, L'Harmattan, Paris, p.107-128.

[2]   Bouckaert Geert (2000b) Trajectories of Modernisation and Reform in Financial Management in the Public Sector. In Theron F., Van Rooyen Andries, Van Baalen Johan (Eds) Good Governance for People: Policy and Management. School of Public Management and Planning: University of Stellenbosch, South Africa, p.123-136.

[3]   Bouckaert Geert (2001) Pride and Performance in public service: some patterns of analysis. In International Review of Administrative Sciences, vol 67:1(2001) 9-20.

[4]   Bouckaert Geert, Ormond Derry, Peters B. Guy (2000), A potential Governance Agenda for Finland. Research Reports Nr 8 (2000) Ministry of Finance, Helsinki, 83p.

[5]   Bouckaert Geert, Timsit Gérard (2000) Administrations and Globalisations. Brussels, International Institute of Administrative Sciences, 36p.

[6]   Bourgault Jacques and Gusella Mary (2001) Performance, pride and recognition in the Canadian federal civil service. In International Review of Administrative Sciences, 67(1), 29-48.

[6]   Felts Arthur, Jos Philip (2000) Time and space: The origins and implications of the New Public

Management. In Administrative Theory & Praxis, 22(3), 519-533.

[7]   Forgacs Imre, Puntscher-Riekmann Sonja (2001) European Integration as an agent of public administration reform – Impact on countries in transition. In Jabès Jak (Ed) Ten Years of Transition: Prospects and Challenges for the Future of Public Administration. NISPAcee, Hungarian Institute of Public Administration, Budapest, p.311-312.

[8]   Fournier Jacques (1998) Governance and European Integration – Reliable public administration. In Sigma, Preparing Public Administrations for the European Administrative Space. Sigma Papers: no. 23. Sigma/OECD. Paris, 119-135.

[9]   Haav Kaarel (2001) European Integration and Public Administration Reform in Estonia. In Jabès Jak (Ed) Ten Years of Transition: Prospects and Challenges for the Future of Public Administration. NISPAcee, Hungarian Institute of Public Administration, Budapest, p.313-330.

[10]   Hesse Joachim Jens (1998) Rebuilding the State: Administrative Reform in Central and Eastern Europe. In Sigma, Preparing Public Administrations for the European Administrative Space. Sigma Papers: no. 23. Sigma/OECD. Paris, 168-179.

[11]   Hood Christopher (1998) Remedies for Misgovernment: changing the mix, but not the ingredients?. In Hondeghem Annie (1998) (Ed) Ethics and Accountability in a Context of Governance and New Public Management. EGPA/IIAS, Brussels, 9-21.

[12]   Jabès Jak (2001) (Ed) Ten Years of Transition: Prospects and Challenges for the Future of Public Administration. NISPAcee, Hungarian Institute of Public Administration, Budapest, 506p.

[13]   Jabès Jak, Vintar Mirko (1995) (Eds) Public Administration in Transition. Proceedings from the Third Annual Conference (Bled, Slovenia). NISPAcee, School of Public Administration, University of Ljubljana, 448p.

[14]   Jenei György (1997) Co-operation in Continuing Education, Training, Research and Consulting between Eastern and Western Europe. In Rouban Luc (1997) (Ed) Citizens and the New Governance, Beyond New Public Management. IOS/ EGPA/IIAS, Brussels, 217-221.

[15]   Jenei György (199X) Establishment of an independent, neutral civil service in the former socialist countries of Central and Eastern Europe. In Simai Mihaly (1999) (Ed) The Democratic Process and the Market, United Nations University Press, 60-74.

[16]   Jenei György, Zupko Gabor (2001) Public sector performance in a new democratic state: the Hungarian case. In International Review of Administrative Sciences, vol 67:1(2001) 77-98.

[17]   Kernaghan Kenneth (2001) Editorial statement. In International Review of Administrative Sciences, 67(1), 11-14.

[18]   Metcalfe Les (1998) Meeting the challenges of accession. In Sigma, Preparing Public Administrations for the European Administrative Space. Sigma Papers: no. 23. Sigma/OECD. Paris, 41-63.

[19]   Newland Chester, Jenei György, Suchorzewski Leszek (199X) Transitions in the Czech Republic, Hungary and Poland: autonomy and community among nation-states. In Kickert Walter, Stillman Richard (199X) (Ed) The Modern State and Its Study. Cambridge Universtiy Press, Cambridge, 1999, 217-244.

[20]   OECD (2000) Government of the Future. Paris, OECD.

[21]   Pollitt Christopher, Bouckaert Geert (2000), Public Management Reform: An International Comparison. Oxford, Oxford University Press, 2000, 305p.

[22]   Pollitt Christopher, Bouckaert Geert (2002) Evaluating Public management Reforms: an International Perspective. In International Journal of Political Studies, Spring 2002, 167-192.

[23]   Sigma (1998) Preparing Public Administrations for the European Administrative Space. Sigma Papers: no. 23. Sigma/OECD. Paris, 192p.

[24]   Sigma (1999) European Principles for Public Administration. Sigma Papers: no. 27. Sigma/OECD, Paris, 28p.

[25]   Todorova Rositsa (2001) EU Integration and Public Administration Reform: The Bulgarian Case. In Jabès Jak (Ed) Ten Years of Transition: Prospects and Challenges for the Future of Public Administration. NISPAcee, Hungarian Institute of Public Administration, Budapest, p.393-405.

[26]   Wollmann Hellmut (2001) Germany's trajectory of public sector modernisation: continuities and discontinuities. In Policy & Politics, 29(2), 151-169.

[27]   Ziller Jacques (1998) EU Integration and Civil Service Reform. In Sigma, Preparing Public Administrations for the European Administrative Space. Sigma Papers: no. 23. Sigma/OECD. Paris, 136-154.

East-West Co-operation in Public Sector Reform
F. van den Berg et al. (Eds.)
IOS Press, 2002

69

Portugal as an Example for Candidate EU-Members

Joaquim Ramos Silva*

1. Introduction

At several levels, the Portuguese experience of the last decades is highly relevant to Central and Eastern European (CEE). First of all, Portugal joined EC/EU in 1986, and became more firmly engaged in structural changes. Previously, in 1974, the country had begun the transition from dictatorship to stable democracy.[1] Moreover, the Portuguese economy had a large gap vis-à-vis the more advanced European partners, and was searching for a real and substantial convergence in a relatively short period. Obviously, all these processes are of interest to new candidates, and a set of lessons has been drawn from the Portuguese case (Silva, 1993, 1997, Lima 2000). In this broad context, we will focus here on the Portuguese experience in the field of public administration, particularly after EU accession.

Concerning this area, and in order to clarify our steps, some preliminary observations must be made. In Portugal, the modernisation of public administration still remains a key point in the process of structural reforms. For a long time and throughout different regimes and epochs, there has been widespread and continuous dissatisfaction over the performance of public administration. After EU membership, despite some significant improvements, this picture has not yet been successfully changed. Also, it must be stressed that international co-operation, particularly at a European level, has played a very positive role in the road to modernisation of Portuguese public administration.

Taking this into consideration, we will emphasise the contemporary reform attempts in public administration, more precisely since the middle of the 1980s. Doing so, we will try to draw some useful lessons for other countries, particularly those of Central and Eastern Europe aiming at EU accession in the near future. Firstly, we give a brief account of their historical background in the 20th century where the lack of an efficient public administration (coupled with isolation from international and European experiences) was a great obstacle to the progress of Portuguese economy. Secondly, we refer to the hope of a fast improvement concomitant with EC membership in 1986 and with the emergence in this decade of a new theoretical and policy environment more favourable to reforms. Consequently, many saw EU membership as an opportunity to seize. Indeed, the campaign for administrative modernisation in 1986-95 was by far the most outstanding reformist step of the last decades in the area, and we will analyse its major achievements and obstacles in

* Joaquim Ramos Silva, associate professor at the Institute of Economics and Business Administration, Technical University of Lisbon (ISEG/UTL) and researcher at Centre of Research on European and International Economics (Portugal).

Many thanks are due to Isabel Corte-Real for the valuable information provided, essential for the writing of this paper. I am also indebted to Frits van den Berg for very useful comments and suggestions. Of course, the author is solely responsible for the views expressed.

[1] Regarding political change towards democracy, similarly to most Central and Eastern European countries, but unlike Spain (Rivas, 2001), in Portugal there was a clear break in the institutions not a gradual evolution.

the following section. Afterwards, we examine more closely one of the greatest problems of the modernisation process: the contradiction between the persistent rise in public spending and the need for highly qualified human resources, which implies higher salaries at least for some categories of top public employees. Finally, we will systematise the main lessons stemming from our analysis.

2. The historical background

The first decades of the 20th century were mainly dominated by the transition from monarchy to republic (1910). At that time, the state apparatus was more concerned with the mere substitution of administrative personnel (namely at the top level) than with substantial improvements in the quality of public services.

Under the dictatorship that ruled the country from 1926 to 1974, the political ideas of the regime stressed the central role of the state in the control of economic and social life. Particularly at the beginning of the self-entitled "New State", strict regulations emerged everywhere, disregarding economic efficiency and competition, and in general, poor public supervision and requirements completed this global negative picture. With regard to public administration policy, Gonçalves (2000, p. 32) pointed out that the reform implemented in the middle of the 1930s (Government-Law 26 115 of 1935) was more motivated by budgetary and financial reasons than a true desire to restructure the sector towards greater efficiency.

Meanwhile, the weak rate of job creation in the private sector (in industry first of all)^{2} diverted many unskilled employees often just arrived from the countryside to public administration. Even in relation to other sectors, they were very badly paid. These features were important in so far as they were echoed in the following decades. Moreover, this historical pattern of the Portuguese case is well illustrated by the often observed negative correlation between the number of public employees (relatively high) and their salaries (relatively low), as shown by the World Bank (1997, p. 10). In turn, this trend was also sustained by relatively more secure jobs in public administration employment, which meant less labour flexibility.

Later on, in the 1960s, despite the continuation of the dictatorial regime and the maintenance of the colonial wars in Africa, the Portuguese economy began a process of deeper integration in Europe. Indeed, Portugal was a founding member of EFTA (European Free Trade Association) that came into force in 1960. Throughout this decade, manufacturing exports quickly became relevant in the structure of Portuguese external trade and foreign direct investment, starting from a very low level grew significantly (Silva, 1990a, pp. 103-4). At the same time, the pace of real convergence with Europe increased, and by the end of the period the economic ties with the African colonies lost their relative importance in the global context of Portuguese external relations.

In these circumstances, when the country finally emerged from a long period of economic isolation, it was not surprising that for the first time, the demands for a better and more efficient public administration also increased greatly. The connection between the requirements for economic development and modern public administration must not be underestimated. The need for correspondence became obvious as a result of the activities of "Working Group 14" created in the middle of the 1960s to evaluate the state of Portuguese public administration, and to propose measures for its reform. In the report of this Working

---

[2] Although Portugal had a strong industrialization process in the 1950s and 1960s, first in the basic industries and later in the export manufacturing industries, unlike many other European countries, it never had a long period of dominance of manufacturing activities in employment and production.

Group, a lot of experiences were studied. In particular, we mention, in Europe, the cases of Italy, Spain, Belgium, Sweden and United Kingdom, and in South America, Brazil and Venezuela.

Moreover, the findings of this report remained an historical landmark. According to Gonçalves (2000, p. 33), we inherited from this Group a "very gloomy diagnosis" of the Portuguese public administration. For instance, in the nineties, about three decades later, many of the flaws pointed out by the report were still observed, and remained largely evident to experts and users alike. Some of its most significant findings were:

• the structures of public administration were rigid, obsolete, highly centralised, and indifferent to the environment;

• repetitious practices and outdated methods, disinterest in new technologies, slowness and apathy;

• the user was nearly forgotten and the public service turned its back on him;

• the human factor was dismantled, civil servants were not motivated, and were poorly trained.

Because of short-term views and subsequent political changes, this acute and incisive diagnosis was not followed by the required policy steps and, in fact, it was forgotten.

Later, during the democratic transition period 1974-1985, public administration grew even more extensively, sometimes in a totally uncontrolled manner (Lopes, 1996, pp. 328-32). Furthermore, as in similar cases of rapid political and social changes, the economic soundness of many public policies was not seriously considered (Silva, 1990b). On the other hand, in the beginning of this stage, some emergency measures like the need for the sudden absorption of 40,000 public employees repatriated from ex-African colonies increased the sector's management problems. To the credit of this period, one should refer to the creation in 1979 of the National Institute of Administration for training and updating the public administration staff as well as for developing research and technical advice. Still more importantly, following the democratisation of the country, the principle of international co-operation was widely accepted for the first time. Public administration, traditionally one of the most closed areas in economic terms,[3] could benefit particularly from this move, although the persistence of short-term macroeconomic imbalances did not allow this to happen in practice.

In the face of all these historical developments, from a long range perspective, it is crystal clear that, for the convergence towards European levels, Portugal needed just the opposite, i.e. a modernised and stimulating public administration. In fact, taking into consideration that the country had only participated timidly in the strong industrialisation process of the late 19th century, and became backward in the European context, the non-existence of an efficient and competitive public administration was one of the most critical points to overcome structural weaknesses . From the USA and Germany in the 19th century until the "Newly Industrialised Asian Economies" in the late 20th century, a relatively more efficient state, and thus a public administration capable of accomplishing its modern tasks, proved to be an indispensable instrument for catching-up (Adelman, 1998, pp. 5-6; Reinert, 1999; Olson, 2000).

Of course, in this paper, not so many lessons can be learned from the long period before the middle of the 1980s, but at least, we must underline the relevance of the historical background for present changes and the link between economic development and public

---

[3] In the conventional textbooks of economics on open economy, public administration was one of the most common examples of the "non-exposed" sector. So, even if this feature is changing in some of the more recent literature, public administration was traditionally de-linked from international effects.

administration. As far as the latter aspect is concerned, economic convergence requires a modernised public administration whose absence will very likely curb the process.

3. The 1980s: EC membership and the new theoretical and policy environment

In 1986, the EC membership at last raised hopes of a better turn in the road to a significant improvement in Portuguese public administration. Not only did conditions exist for a more intense and regular international co-operation (first of all, with other EU Member States), but also the intellectual context was far more favourable than before to tackling many of the enduring problems of the Portuguese public administration. However, despite some significant progress in several areas, a clear shift was not observed. Some authors, despite their general positive appraisal of the early accession period for Portugal, think that the situation had even deteriorated in public administration, at least during the first years of membership.[4] In any event, the advances as well as the stalemates of this phase will be more closely examined and discussed in the next section.

Furthermore, it must be noted that stimulation for reform in Portuguese public administration came not only from the level of international co-operation within the EC/EU. As detailed below, the theoretical and political atmosphere was changing in favour of reform in the public sector. In particular, an increasing number of economists and other social experts realised that there was a bloated public sector, too much regulation, and deep indifference towards the rise in prices.[5] To overcome the crisis, it was believed that these trends should be opposed through policy measures. In economics, the rising relevance of the public-choice approach was also representative of this move. All this put the role of the state (whose increase was no longer good *per se*) under closer scrutiny than before in the name of efficiency, competitiveness, and other similar criteria (Krueger, 1990, Breton 1996). In policy terms, it led to fresh developments like the "new public management" (McCourt and Minogue, 2001), the "re-invention of government", and other comparable formulae.

On the whole, this move opened new ways to deal with problems like those the Portuguese public administration had known for a long time. In this sense, the careful preparation and implementation of management and organisational reforms, often inspired by market logic were much needed. Moreover, in the framework of these new public policies, a set of targets was of the highest importance. Following Christensen and Lægreid (1999, p. 175), we mention some of them:

- measurement and evaluation of results;
- quality system management;
- wages and budgetary flexibility;
- simplification of rules and deregulation;
- increased consumer/client participation;
- contract systems, and the transfer of tasks to private firms.

After EC membership, not only the new international environment, namely in terms of co-operation, but also the global changing theoretical environment were both important for policy purposes. Undoubtedly, they stimulated effective steps towards reform in the

---

[4] This is the case of Borges: "After examining the areas where some progress has been achieved in the last years ... we have now but to approach the most serious problems where practically there was no advance at all, or still worse, where there was some receding. Among these areas, *the imperative need for a profound reform in the public administration has a greater seriousness* ... " (1991, p. 95).

[5] See for instance, Eichner, 1985, pp. 208-214.

Portuguese public administration. However, its successful implementation was not guaranteed, and required the prior identification of substantial obstacles lying ahead, particularly those of a political and ideological order. In brief, those involved in the process must bear in mind that external factors are a powerful help but they are not enough for the accomplishment of reform.

4. The campaign for administrative modernisation in 1986–1995 and later developments

In the long run, it is clear that the first decade after EC membership stands out as the period when modernisation of public administration was most fostered. The major achievements of the period have been presented in several qualified publications (OECD, 1996, Corte-Real et al., 2000). We begin by observing that, following the suggestion of Corte-Real (1999, p. 54), instead of reform, it is perhaps more appropriate to characterise it as *administrative modernisation, a continuous process of management and innovation which attended to citizens and firms, as well as to society.*[6] In this spirit, at the beginning of the period, it is worth recalling that the government had created a Secretariat of Administrative Reform to manage this process of change.

It must be stressed that the Portuguese strategy for the modernisation of public administration was in many aspects similar to that of other OECD countries,[7] and was the result of prior contacts and co-operation: "After forty years of isolation Portugal was craving for information on what was happening outside and was very keen to link itself up with the world at large. This urge impelled Portugal to successfully draw on foreign experience in administrative change and improvement. Actions of other administrations were closely observed, studied and carefully re-interpreted and were used as inspiration for innovative solutions to national problems" (OECD, 1996, pp. 25-6).

We cannot give a full account here of all the measures taken in this period. So, we refer to some of the most relevant:[8]

• 1987: *Commission Enterprises-Administration.* This commission is still in operation today and has three main roles: maintaining dialogue between enterprises and public administration; preventing new bureaucratic practices by examining draft legislation before it is approved; and proposing simplification measures in order to eliminate unnecessary bureaucracy.

• 1989: *The New Payment System.* This reform introduced the principles of modern payment in the Portuguese public administration, clearly inspired by the practices of the most advanced countries where the career system prevails.

• 1991: *INFOCID – Information for the Citizen.* For the first time, a well-organised flow of information to the citizens was established, using a database accessible all over the country through multimedia kiosks and later on the Internet. One of its most important aspects has been that it brings together more than 30 information providers in areas such as education, youth, employment, etc., and makes information accessible at client contact points.

• 1991: *The Code of Administrative Procedure.* This is probably the greatest achievement of the period; it had been promised since the 1960s. The code provides a framework for the

---

[6] However, in the context of this paper, we use the two terms *reform* (in public administration), and *administrative modernisation*, without rigorous distinction.

[7] For more details on this subject, see OECD, 1996, p. 25.

[8] A great deal of the following information is extracted from Corte-Real, 2000, Gonçalves, 2000, Rocha, 1998, and OECD, 1996; for more details see these sources.

relationship between the administration and its citizens. It reinforces procedures and practices related to the principles of access to information, law enforcement, transparency and participation in the decision-making process. The code ensures the rights of citizens and increases the efficiency of the administrative process in public services. At the same time, a Public Service De-ontological Charter was established, imposing some obligations on civil servants such as the delivery of quality service, exemption, competence and proportionality, courtesy and information, drive and dedication.

• 1992-93: *PROFAP – Vocational Training Programme*. This was the first vocational training programme customised to the objectives of administrative modernisation. Among other aspects, the setting up of this programme was associated with the definition of the principles applicable to the training of civil servants and the redefinition of the bodies in charge of training in the public administration. Between 1991/92 and 1999, there were more than 200,000 trainees.

• 1994: *Renewing Administration – A Challenge, A Commitment*. This report of the Commission for Quality and Rationalisation of Public Administration had two major concerns. Firstly, to contribute to the withdrawal of the state in fields and sectors where citizens and enterprises provided services at a lower cost. Secondly, to acknowledge that public expenditure was subject to constraints and that public resources were scarce. As a consequence, public administration would seriously have to aim at improving its own efficiency.

Under the effect of this new policy, by the middle of the 1990s, the image of the Portuguese public administration had improved somewhat. In particular, the gap with the customer had been clearly reduced in some services. Neves and Rebelo (2001, p. 115), showed by using an index on the quality of bureaucracy (1 up to 6, the highest level), that the Portuguese position was much better in 1998 with 5 (5.6 for EU) than in 1984 with only 3 (5.3 for EU). From a more critical point of view, Rocha (1998, p. 85) nevertheless recognised: "If there is any area of improvement under the new public management, it has come in the public sector's enhanced image among citizens. This development is primarily attributable to the adoption of new forms of relationships between administrators and the public."

Regardless of the success of each measure, the list given above is not an agenda proposal for CEE countries, still less a desirable sequence. It is only a representative programme of the Portuguese experience that must be taken into consideration and analysis by new EU candidates.

Another major innovation brought about by the administrative modernisation of this period was the evaluation of the entire process by an outside and independent technical staff. This was done in the OECD report, *Putting Citizens First, Portuguese Experience in Public Management Reform* (1996). This work has been particularly relevant to the internationalisation of this experience. Still more important, as with many issues linked to the modernisation of public administration, its results in particular, will likely remain controversial at the political domestic level. Thus it is essential to guarantee the informed judgement of credible outside bodies, and this is certainly good practice.

We must now mention some of the most serious flaws in the modernisation process of public administration. To begin with, it produced uneven results. Moreover, in core areas, particularly in health, education and justice, powerful lobbies refused to adjust to the needs of modernisation, and easily blocked the thoroughness of the reform under various pretexts.[9] Since then, the situation in these areas has worsened, but for the Portuguese

---

[9] See the case of the judiciary in Rocha, 1998, p. 84.

customer they were fundamental for generating a sustainable feeling that the state of things had at last changed in the public administration service as a whole.[10] It is appropriate to blame these pressure groups for their egoistical behaviour, but this is not enough. To overcome this kind of obstacle, an in-depth and broader explanation of the modernisation process was required, at least in so far as the great majority of the population had something to gain from it. In addition, the systemic effects of modernisation, namely in welfare, productivity, and competitiveness, should have been given greater attention and not only its local, temporary and partial effects in a restricted number of public departments.

Finally, regarding these measures, another lesson must be taken seriously into consideration. Even in the case of the best and the most advanced reform legislation, it is absolutely necessary to establish the mechanisms of its enforcement, and to follow closely the process towards full implementation. In the Portuguese experience, as emphasised by Rocha (1998, p. 83), these preliminary conditions for success were missing. It is worth remembering that in Portugal, as well as in many CEE countries, there is a potential gap between reality and legislation; thus, a greater concern with the enforcement of law is particularly required.

After the general election in October 1995, another government took office by the end of that year. The main steps of the former period were not questioned but new broad initiatives were not taken either. On the positive side, the government created the *Citizen Shops* (Lojas do Cidadão) in 2000, perhaps its most important initiative in the field of public administration. The main idea underlying *Citizen Shops* was to bring together at the same location a large number of public services to provide easy accessibility and simplicity, allowing the citizen in his daily life to do multiple operations. However, as this initiative is still in the early stages, it is too soon to evaluate its success. Also, a greater integration of information technology into public administration has been announced for the coming years. Again, as mentioned above, following up this government decision (enforcement) will be essential.

On the negative side, there has been a continuous rise in public spending and a substantial increase in the number of public employees.[11] More seriously, public accounts and other major indicators of the sector have not been transparent; so, parallel institutes were set up without clear control or supervision - and at least one of them was investigated by a parliamentary commission in mid-2001. In addition, despite the fact that this is a subject traditionally disputed among political parties, some experts (Gonçalves, 2000, p. 37) also share the view that since 1995, there has been increasing politicisation in the recruitment of public administration staff to the detriment of technical preferences. Risks of this kind may also be considerable in CEE countries and may compromise the progress of any reform. The need to monitor the whole process through clear and open rules (in terms of accountability, for instance) and on the basis of technical criteria must therefore be highly stressed.

---

[10] According to an enquiry of Eurostat recently published, within the European Union, the Portuguese population was the most unsatisfied with health services (largely public) 72,7% of the total. The corresponding number for EU was 27,1% on average. After Portugal, Greece with 64,8%, and Italy with 50,4%, occupied the second and third places in the ranking of dissatisfaction. The most satisfied were the Dutch with only 6,6% unsatisfied (in the weekly *Expresso*, Lisbon 2001/06/16).

[11] The *media* have recently put forward several figures (in general, about 800,000), but there is not yet a credible estimate of the increase of public employees between 1995 and 2001. In 1994, the number of employees in the public administration was estimated at 623,537 (464,314 in 1986), representing about 14% of the workforce (OECD, 1996, p. 124); these figures did not include employment in public enterprises but only in the public administration, central and local. In our view, this has been a great flaw in Portuguese public administration, for accurate statistical data concerning all aspects of its activities, including employees, is a prerequisite for any true reform.

To sum up: after EC membership, particularly in 1986-1995, Portuguese public administration underwent some significant changes. Progress was mainly felt in the establishment of a framework involving the relationships between citizens and enterprises and the public administration, and to a certain extent, the bureaucracy was reduced. At the same time, some structural frameworks, that had been expected for a long time, finally came to fruition. There were also advances towards the introduction of new information and communication technologies into the public administration. The contribution of European and international co-operation has been far from negligible in this evolution. However, basic areas of public service (such as health, education, administration of justice, social insurance) remained essentially untouched by these developments while citizens and enterprises hardly realised that the situation was really changing. In some respects, the situation has even worsened. This has mainly been due to several reasons: opposition to reform on the part of powerful conservative lobbies located in strategic areas; insufficient exploration of the systemic effects of administrative modernisation; and a lack of enforcement of legislation, which wrongly led people to think of linear implementation as the correct way forward.

5. The continuous rise in public spending and the salary issue

Referring to the Portuguese case, in a rationale that became very common in the nineties, Borges pointed out " ...we have the feeling that public administration is managed in a context of inevitable increase of spending, without great efficiency concerns" (1991, p. 95). In Portugal, unlike other European countries, in the last two or three decades, it was not possible to stop, or at least to slowdown substantially, the rise in public spending. At the beginning of the nineties, in spite of the fact that Portugal was one of its less developed countries, its total public expenditure was already above the EU level (Lopes, 1995, p. 326), and the increase continued throughout the decade (Silva, 2000, p. 228). At the same time, as mentioned earlier, the performance of public administration remained poor and the users were highly disappointed with large sections of the public services. Thus, the objective of "a better service at a lower cost" seemed particularly hard to reach in the Portuguese context. Moreover, the full implementation of the New Payment System significantly contributed to the increase in public spending (it resulted "in an increase of the general government wage bill from 12% of GDP in 1989 to 14.0% in 1992", European Commission, 1997, p. 69)[12] but had no major impact on efficiency. Thus, a decisive dimension of the reform process was missing, the increase in salaries concomitant with the New Payment System had neither been linked to results nor evaluated, even in the medium term.

A necessary condition for the improvement of public services through greater efficiency and productivity lies in the recruitment of more qualified human resources. This can lead to higher wages, at least for some categories. Wage flexibility can also be an important support for reform. As mentioned in the historical background section, Portuguese public employees were badly paid but had relatively secure jobs. However, as a politically sensitive question, in the context of modernisation, there was no clear approved scheme that benefited meritocracy and technical expertise through salaries. Moreover, a considerable

---

[12] "In just two years, from 1989 to 1991 total public expenditure soared from 38,2% of GDP to 45,1%" (European Commission, 1997, p. 69). In 1991, there was the highest annual increase of public spending of the nineties – more than 10% in real terms. Obviously, other factors than the New Payment System also contributed to the increase but its role was far from negligible (for more details, see European Commission, 1997, p. 69).

gap remained between the salaries of top employees in the public and private sectors to the detriment of the former. On the other hand, to overcome resistance to reform in large areas of public service, the biggest increases went to political appointees rather than to technical experts (Rocha, 1998, p. 85). Hence, the wage policy was not responsive to basic aspects of the administrative modernisation. Considering how wages were increased, it was not surprising to note that no visible improvement was observed in many of the services provided, and that as before, public spending continued to rise.

The salary issue is one of the most relevant in the context of a true reform in the public administration. In particular, sustaining relatively higher salaries for some categories of experts and top managers can be an important tool for strengthening the reform. Whatever the increase of salaries and the categories covered, the poor outcomes of the Portuguese case also show the need for good control and appropriate timing of this process. The better organised groups can easily take the "lion's share". A stronger link between higher salaries and higher productivity or, at least, better performance must be emphasised and closely monitored. On the other hand, taking into account the great complexity of this issue, a broader co-operation between experts in several fields (public administration, economics, along with other social sciences) seems recommendable to deal with this very difficult and hard problem. These are the most relevant lessons taken from the analysis of this fundamental but troubling point.

6. Concluding remarks

As stressed in the beginning, Portugal is a good case study for EU candidates of Central and Eastern Europe. As far as public administration is concerned, Portugal has accumulated a rich experience in the three last decades, particularly since EU accession in 1986. From an historical point of view, after a long period of stagnation, things started to change. Obviously, there are positive and negative lessons to be learned from this experience. Some of them were developed in this paper.

The most pertinent observation is perhaps the recognition that EU membership represented an historical opportunity for reform in the field of public administration. This period, particularly the years 1986-1995, was an era of significant achievement. Modern basic principles, such as those concerning the payment of public employees or administrative procedures, were at last institutionalised, and new directions were seriously taken (e.g. the supervision of independent regulatory bodies, the transfer of many services to private firms or working in close association with them and the broad introduction of information technology). International and European co-operation played an important role in this process, but due to historical lags, this form of co-operation must be enlarged and deepened. During the last two decades, the period in which reform in the Portuguese public administration has most advanced, international co-operation has been a significant stimulus and a great source of inspiration.

In spite of the improvements, it was not at all possible to radically change the anchored view of an inefficient Portuguese public administration or even to fill the gaps in its performance in relation to the level of economic development. External but also internal contradictions have neutralised many valuable aspects of the campaign for administrative modernisation and contributed only very partially to its success. In the light of other contemporary experiences, the most significant failure of the Portuguese case was perhaps the fact that the recorded improvements were not accompanied by a slowdown, but an increase in public spending.

In the context of Portuguese EU membership, the appraisal of reform in the public administration is a mixed one. After a long period of stagnation, substantial improvements are evident in several fields, particularly with regard to the image of Portuguese public administration among its citizens. However, the design of the process failed to perceive or evaluate the resistance of anti-reformist lobbies in crucial areas of the public service. For all these reasons, the Portuguese experience may be of great interest to EU candidates from Central and Eastern Europe, especially as these countries are likely to have similar problems.

References

[1]   Adelman, I. (1998), "The Genesis of the Current Global Economic System", *Handbook on the Globalization of the World Economy*, Ed. A. Levy-Livermore, Edward Elgar, Cheltenham/UK, pp. 3-28.

[2]   Borges, A. (1991), "A Economia Portuguesa de 1985 a 1991: Estabilização, Crescimento, Reformas Estruturais e Equidade", *Portugal em Mudança*, Imprensa Nacional, Lisbon, pp. 41-103.

[3]   Breton, A. (1996), *Competitive Governments, An Economic Theory of Politics and Public Finance*, Paperback edition, Cambridge University Press, Cambridge.

[4]   Christensen, T. and Lægreid, P. (1999), "New Public Management - Design, Resistance, or Transformation? A Study of How Modern Reforms Are Received in a Civil Service System", *Public Productivity & Management Review*, Vol. 23, n° 2, December, pp. 169-193.

[5]   Corte-Real, I. (1999), "Reforma da Administração Pública", in *As Grandes Reformas para o Século XXI*, Associação Industrial do Minho, Braga, pp. 51-66.

[6]   Corte-Real, I., Nomden, K., Kelly, M. and Petiteville, F. (2000), *Administrations in Transition, Modernisation of Public Administration in Four Countries: Portugal, the Netherlands, Ireland and France*, Current European Issues, European Institute of Public Administration, Maastricht.

[7]   Eichner, A. S. (1985), *Toward a New Economics*, The MacMillan Press, London.

[8]   European Commission (1997), "Portugal in the Transition to EMU", *European Economy*, Reports and Studies, n° 1, Brussels.

[9]   Gonçalves, J. D. M. (2000), "A Reforma Administrativa em Portugal: Os Primórdios, a Teoria, a Panorâmica e a Finalidade", *Reformar a Administração Pública: um Imperativo*, Forum 2000, Instituto Superior de Ciências Sociais e Políticas, Technical University of Lisbon, Lisbon, pp. 31-41.

[10]   Krueger, A. O. (1990), "Economists' Changing Perceptions of Government", *Weltwirtschaftliches Archiv*, Vol. 126, n° 3, pp. 417-431.

[11]   Lima, M. A. (2000), "Portugal in the European Union: What Can We Tell the Central and Eastern European Countries", *The World Economy*, Vol. 23, n° 10, November, pp. 1395-1408.

[12]   Lopes, J. S. (1996), "A Economia Portuguesa desde 1960", *A Situação Social Portuguesa*, Org. António Barreto, Instituto de Ciências Sociais, Universidade de Lisboa, pp. 233-364.

[13]   McCourt, W. and Minogue, M. (2001), *The Internationalization of Public Management, Reinventing the Third World State*, New Horizons in Public Policy, Edward Elgar, Cheltenham, UK.

[14]   Neves, J. C. and Rebelo, S. (2001), *O Desenvolvimento Económico em Portugal*, Bertrand, Lisbon.

[15]   OECD (1996), *Putting Citizens First: Portuguese Experience in Public Management Reform*, Public Management Occasional Papers n° 13, Paris.

[16]   Olson, M. (2000), *Power and Prosperity, Outgrowing Communist and Capitalist Dictatorships*, Basic Books, New York.

[17]   Reinert, E. (1999), "The Role of the State in Economic Growth", *Journal of Economic Studies*, Vol. 26, n° 4/5, pp. 268-326.

[18]   Rivas, X. L. B. (2001), "Bases Analíticas para la Comprensión de las Políticas Sociales en la Transición Democrática Española", *Políticas Sociais e Transição Democrática: Análises Comparativas de Brasil, Espanha e Portugal*, Ed. R. S. Santos, Mandacaru-CETEAD, São Paulo-Salvador, pp. 53-89.

[19]   Rocha, J. A. O. (1998), "The New Public Management and its Consequences in the Public Personnel System", *Review of Public Personnel Administration*, Spring, pp. 82-87.

[20]   Silva, J. R. (1990a), "Luso-American Economic Relations and the Portuguese Membership of European Community", *Portugal: An Atlantic Paradox, Portuguese/US Relations after the EC Enlargement*, Institute for Strategic and International Studies, Lisbon, pp. 77-139,

[21]   Silva, J. R. (1990b), "Economic Policy for Democratic Transition", Working Paper 3/90, Department of Economics, ISEG, Technical University of Lisbon.

[22]   Silva, J. R. (1993), "Some Theses on Transition and Integration of Eastern European Countries", *Estudos de Economia*, Vol. XIII, n° 4, July-September, pp. 429-433.

[23]   Silva, J. R. (1997), "Five Years of Reform's Implementation in the Eastern Countries", *Issues in Transformation Theory*, Eds J. G. Backhaus and G. Krause, Metropolis Verlag, Marburg, pp. 127-139.

[24]   Silva, J. R. (2000), "The Portuguese Economy in the Light of Irish Experience: A Comparison of the 1990 Decade", Issues on the European Economics, Recent Developments, Proceedings of the 3rd Conference on European Economy /December 10-11, 1999), CEDIN/ISEG, Lisbon, pp. 221-242.

[25]   World Bank (1997), *L'État dans un monde en mutation*, World Development Report 1997 (French edition), Oxford University Press/World Bank, Washington.

East-West Co-operation in Public Sector Reform
F. van den Berg et al. (Eds.)
IOS Press, 2002

81

From Co-operation to Integration – the Case of Poland

Jacek Czaputowicz*

Until the end of the 1980s the Communist Party managed almost every area of political, economic and social life in the states of Central and Eastern Europe. The state used to be the owner of the majority of real estate, enterprises and entities providing services. Administration consisted of a strictly hierarchical structure, where employment and career opportunities were determined by the criterion of loyalty, rather than skills or qualifications. The structures and staff in public administration where ill-adapted to market economy. As a result of systemic transformations which occurred at the junction of the 1980s and 1990s, public administration was faced with new challenges such as unemployment, the necessity to intervene on the market of agricultural goods, or industrial restructuring. Deep systemic changes accounted, among other factors, for the need to introduce centrally managed change to the old state administration model. Departure from the centrally managed system, adopting a multi-party system, developing institutions of local and professional governance put employees in public administration in Poland in a situation marked by contradiction and conflict- in most cases they felt unprepared. Another important factor was the process of European integration. The response to such challenges included the modernisation of public administration and the establishment of the Civil Service.

1. The Civil Service in Poland

The first Civil Service Law was adopted on 6 July 1996. To implement the tasks ensuing from the Law, a central organ of Government administration was established, i.e. the Head of the Civil Service. To assist the Head of the Civil Service in task implementation, the Office of Civil Service was established on 6 January 1997. In all units of Government administration, Director-General positions were created, with responsibility for the proper functioning of the office, implementing staffing policy, and implementing Civil Service tasks in the office.

However, the Law of July 1996 was from the beginning subject to many doubts and criticism. Among the requirements criticised we find the requirement of long-term employment, which created a barrier to young people entering the Civil Service, and practical aspects of the Law's implementation which manifested themselves in the process of recruitment for the Civil Service and staffing of positions influenced by political factors. In addition, appointed Civil Servants were offered remuneration considerably higher than those offered to Government administration employees. Practically speaking, this meant there was no possibility of achieving increased work effectiveness and stimulating improvement in qualifications. Immediately after the nomination of the new Cabinet in

* Dr Jacek Czaputowicz, Deputy Head of Civil Service, Lecturer at the Warsaw School of Economics (Poland).

November 1997, Prime Minister Jerzy Buzek, as the Constitutional head of the Civil Service Corps, suspended the controversial qualification procedure for the Civil Service. Work on a new bill was initiated.

The Civil Service Act of 18 December 1998, came into effect on 1 July 1999, and introduced a coherent organisational and legal system for the Civil Service, in keeping with the standards of an apolitical, impartial and professional Civil Service, adopted by the EU and OECD member states. The Act first defined in the first place coherent and unitary principles regarding public service for all employees in Government administration, such as the necessity to meet formal requirements, service privileges, principles for recruitment and selection, promotion and periodical employee assessment, as well as permanent upgrading and the requirements of professional ethics. Secondly, the adoption of the Act made it possible to harmonise regulations dealing with employees in Government administration with the requirements of the new Constitution of the Republic of Poland adopted in 1997, and the EU legislation. Thirdly, the Act created a legal framework for preparing Polish administration for the new tasks assumed by the state in connection with integration, globalisation of world economy, and systemic reforms taken in hand by the Polish Government, in particular the reform of the public administration system, implemented between 1998 and 1999.

Polish specificity consists, for example, in the fact that the Civil Service Corps does not incorporate employees into local Government administration, and those state institutions which do not report to the Prime Minister (such as the Chancellery of the Parliament, the President's Chancellery, Ombudsman's Office, and others). The reasons for such exclusions is the issue of supervision.

The Civil Service Corps in Poland incorporates more than 118,000 people, employed in official positions in Government administration, including ministries, central and voivodship offices, as well as units subordinated directly to central administration, voivode or poviat. The latter group, subordinated to voivode or poviat, comprises inspection offices and other units providing support to the heads of particular services, inspections and guards at voivodship and poviat levels. It is noteworthy that tax administration which is related to the Ministry of Finance (tax offices, tax chambers and offices of tax control) accounts for 42% of the Civil Service employment.

Figure 1. Employment in the Polish Civil Service

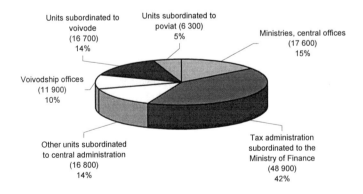

Total – 118,300 employees (year 2001)

The Civil Service Act introduced the requirement of periodical assessment to be carried out by the in-line manger, at least once every two years. It is expected to prove decisive for employee promotion to higher levels and influence individual professional career development. It is assumed, on the basis of experiences in Western state administrations, that periodical assessment will be carried out on the basis of measurable effects of a civil servant's work. Thus, it is going to take into account each employee's input in the performance of statutory tasks of a given organisation and long-term office objectives.

Under the Act the members of the Civil Service corps are obligated to develop professional knowledge. An important measure is the introduction of the individual professional development programme (for each Civil Servant) which also incorporates the training plan as well as the annual provision, announced by the Head of the Civil Service, of a central training plan, which covers training priorities for the Government administration in a given year.

The Civil Service Act introduces basic standards of professional ethics for employees in the Government administration: the principle of impartiality, political neutrality, honesty and professionalism.[1]

Collecting all the standards and ethical requirements in a single document should make it easier to interpret particular situations which occur in Civil Service practice, prevent conflicts between superiors and their subordinates. The implementation of the code might in consequence influence the effectiveness of the work of public officials. The rules of professional ethics will include such obligations as professionalism of activities performed, accountability for decisions made, apolitical behaviour and an impartial approach to professional tasks, identifying professional activity with public service performance as well as honest application of the laws in force, adopting the principle of openness in implementing procedures, an open approach to public opinion, keeping secrecy and confidentiality as well as honesty in personal and professional relations[2].

A career path in the Civil Service covers four stages: recruitment, preparatory service, qualification procedure for Civil Service employees applying for an appointment, and competitive examinations for senior staff positions.

Civil Service recruitment is carried out in a decentralised system, where the leading role is played by Directors-General in Ministries, central and voivodship offices. They are in charge of recruitment for the basic category of Civil Service employees. Announcements of vacancies in the Civil Service are published obligatorily in the Civil Service Bulletin. Between July 1999 and December 2000, 11,500 such announcements were published. Usually a few to several candidates apply for each position. This situation has a motivating influence on people already employed in administration.

The second stage is a six-months preparatory period. This period is aimed at ensuring the preparation, in theory and in practice, of a person employed for the first time in public administration,, to ensure that they will perform their service duties properly. At the end of the preparatory service, the Director-General of the office, on the basis of positive assessment confirmed by the examining commission, will conclude an open-ended employment contract with the employee.

---

[1] For the issues of ethics in Civil Service, see B. Kudrycka *Neutralnosc polityczna urzedników* [Political Neutrality of Civil Servants], Warsaw 1998; *Etyka w urzedzie - efekt kultury czy prawa ?* [Ethics in Office. Is it about culture or the law?], VII Conference of Graduates from the National School of Public Administration; Witold Krajewski *Legal Regulations dealing with Ethics in the Civil Service in Poland*, "Sluzba Cywilna", Warsaw, Autumn-Winter 2000/2001, pp. 97 - 121.

[2] Project of the draft code of ethics developed by the team appointed by the Head of Civil Service and chaired by Prof. B. Kudrycka, is available on www.usc.gov.pl/pl/informator/j_ke/kodeks_projekt.html (in Polish).

Figure 2. Career Path in the Civil Service

Rules for organising examinations for the privileged category of Civil Servants are defined in the "Regulation by the President of the Council of Ministers" of 3 November 1999, on the organisation and application of detailed rules for competitive examinations for senior positions in the Civil Service. Access to this category is limited to employees in public administration with at least two years of employment, completed university-level education and a good command of at least one foreign language. Appointment guarantees stability of employment and the right to a financial bonus, which will be increased depending on the duration of employment in the Civil Service. Note that meeting the requirement of a good command of a foreign language is a difficult challenge in becoming a Civil Servant.Only a Civil Servant can apply for a senior position in the Civil Service (until 30 April 2004, this right can be enjoyed by every citizen). Competitive examinations are held with a view to staffing approximately 1600 managerial positions in Government administration, those of Directors-General, Directors of Departments, and their deputies. Announcements of competitive examinations must be published in the Civil Service Bulletin.

2. Convergence of Civil Services in the EU

It is recognised in the EU Member States that the Civil Service or, in the broad sense of the term, public administration, is a domain of the sovereign state. Hence at the European Community level there are no regulations dealing with public administration and Civil Service in EU Member States. In keeping withthe principle of subsidiarity, every state shapes its own administration and the rules for its functioning.

Yet, there clearly exists a tendency to europeanise public administration, which is manifested by building thematic connections between public administrations of the Member States and the EU. This leads to standardisation of Civil Services in Member States.[3] Europeanisation is also expressed by introducing unitary principles, behaviour, and procedures. Those principles usually incorporate the rule of law, openness, transparency and accountability, effectiveness and efficiency. These are reflected in the internal legal systems and confirmation in the case-law of the European Court of Justice. Common principles have led to a certain convergence among the Member States. Some authors in fact refer to the coming of the European Administrative Space.[4]

---

[3] See: P. Ahonen and others: *Public Administration in the New Millenium: Some European Scenarios*. EIPA, Maastricht, 17 February 2000, p. 9.

[4] For a broader reference, see: European Principles for Public Administration, SIGMA Papers, Paris 1998, No 27.

Europeanisation of the public administration goes deeper when similar and repeated problems occur, ensuing from policies pursued at the EU level. European Union Member States had to establish procedures and mechanisms to monitor the implementation of decisions made by Community institutions. Effective administration in the area of implementing the European law requires the Member States to modify their internal administrative structures so that decisions made by European institutions may become effective. For example, the distribution of resources under structural funds requires the application of specific procedures and the setting-up of appropriate institutions, which by their nature will be similar across Member States because they mustimplement the same tasks.

It is broadly understood that one of the conditions for meeting membership requirements by candidate countries is the construction of proper administrative organisations. This activity is covered by special European Union assistance.

In the EU, co-operation among institutions responsible for public administration is informal in character. At the European level there exists no Council of Ministers for Public Administration, as opposed to other sectors (finance, agriculture, environment, etc.) Nevertheless, for a few years now, informal meetings of Ministers responsible for public administration and the Civil Service have been held. In Strasbourg on 7 November 2000, the 8th meeting of Ministers responsible for Public Administration and Civil Service in the EU Member States was held; five resolutions were adopted, providing support for activities in favour of modernising management in the public sector. Detailed resolutions dealt with dialogue between Government and trade unions, e-Government, better regulation within the European Union, and the quality and benchmarking of public services in EU.[5] A decision was also taken to establish working groups to monitor and implement the adopted resolutions and decisions with regard to the organisation of regular meetings to be determined under each subsequent Presidency.

A new window of quality was opened up by the first meeting of representatives of the Presidency and the EU Commission with the Directors-General responsible for Public Administration and Civil Service in candidate countries, held in Brussels on 16 November 2000. This fact clearly shows the EU is interested in the process of adapting the public administrations of candidate countries to Community standards. According to Neil Kinnock, the meeting aimed to encourage mutually beneficial co-operation between EU Member States and candidate countries.

The different fields of co-operation between the Directors-General responsible for public administration in the European Union were presented to the representatives from candidate countries in the meeting in Stockholm on 23 May 2001. The three core-areas were: innovative public services, human resources, and public governance. The Innovative Public Services Group was established to promote best practices and excellence in EU public administrations through various initiatives (such as Common Assessment Framework and European Benchmarking Network). The aim of the working group on E-government wasto analyse the impact of information technologies on the organisation and quality of work within administrations. The goal of the working group on European Training Programmes was to co-operate rigorously with the directors of schools and institutes of public administration in the EU Member States in order to develop training activities in EU related matters. A dialogue with the candidate countries remains a priority[6].

Similar meetings of this type are important for candidate countries because they give them an insight into the processes which occur in public administrations of the EU Member

---

[5] Resolutions are available on www.fonction-publique.gouv.fr/lactualite/lesgrands dossiers/europe.
[6] The next meeting in this co-operation framework is due to take place in Brussels on 16 November 2001. It will be devoted to strategies on training in the context of the enlargement.

States and help them to adapt their administrations to EU standards. In spite of the fact that the European law leaves the regulation of public services to the EU Member States themselves, candidate countries are expected to follow common rules such as legality, transparency, responsibility, accountability and effectiveness. Public administration should be characterised by the sense of service, political neutrality; while a key role should be played by the act that regulates the shape and functioning of the Civil Service.

3. Poland's Co-operation with its EU Partners under the PHARE Programme

The quality of public administration and the Civil Service is perceived by the European Commission as one of the factors which determines the degree to which the state meets the requirements of European integration. The Commission in its document entitled "Partnership for Accession", issued in autumn 1997, recommended improving the qualifications of administrative employees in the sphere of EU problem studies, effectiveness of public management, developing a strategy for the versatile training of Civil Servants, and guaranteeing equal access to the Civil Service to all citizens. Poland addressed these postulates in The National Programme of Preparation for EU Membership of July 1998. This programme is modified on an annual basis as each set of tasks is completed and new needs appear. The EU is consulted about changes. The latest version of the programme, developed in 2000, directly addresses the structures of public administration, lists the guarantee of equal access to the Civil Service (under priority 30.4) and the preparation of regional administration for participation in selected areas of European Community policy, as well as Community projects and funds (priority 30.6)[7].

In assessment by the Commission all candidate countries must meet political criteria for EU membership, yet progress in establishing and strengthening institutions, whose task consists in implementing and applying community law, is not equal[8].

As in previous years, candidates strive to overcome problems relative to low effectiveness of the administration and judiciary, which in some cases result from a failure to adopt the necessary legal framework. Modern Civil Service Acts, which in the Commission's opinion constitute the foundation for the proper functioning of an efficient public administration, free of all political influences, were adopted exclusively by Hungary and Poland. Progress in modernising public administration in Estonia and Slovenia (with the Government draft legislation failing to reach the Parliament by November last year) as well as in the Czech Republic, (where the relevant law will come into effect at the earliest in 2002), was recognised as limited.

In the course of work on the Interim Report on Poland's Progress on the Way to EU Membership as well as the report itself of 8 November 2000, the European Commission confirmed that the direction of change in the Civil Service was correct. At the same time, the Commission expressed its concern that the slow pace of implementation of the Civil Service Act, seen in the low number of appointments to Civil Servant positions, does not guarantee political independence and stability of appointments, or efficient functioning of the Civil Service. The Commission also highlighted the issue of pay levels, which is important to guarantee recruitment and retain a corps of experienced servants. Frequently, the salaries offered at the local level exceeded those in central government institutions. Pay

---

[7] The National Programme of Preparation for EU Membership of 26 April 2000 is available on www.ukie.gov.pl.
[8] Interim reports dealing with progress made by particular candidate countries on the way to EU membership are available on the homepage of
www.europa.eu.int/comm/enlargement/report_11_00/index.htm#reports.

levels in different sectors of Government administration also vary.

The need to permanently improve the Civil Service system is recognised in Poland. In December 2000, a conference was held at the Chancellery of the Chairman of Ministers on The Civil Service Act – this represented two years of expectations and experiences, in which representatives of Government administration, Parliamentarians and research workers carried out an assessment of the functioning of the Civil Service Act, and presented draft amendments[9]. The Civil Service Council acknowledged that it would be advisable to begin work to amend selected sections of the Civil Service system. The Council suggested introducing another Civil Servant category for persons of lower qualifications, and, in consequence, establishing various qualification procedures. The Civil Service system should also cover chairmen and deputy chairmen in central offices, as well as heads of merged services, inspections and guards at the voivodship level. At present, only employees in those organisations are included in the Civil Service Corps. Tasks, instruments, authorisations and accountability for creating pay systems in the Civil Service should be devolved to the Head of the Civil Service. The Council also recommended reducing the number of jobs to be staffed exclusively on the basis of competitive examinations. In addition, the system for educating and training Civil Service Corps members required structuring[10].

Twinning partnership is perceived by the EU as a tool for strengthening administrative capacity in applicant countries. The preparation of the civil service for co-operation within the civil services of the EU Member States is one of the objectives of the Polish government during the accession process. Under PHARE 1999, 17 twinning co-operation projects are being implemented in Poland, 3 of which directly focus on strengthening public administration. The first project deals with customs administration. It is aimed at full implementation of the acquis and the improvement of customs administration effectiveness. The second one covers tax administration and is intended to support the adjustment of Polish law in the field of VAT, personal and corporate income taxes as well as the strengthening of tax administration.

The third project deals with developing human resources in the civil service. The project is called Strengthening Administration and Human Resources in Preparation for EU Membership[11]. This project is implemented in twinning co-operation between the Office of Civil Service and the consortium led by the Office of Prime Minister of the United Kingdom in co-operation with the Danish School of Public Administration and the Spanish National Institute for Public Administration. On the Polish side the project is implemented by the Office of Civil Service in close co-operation with pilot offices, including Prime Minister's Chancellery, 9 core Ministries and 2 Voivodship offices.

The project is not specifically focused on any Community acquis. It concentrates on the idea that to implement the acquis is no longer enough to acquire knowledge of EU laws, regulations and institutions, but it is essential to design and put into practice management standards and procedures so as to increase the quality of services performed by civil servants.

The project includes three components: the first one is designed to strengthen management in public administration, the second one will develop a data base in order to facilitate effective staff management across the civil service, and the third one will carry

---

[9] See "Ustawa o Sluzbie Cywilnej - dwa lata oczekiwan i doswiadczen. Konferencja" [The Civil Service Act – two years of expectations and experiences. Conference]. Papers and discussion, Chancellery of the Chairman of the Council of Ministers and the Civil Service Council, December 2000.

[10] See Resolution 41 by the Civil Service Council of 14 March 2001, concerning changes in the civil service system. Bulletin of Civil Service, No 7(63), 1 April 2001.

[11] More details on the project implementation are available on www.sluzbacywilna.gov.pl (in Polish).

out an information and promotion campaign for the civil service. Project implementation was initiated on 2 October 2000, and will continue until September 2003. It is clear that the project is still in the initial stage of implementation.

The project is part of the general process of reforming the civil service. It assumes that the Office of Civil Service will be converted into a strategic and policy-making centre in charge of managing human resources in the civil service. It is expected that actions which have already been initiated will lead to developing the mission statement, strategic plans and quality targets in each pilot office.

In the first component, most of the activities focus on human resource management. The project is planned to yield a general Human Resources Management Strategy for the Polish civil service as a whole and for particular pilot offices. Human resources management tools will also be improved, especially job descriptions, the job evaluation scheme, recruitment systems, periodical civil servant assessment and the drafting of career paths. The development and implementation of the Assessment Centre for Polish Administration is also planned in order to modernise and improve the effectiveness of recruitment tools. A Recruitment Manual to guarantee an honest and consistent approach to recruitment at all levels along with a Management Manual for the Polish civil service are being drafted. Recently the pilot training on improving human resources management tools was provided to trainers who will deliver further training in the cascade system.

Under the second component a data base containing information on the civil service corps will be developed, implemented and made available for use. It will permit the effective monitoring of the systems of civil service staff management and training.

The third component of the project envisages carrying out an information and promotion campaign and opening the Civil Service Information Centre. It is very important for Poland to make information on the civil service widely available to the general public as well as to deepen common understanding of the civil service idea.The project should react to new problems occurring in the course of its implementation. For example it has turned out that in Poland strategic and business management is poorly known among the civil servants. Therefore major emphasis has been placed on the training of directors in this area. The Office of Civil Service held a conference and workshops on strategic and business planning for Directors-General as well as Directors and Deputy Directors of Departments in pilot offices. At present people are working on mission statements and strategic plans in six pilot offices. It seems that providing additional training on strategic management is a good example of rapid reaction to new challenges appearing in the course of project implementation.

As a result of many meetings between short-term experts and employees in pilot offices a report appeared on the motivation system. It recommends the delegation of responsibilities as well as the clear definition of competencies in pilot offices. An increasing role should be played by training units in the offices.

Recommendations on the pay system stress the need to reduce the disproportions in pay levels in and between offices. This outside view of our partners from EU Member States is a valuable contribution to our reform programme.

Twinning projects are undoubtedly important and valuable tools for strengthening the administration in Poland. They allow us to accelerate the building of our modern Civil Service. One very important aspect consists in the fact that the project is implemented in more than one office. Thanks to close co-operation among 13 pilot offices it is possible to establish good practices which, in the near future, will be available for use by the remaining offices in Government administration. Thus, its results will cover the whole public administration.

The experiences collected so far prove that it is necessary to be realistic about the direct results of the twinning project[12]. Change in public administration is in the first place a question of organisational culture rather then procedures. This change requires much time in order to eliminate bureaucratic habits inherited from the period of centrally planned economy.

There is a belief that twinning co-operation will become a catalyst for desirable change by improving public administration. Thanks to twinning projects Poland has the opportunity to become familiar with detailed solutions from the EU Member States as well as to select and then adopt those which are most adequate for our country.

An important advantage of twinning co-operation is participation of civil servants from EU Member States, not consultants from outside the public administration who often do not understand the specific nature of the initiative. In consequence, an international network of co-operation between public officials from Poland and other European countries is being created in a natural way. We hope that this kind of co-operation will continue after Poland's accession to the EU. Therefore twinning co-operation for strengthening public administration is of great value to our country.

4. Convergence of the Polish Civil Service System with the EU Models

In general, it is possible to distinguish two Civil Service models existing in the European countries.

The first model is a traditional career system, also referred to as the closed system. It is characterised by the division of Civil Service into levels, grades and corps. Recruitment is usually done to fill the lowest positions while promotions occur as a result of appointments, at times preceded by internal competitive examinations. Employees' entitlements (pay levels, duration of vacation) are closely linked to the grade held. The starting point for the model is the assumption that public administration pursues objectives different from the private sector, hence employing different recruitment criteria, evaluation and employee assessment systems, taking into account the nature of tasks performed. This model reflects Continental mind-sets, for example the German and French legal approach, with a marked recognition for administrative procedures and hierarchies. Among the weaknesses, it is possible to enumerate a lack of motivation to improve work quality combined with a rigid remuneration system and lack of competition, high Civil Service costs as a result of guaranteed employment and pay levels, as well as low adaptability to the EU situation in which a free flow of labour is possible.

The second model is referred to as the position system or or the open system. Recruitment is carried out for particular vacancies, frequently by holding open competitive examinations for senior staff positions. In this system employment is frequently based on contract. The basis for employee assessment, which determines promotion and career, is individual professional achievement and not membership of a particular Civil Service group. The system is characterised by flat hierarchical structures, closeness between the administration and the citizen, and result-orientation. Close connections between the public and private sectors are expressed, for instance, in terms of a mutual labour flow between the two sectors and the application of similar selection and assessment criteria. Managing skills are more important than formal qualifications. This model is more typical of Anglo-Saxon and Scandinavian countries. The weaknesses include weak connection between the servant, the organisation and work performed; great vulnerability to external factors, not always related to the interests of the state; and low effectiveness in long-term activities, in

---

[12] Important remarks and recommendations can be found in the reports of the short-term experts, which are available on www.sluzbacywilna.gov.pl/raporty.htm.

particular those which require keeping state secrecy. The career system in its purest shape occurs in France, while the position system is usual in Great Britain. The characteristics of both models are presented in Table 1.

Table 1. Two Models of Civil Service in Europe

Closed System	Open System
Recruitment only to entry positions	Recruitment also to mid-career jobs
Specific diplomas and educational background for specific careers	No specific diplomas, but specific skills set as requirements for the particular post
No recognition of professional experience outside the public sector	Recognition of professional experience outside the public sector
Formal recruitment procedures	No specific formal selection methods
Training periods for beginners	No training period for newly recruited staff
Permanent tenure	No permanent tenure guarantee
Statutory remuneration scheme	Individual payment based on collective agreements
Set progression on the salary scale	No set progression
Seniority system	No seniority system
Special regulations for labour negotiations	Same negotiation position as in the private sector

Source: A. Auer, Ch. Demmke, R. Polet, Civil Services in the Europe of Fifteen.
EIPA, Maastricht 1996, p. 137-138.

The open and closed models rarely occur in pure forms. The countries characterised by the typical open system include Sweden, the Netherlands and Great Britain, while the closed system occurs in Belgium, France, Germany, Greece and Luxembourg. The remaining seven EU member states combine the elements of both systems with one or the other prevailing[13].

How does the Polish Civil Service system compare to other models existing in the EU Member States? Is it a closed (or Continental) career system, or an open system? Let us look at specific elements of the system, following the order presented above in Table 1.

Recruitment in Poland applies to positions at all levels of the Civil Service. Announcements of vacancies do not solely cover lower-level jobs, but also middle- and upper-levels, including Directors' positions, also staffed by means of competitive examinations. Hence, this is as an open-system solution.

Requirements
In order to fill a particular Civil Servant position it is necessary to have formal education usually at university level, and for a lower job, secondary education. Yet this is not a sufficient requirement since the recruitment is open and competitive; it is designed to find people with the skills necessary for a given job. Each time requirements are indicated in a job description; real skills necessary to perform a given job are taken into account, not simply particular certificates and diplomas. Such skills are frequently checked by adequate tests. Hence this is an open-system solution.

Professional experience outside the public sector is taken into account while calculating the time-related employment bonus in the Civil Service, the anniversary bonus and the one-time exit bonus on retirement. Solely for Civil Servants is the duration of employment in public administration taken into account for the Civil Service bonus based on grade, additional holiday leave and the additional leave allowed to improve one's health.

---

[13] See A. Auer, Ch. Demmke, R. Polet, *Civil Services in the Europe of Fifteen*, EIPA, Maastricht 1996, p. 131.

Recruitment procedures
Recruitment for the Civil Service lies in the hands of the Director-General of the office, including the selection of particular recruitment procedures applied in a given office. The Director-General has to guarantee the openness and competitiveness of selection, as well as access to information on vacancies in the Civil Service, by providing the necessary information inside the office, and publishing the announcement in the Civil Service Bulletin. Recruitment for vacant managing positions stays in the hands of the Head of Civil Service. It is assumed that in future only Civil Servants will be eligible for those positions. Applicants taking part in a competitive examinations will be required to show knowledge indispensable for task performance in a given position, the appropriate predispositions and attitudes as well as managing skills. Existence of recruitment procedures is characteristic of the closed system.

Preparatory service
Every person employed for the first time by the Civil Service spends a six months' preparatory service in the course of which they gain the knowledge and skills necessary for functioning in the state administration for a given office[14]. The curriculum consists of 160 hours of lectures and exercises, covering administrative law, public finances, European integration, public official's status and culture of office work. In the course of the preparatory service the employee is employed for a fixed period of time. The passing of an examination at the end of this period brings the preparatory service to a successful conclusion and is the basis for signing an open-ended contract. The preparatory service is a solution typical of the career system, i.e. the closed system.

Guarantee of employment
There is a difference in the status of the Civil Servant as compared to the employee in the Civil Service. Civil Servants are people who meet particular requirements (including university-level education and a good command of a foreign language) and have passed the qualification procedures. Civil Servants remain in protected employment. Today they constitute a small group[15] in comparison to the pool of Civil Service employees, whose employment contracts are open-ended (a considerable number of people appointed under the 1982 Act, whose employment in the transition period until 2004 is protected, are not taken into account here). Thus, it is possible to say that the full guarantee of Civil Servant employment comes from closed-system solutions while for Civil Service employees open-system solutions are applied.

Pay system
The pay system is directly regulated by the Civil Service Act and the Regulation by the President of the Council of Ministers, issued on this basis[16]. The principles adopted in the regulations define the level of base pay for every Civil Service corps member: the base amount, as determined in the Budget Law, is multiplied by an individual co-efficient. Yet, the system grants considerable freedom in determining individual salaries, since particular positions are ascribed to a wide range of positions, whereas pay levels are broadly determined. This legal regulation of pay levels is a solution typical of the career system.

---

[14] The detailed curriculum for the preparatory service was published in the Civil Service Bulletin, No 3(35) of February 2000, and on the Office website.
[15] The total number of civil servants stood at 830 persons at the end of September 2001.
[16] See Official Journal No 89 of 30 October 1999.

The principles for increasing pay levels

The amounts of pay increases are determined in the Budget Law. The system provides for an automatic pay indexation, taking into account inflation. A problem for the Polish administration is the differences between salaries received in similar positions but in different offices. In the course of work on the reform, it is claimed that broader and more flexible principles to determine pay levels should be introduced, based on the assumption that pay systems should create conditions to favour linking levels of employees' remuneration with the quality of their work[17]. It is also considered that the systemic increase in pay levels should not exceed 50% of the planned inflation indicator. The remaining 50% of the increase should be used to create a system of motivation-based pay increases, while the increase in pay over the inflation level should be used to correct disproportions between average pay levels in particular offices. The Polish system of pay increases is then similar to the career system, yet new suggestions favour the introduction of mechanisms characteristic of the open system.

The seniority system

This system assumes that the levels of remuneration should depend on the importance of a given position for the functioning of the organisation, accountability and the results achieved. There is no direct link between base remuneration levels and the employee's age or duration of employment. Hence this solution could be identified as an open-system solution. Yet, in the practice of the Polish administration, the seniority system is attractive, since it is difficult to reduce the remuneration of an employee with considerable seniority in a situation in which the value of his/her work is overestimated. Looking at the scarcity of resources in the hands of Directors-General, it is also difficult to increase the remuneration of young employees, the value of whose work is underestimated. Changing this practice will require time.

Negotiating employment conditions

There are no mechanisms allowing for conditions of employment to be negotiated. Employment relationships in the Civil Service stem from the public law. They are single-handedly defined by the Act and cannot be amended by way of signing any agreement between the employer and employee organisations. This solution is characteristic of the career system.

In sum, we can say that a mixed Civil Service system exists in Poland. Components characteristic of the closed-career system include preparatory service, protected employment for Civil Servants, statutory pay indexation and employment rooted in the public law. While the components of the open position system include recruitment to all levels, staffing senior positions by way of holding open competitive examinations, rewarding competencies proper to a given job, linking remuneration to accountability level and the outputs achieved. The peculiarity of the Polish system lies in the fact that the principles proper to the career system are applicable to a greater extent to Civil Servants, while the principles characteristic of the position system are applicable to Civil Service employees who definitely outnumber their colleagues in the Civil Service Corps.

---

[17] Analiza systemu wynagrodzen w sferze budzetowej [Analysis of pay system in the budget sector], Cross-Ministry Team for Developing a Complex Analysis of the Pay System in the Budget Sector, February 2001.

5. Conclusion

It is necessary to conclude that the Polish model of the Civil Service meets EU requirements. Open and competitive selection and the principle of employee assessment based on merit have already been established. At the same time the Civil Service system in Poland requires permanent up-grading both in the context of EU integration and the effectiveness of public sector management. There is also need to watch carefully the processes which occur in the public administrations of EU Member States – for they have accumulated greater and more diversified experiences from functioning under democracy over a longer period of time and may indeed provide a useful pattern for candidate countries. Co-operation under the PHARE Programme has successfully served as an effective instrument in assisting the Polish Civil Service to adjust to EU standards and in supporting its integration into the European Union.

East-West Co-operation in Public Sector Reform
F. van den Berg et al. (Eds.)
IOS Press, 2002

95

Learning Co-operation from Non-co-operation: Two Cases of Public Administration Development in Central and Eastern Europe

Pertti Ahonen*

Abstract. This is a study with a phenomenological leaning, it includes two case studies on institutional and capacity development in a Candidate Member State to the European Union. For reasons of research ethics the cases will remain anonymous. A special type of correlation exists between the phenomenological orientation, which helps fix one's attention on extremes and paradoxes, and the cases, which pose problems in ensuring sustainable east-west co-operation. The analysis of the cases brings forth consultant isolation, heavy politicisation of issues, institutions and procedures, and the consequences of rapid, hard-to-manage change. The cases reveal an oversupply of institutional and capacity development services and mutual crowding out by consultants. Various organisations turned out to be very different as to their readiness to co-operate; the organisations that most needed capacity development were the least keen to receive it and vice versa. There are several lessons to be learned. Large, complicated projects funded by multi- or bi-lateral donors may remain more symbolic than substantive; they showcase good intentions but leave much to desire in their implementation. Instead of the "solitary confinement" of individual project experts, teamwork, albeit no panacea, turns out to have definite advantages. Unilateral improvements to project principles and cycles in the EU and the Member States would remedy part of the problems. However, there are no simple solutions to problems arising from the political necessity of involving partners from many Member States in EU projects. Moreover, while "hard" aspects can be managed, such as "injecting" the *acquis communautaire* into each Candidate Member State, it is harder to deal with "soft" aspects including sustainable east-west co-operation. Ultimately, we not only need to multiply and make known success stories as "best practices" and "benchmarks", but we must also probe cases to verify whether stories of failure or near-failure also have existential lessons to teach us.

1. Setting the Scene

A distinction between an "east" and a "west" has continued to beset Europe although, in comparison to Asia, all Europe is definitely part of a geographical west. The focus of this study is on certain *intellectual* aspects of east-west *co-operation partnerships of institutional and capacity development*. The *purpose* of this study of two cases is to

* Dr. Pertti Ahonen, Professor of Public Management and Policy, European Institute of Public Administration, EIPA (Netherlands)

highlight an unexpected and paradoxical feature. Although both cases involve structured co-operation in terms of Jenei *et al.'s* [1] scheme, this co-operation turned out to be deceptive in many respects. The CEE country involved is one of the EU Candidate Member States.

This is a study with a phenomenological approach. Each application of such an approach is a humanistic enterprise that cannot be accomplished "by the book", and books on phenomenological methods are only compromises [2]. Phenomenological approaches *reduce* phenomena to their barest elements. Without reduction, we encounter only bland or chaotic everyday experience or remain under the spell of the received views of the latest "fads" and "buzzwords" [3]. Phenomenological approaches take into account *personal experience*. Each human being has a good grasp of his or her situation and therefore *foreknowledge*. This has been strongly emphasised, for instance, by *Anthony Giddens* [4]. However, mere foreknowledge is not enough, but the "hermeneutics of suspicion" [5] is needed as well in order to penetrate beyond everyday appearances and the received views.

Phenomenological approaches fix attention on *boundary situations* [6]: extremes, crises, paradoxes, irreconcilable contradictions, and absurdity. The phenomenological investigator is certainly not looking for "trouble" where it is not. However, very frequently things do not go smoothly, we meet resistance from things and people, and our projects run into jeopardy [7]. Although we learn from the smooth-running "best practices", we also learn from what resists our efforts. If we only read and write success stories, we maintain a world paradoxically analogous to the previous Soviet empire, which did not allow the slightest criticism of its assumed "best of all possible worlds".

A phenomenological approach implies what are nowadays called *"qualitative methods"*. In the same vein, it implies *case study research"* [8], although the 19th century term "ideographic study" would be more fitting. This is a clinical study, and ethical considerations required anonymity.

2. Outline of the Two Cases

2.1   The First Case: Creating Follow-Up Capacity to Government Reforms

The history of the first case starts in 1997 soon after the CEE country in question had received feedback to its membership application from the European Commission. The project was defined under the EU-Phare programme, with the target of rendering assistance towards the target country's membership preparation by means of *institutional and capacity development*. The project purpose was to strengthen certain parts of the target country's administration that the Commission judged to be substandard. The project revolved around a set of key *reform programmes* that the government of the target country had launched. The project objective was to help the target country to create *follow-up capacity* to those programmes, to find out about the achievements of the actual follow-up measures, and to help the country stabilise sustainable follow-up capacity for the future. From the outset the project setting was very *complicated*, because the project targeted several ministries, the Prime Minister's Office and a set of other organisations.

The European Commission organised a *competition* for the project, and a *consortium* with several members from several Member States won the contract. The *main partner* did not come from the same country as the *host organisation* of the *individual consultant* whose experiences the cases chart. The focal consultant had a role defined in the master plan of the project. The project plan prescribed a *strong division of labour* between the individual consultants, and little if any *team work* was presupposed. A local individual consultant contracted by the consortium's main partner was supposed to help with the fieldwork of our target individual consultant. The consultant was no part of any earlier stage of the project implementation, and he arrived only after the project activities assigned to him had started. There was some early *sharing of documentation*, however, such as the inception report. Our individual consultant was involved with the project for about six months and made several field trips.

The very purpose of the activities carried out by our individual consultant was, *first*, one of fact-finding to collect sufficient background information to organise the first seminar. *Second*, the consultant was supposed to prepare a background study on policy reform follow-up activities in selected EU Member States and present the preliminary results to the first seminar. *Third*, another seminar would deliver ever-increasing final results, including preliminary recommendations that combined analysis results from the target country and comparable experiences gained in the Member States. *Fourth*, a further seminar was supposed to continue along the same lines, and *fifth*, a final seminar was to confirm the results.

In actual practice, the situation was not as simple as presumed in the project planning documents. The project start and implementation had been *delayed*, and the acute need to establish reform follow-up became questionable, especially because the reforms had almost been completed by this stage. Moreover, the *citizens* had a negative attitude towards a few of the reforms, which made the government hesitant to pursue the follow-up. Finally, the government had launched plans for *major reorganisation* both in the fields related to the reforms and in those administrative departments that were charged with following up the reforms. In this situation of *panta rei*, everything flowing, the project lacked a fixed anchorage.

2.2. The Second Case: Analysing and Evaluating in Order to Plan Capacity Development

In the second case, a Member State government had agreed with the Candidate Member State government to establish a capacity enhancement programme in view of the candidate's imminent Community membership. As in the first case, a *competition* was held, and a consulting organisation at the head of a *consortium* had won the contract. Our target *individual consultant's organisation* was again part of the consortium. A set of tasks was assigned to this person. The tasks involved *analysis* and *evaluation* of the situation in quite *a few organisations* of the target country's national government with a view to organising subsequent training to enhance the capacity to deal with European affairs. In the target country, there was a European Affairs Committee with high ministerial representation and a permanent organisation, the Office of European Affairs, feeding to the Committee and co-ordinating the management of European affairs in the various national government organisations. The overall organisation structure was a prototype for the EU affairs administration that would take over on the target country's membership. As in the first case, the *project setting was complicated* and, what is more, it was made up of an even higher number of organisations than in the first case.

Our individual consultant was supposed to carry out the analyses and evaluations according to a structured *scheme* and *report* without delay while still in the field. For about two months, the consultant made a few field trips to the target country for the analyses and evaluations. During the trips he was also in contact with representatives of the main partner in the project consortium.

3. Analysing the First Case

3.1 "A Glass Bubble", Politicisation, and Rapid Change

One spring day our focal consultant arrived at the capital city of the target country for the very first consulting mission. The first weekday the consultant appeared in the project office that was supposed to provide support for the mission. It soon turned out that the local consultants were very busily engaged in other projects and could not give our consultant's project high priority.

Soon interviews ensued to establish the groundwork for the activities that our consultant was supposed to carry out later. When the consultant compared these interview experiences with those in previous projects in other countries, he could not help noticing that this time the meetings were few and he did not have his usual say in the matter in order to access interviewees. On occasion, the locals interviewed spoke quickly in the local language without any explanation to our individual consultant. This appeared substandard compared to the situation one might expect if an interpreter had been engaged. In a few the interviews, the consultant felt isolated, as though in a *glass bubble,* in the absence of a command of the local language and because the meetings typically had not been organised much beforehand to enable good preparation by all concerned. It turned out that there were almost no possibilities for *checking* any information even when it remained in doubt during an interview. Because the interviews were limited in number, cross-checking was also ruled out.

Some written *material* was available, but it was scant in comparison to what our focal consultant had been accustomed to on prior missions. Our focal consultant was frustrated by the shortage of material, despite the fact that his basic duty was not to analyse circumstances in the target country but bring experiences gained in the EU countries to the attention of the local civil servants. Yet he felt that to *contextualise* the EU experiences, he should indeed know more about the country that would receive the benefits of comparative knowledge.

Our consultant noticed that the general atmosphere in the field covered by the project was *politicised*. Caution and reluctance to commit themselves and, on occasion, reluctance to co-operate, could be understood to a certain extent, considering that background. Very many senior civil servants were evidently worried about losing their jobs, should the opposition come to power in the next elections. Although the position of career civil servant had been defined in the target country, these civil servants were still few in number, and therefore many civil servants were in some danger of losing their jobs. This was an experience that our focal consultant had also found in previous assignments in other countries.

Another aggravating factor was that one of the main functions covered by the project was being *reorganised*. The situation was further aggravated by uncertainty as to whether anything would happen after all. The government had made additional public plans, but there was even more uncertainty as whether these would lead to actual changes. Should any real changes happen, the project would run the risk of being *outdated* and *ill-timed*. An *absurd* feature turned out to be the reluctance of the final donor to allow changes in the project even if many of these had become well established between the project idea and its implementation eighteen to thirty months later.

3.2 Eager EU Experts Planned Training for Over-Trained Locals

The project was supposed to consist partly of *training* the locals and the training was to generate *material* on the basis of which the project would draw its final conclusions. The intermediate and the final results of the project were to be delivered in training seminars. In the course of the project activities, there should be vigorous *learning* in the target country, based on experiences gained in established EU Member States.

In the first seminar, a good number of participants showed up, although the training room was not overfull. However, many of the participants left early and were replaced by other participants, some of who also left early. This was in part a *technical problem* brought about by the proximity of the training quarters to the centre of the capital city. A feeling of being inside a *glass bubble* followed again, albeit less acutely, for our focal consultant because of the consecutive translation which also slowed down the pace of presentation. Our focal consultant again felt he was in a glass bubble though not so keenly as before, he attributed this impression to the consecutive translation which slowed down the pace of presentation.

The participants who attended turned out to be reasonably *interested* in the theme, although they kept to the point about as often as they digressed from it. In this respect the experience was better than those the consultant had encountered on other occasions. The highest-ranking participant was behind many of the conclusions to be drawn from the seminar.

During the last project seminar, our consultant ended up experiencing further *absurdit*ies. Both among local and EU consultants, the *contributions* tended to treat *general* issues that seemed to have little to do with the project theme, although the project had been ongoing for quite some time and empirically grounded conclusions and recommendations were called for. *Was this all just talk?* Our focal consultant had to conclude that to a considerable extent the project remained *symbolic*: the important point was not what it contributed but that it had been set up in the first place and that it was actually implemented at least in one way or another.

4. Analysing the Second Case

4.1 From Cordial Co-operation to Reluctance and Rejection by Some Target Organisations

During the second project, one of the consultant's task was to approach comparable organisations. *Ex ante* there were no signs that a *"tale of degradation"* would ensue. In the *first organisation* all went well: a good relationship with the management ensued, the workforce appeared reasonably motivated, there was evidence of skill and toil, and a willingness to dedicate time for a reasonably co-operative partnership with the consultant. There was also reference to what some organisation members saw in their mind's eye: themselves strutting around in the Brussels corridors of power as permanent European civil servants.

At the back of the consultant's mind, the nightmare lurked that things might not be equally well in the other organisations. To put it biblically: *what if it is the "healthy" who are looking for healing only*, not those in need of measures of institution and capacity development? As a matter of fact, there appeared the first sign of what was soon to be perceived, because a fourth organisation declined all interviews and denied access to any consultant.

The *second organisation* turned out to be a harder case. It took a few days before even the first interview could take place. Even then, the civil servant being interviewed was not allowed enough time to reasonably complete the interview. Our focal consultant continued efforts to gain access to the core of the second organisation. The section of the organisation where he gained admittance had only recently moved from the core to another part of the organisation.

Finally, our consultant was able to have a chat with the head of the focal part. This person's views contributed to a sense of *absurdity* in that *the target section of the second organisation should clearly and definitely have been included*. However, in the interviewee's opinion, the *need* for institutional and capacity development *was so grave* and the employees were so overworked, *that it was not feasible* to satisfy the need for development. He also pointed out that for various reasons, including lack of institutional and capacity development activities, too many employees were likely to leave during the next year anyway.

Our focal consultant carried out only a handful of interviews in the section of the second organisation to which he gained access. Even this proceeded slowly because of the considerable workload of the employees. Fortunately as it turned out, our focal consultant came across another expatriate consultant, who was making his last trip to the target organisation to wrap up a twinning project carried out bilaterally between the target country and a donor country. Our focal consultant received the impression that the twinning had worked well and that permanent ties had most probably been created.

Trying to "enter" the third organisation turned out to be a *Via Dolorosa*. Our consultant's "frustration quotient" soared, proving the trite dictum that the wrong kind of stress is of two kinds: one from too much work, while the other stems from the inability to get work going, let alone done.

The focal consultant was able to arrange a very short meeting that with the departing key expert in the third target organisation. The interviewee had been proposed to the consultant as the real *"brains"* of the organisation. After that,, there were no signs of further interviews, which our focal consultant was not in a position to arrange himself. After *a few days lost* a local contact person was able to organise a discussion between our consultant and *two high-ranking representatives of the target organisation*. It was confirmed that a recent organisational reform had led to the separation of the organisation from its previous host organisation and to an independent organisational status. However, the new organisation had been started *without a budget*, which had been made available only months after the body was set up, and only a few days before the very date of the discussion. Given that the *recruitment process* was lagging, only a handful of the target personnel were sitting in their offices.

The pain expressed by our focal consultant was partly ethical. First, there were personal *pangs because he was not able to do his job well or even do it at all.* Second, *there were pangs because donor* money *was being* wasted *in the vain efforts to gain access to the third organisation, not to mention the fourth one. All was legally right, money legally allocated was being legally expended, but substantially things were wrong.*

4.2 Inter-Consultant Crowding Out

As regards the second project, our focal consultant had been advised that one of the few other individual consultants who were dealing with the same organisations was around. It turned out that the other consultant had acquired a profound experience of the absurdity common to consultant work. The latter pointed out that *individual consultants swarm around*. The *same civil servants* were approached again and again, the same questions were posed again and again, and those civil servants most under fire were unable to progress with their work because of the incessant interviews.

The consultant colleague pointed out that there was *hardly any co-ordination* between the work of the various "donors", if this word can be used both of the European Commission and the governments of each Member State and other multilateral and bilateral actors. Although formal co-ordination exists, the life cycles of projects and the planning and presence cycle of donors varies, often times the projects have related foci.

After the meeting our focal consultant felt that he had indeed received a *partial explanation* for his impression of the absurd. Indeed, it hardly makes sense if EU consultants, probably rather expensive for those who ultimately pay the bill, and in any event paid many times more than the locals, swarm around in such numbers that they crowd each other out, consume a substantial part of the working time of the local target civil servants, and probably contribute to the rise of further projects, which demolish further chunks of scarce time.

4.3 Forced Feeding of Training?

In the three-organisation project, our focal consultant traced another individual consultant. The other consultant was a relative long-termer. The encounter became a revelation that one of the target organisations was in rather bad shape. This confirmed the focal consultant's own experiences.

The other consultant sarcastically pointed out that should the substantial amount of training provided work, the *target country would have Europe's best expertise* in the field it covered in one of the policy areas of the EU. However, the other consultant doubted if much of that training would be relevant, once the target country indeed becomes an EU member. He doubted if most of the civil servants having received that training would still be anywhere near their present jobs. He also doubted whether the theoretical and case-oriented training would really have taught the target civil servants to run the procedures of which they should take charge.

5. Conclusions

5.1   Summary of Results

The *final table* (Table 1) summarises the two case analyses. The table is organised according to the central foci of the study. The table also includes a column where the author has recorded previous experiences to compare them with those of the two cases analysed.

The results do not reveal a world apart from what other studies have covered. Some of the experiences in the two projects refer to *technical* and *organisational* problems that can be relieved by the appropriate means. An example is the *"glass bubble"*, metaphorically used to characterise the situation of the consultant with only scant access to interviewees and placed behind a linguistic wall. Despite the slowness of the procedure, an interpreter may be a worthwhile investment to put the expensive consultant expertise to full use. Another example is the undoubted justification for allowing *adjustments in project* in so far as the situation changes, or in projects that are carried out on the basis of bygone reasons.

There were also combined problems of phenomenological *"dead objectifications"* and technical and organisational faults. Here, complicated structures and chains of project implementation were typical. From the phenomenological point of view, formal procedures may overwhelm human beings and reduce their possibilities for fruitful, creative interaction. In the technical perspective, we are dealing with problems that have been tackled in *implementation research* and related efforts ([9], [10]).

The phenomenological approach played a role in both project analyses in helping *reduce phenomena to their essentials* and in focusing on extreme situations, crisis, and absurdity. There was no need to look far for such features, and the experiences greatly boosted the consultant's knowledge. It was especially true in the first case where the *smooth*, legalistic *surface* of project implementation turned out to *hide substantial problems* with meaning, commitment on the part of the beneficiaries, lack of co-operation and lack of project timeliness. In the second case, the individual consultant encountered very different organisations in his personal small *Via Dolorosa*. He had every reason to adhere to a "hermeneutics of suspicion" and not to believe literally in what the project documents and the lofty political principles behind them said. His two consultant colleagues were no lesser instinctive users of the same type of hermeneutics.

5.2 Seven Lessons Learned

The analysis or the two cases suggests a set of *lessons*, some of which are summarised in the final table. *First*, there are projects funded by multi- and bi-lateral donors in the CEE countries with an import more *symbolic* than substantive [11]. Even where the symbolic character of some projects is more or less intended by the donors, this is not easy for an expert consultant whose loyalty is towards a specific field of expertise and not towards successful public relations activities. A consultant who wants to preserve his or her integrity may find it hard to work for projects that are ends in themselves and a matter of prestige instead of being able to achieve improvements. Where a consultant can do otherwise, he or she might consider dropping out of projects that are symbolic only, or not committing him- or herself to such projects at all.

Second, although no one questions the necessity of built-in legal and regularity safeguards in complicated projects with stakeholders in numerous countries, *formalism for formalism's sake* is a risk. There is also the related risk of *"dead objectifications"* emerging as obstacles to interaction between human beings, to their creativity and to improvements they may be able to bring about. *Flexibility* appears as a countervailing power to the objectifications, although there is no blueprint for how to nurture during-project flexibility from the project initiation phase onwards. The second set of lessons relates to observations made within the EU institutions themselves, i.e. that formal legality and regularity are not enough. However, in the two projects the wider concerns of efficiency, effectiveness, relevance and sustainability did not come to the fore [12].

Third, the two cases suggest that the performance of an individual consultant is particularly vulnerable if he or she is left to work alone. The focal consultant had good personal experiences of *teamwork*, and teamwork appears as a welcome alternative to the *solitary* efforts in the two project cases. Teamwork is no panacea, but in comparison to the "solitary confinement" of individual expert consultants during field missions, teamwork may have its strengths. Teamwork might also better enable encounters between the EU and the CEE consultants and upgrade encounters between the EU consultants and the domestic experts working in the actual practice of CEE public administration. Finally, teamwork might, better than vulnerable solitary work, enable the building of strong relations, and not merely passing o-operation.

Fourth, the two cases do not raise the least concern regarding the ability or willingness of the CEE partners to engage in co-operation. However, there is a lesson to be learnt. In the two cases analysed, the burden of proof makes the scales tilt towards the EU partners, and even more to the donor arrangements that were not particularly conducive to in-depth co-operation. In the two cases, *unilateral improvements* carried out by donors could lead to substantial improvements increasing the chances of accomplishing sustainable co-operation ties.

Fifth, the two cases refer to general problems in *European projects* in the CEE countries. Although phenomenological studies are not studies to be generalised, they may still suggest what to study in other contexts. A European project may involve the need to create project consortia with members from several Member States. Quite often a certain turn-taking seems to prevail to allow consulting agencies from different countries to win projects. This may be an aspect of European democratic equality, but it is not an aspect of efficiency and effectiveness. Improved allocation of projects to project consortia and improved constitution of such consortia is another lesson from the two-case study.

One may also ask if the other practice, also dictated by European democratic equality, of *spreading widely experiences and practices in the Member States in the CEE* is always worth the effort. Instead, the Candidate Member States might benefit more from support for analysing their own situation and their own prospects. After all, it hardly makes sense to turn the CEE countries into showcases of existing solutions in the existing Member States or, for that reason, the United States. There is also the related lesson that both *multi-lateral* (i.e. EU) and *bi-lateral* (i.e. Member State) *projects in the CEE with strong European features* may be *particularly prone* to complications *and management problems* in their project cycles, their implementation structures and chains, or both. Most EU resources used in such projects stem ultimately from the European taxpayers, either directly or indirectly, and there is every reason to ensure that the taxpayers' money is not wasted.

Sixth, there are aspects of "European" projects to be implemented in the CEE countries that are likely to be easy, whereas there are aspects that are likely to be difficult. Likewise, on the scale of individual projects some parts are likely to be on the easy end of the scale, and others on the difficult end. The two cases suggest that it is almost too easy to organise training as such. Moreover, the more technically oriented the training is, such as legal training to enable the absorption of the *acquis communautaire* in the Candidate Member States, the easier its technical organisation is likely to be. As a matter of fact, in the second case it was possible to ascertain that the absorption of *acquis* was well under way in the most successful of the three target organisations. However, the *"softer"* aspects a project or its parts should handle, the harder the challenges are likely to be.

Seventh, the ultimate lesson suggested by this two-case study is that stories involving aspects of *failure* are no less instructive than success stories. This is hardly a point that can be proven to anybody who is diametrically opposed to the above opinion. However, whoever applies a phenomenological approach sees that learning also flows from the experience of failure, frustration and even suffering. Let us assume that a project seems to be an excessively formalistic enterprise or an excessively symbolic act and that it is greeted with some apprehension by its intended recipients. We can ask ourselves if such a project does not teach us more and not less than a project that calls nobody's peace of mind into question but runs as sheer smooth routine without anybody seeing the point of questioning anything.

References

[1]   G. Jenei, L.T. LeLoup and F. van den Berg, East-West Cooperation in Public Administration: A Framework for Assessment. To be published in: G. Jenei, L.T. LeLoup and F. van den Berg (eds), East-West Cooperation in Public Adminstration: Lessons, Assessments, and Prospects after a Decade, IOS Press, Amsterdam, 2001.
[2]   C. Moustakas, Phenomenological Research Methods. Sage, London, 1994.
[3]   D. Collins, Management Fads and Buzz words: Critical-Practical Perspectives, Routledge, London, 2000.
[4]   A. Giddens, Central Problems in Social Theory, University of California Press, Berkeley, CA.

[5]   H.L. Dreyfus, Being-in-the-World: A Commentary on Heidegger's Being and Time, Division I, MIT Press, Cambridge, MA 1991, p. 345.

[6]   K. Jaspers, *Philosophie,* II, *Existenzerhellung,* 4. ed., 1. ed. 1931, Springer-Verlag, Berlin 1973, p. 201 and onwards.

[7]   M. Heidegger, Sein und Zeit, 1. ed. 1927, Max Niemeyer Verlag, Tübingen 2001. English translation, *Being and Time,* Harper & Row, New York, 1963 In the text, the first page number refers to the German and the second to the English edition, § 40, pp. 184-191/186-189.

[8]   R.E. Stake, The Art of Case Study Research, Sage, London, 1995.

[9]   J.L. Pressman and A.B. Wildavsky, Implementation, 3. ed., University of California Press, Berkeley, CA, 1983.

[10]   S.D. Sieber, Fatal Remedies: The Ironies of Social Intervention, Plenum Press, 1981.

[11]   M. Edelman, Constructing the Political Spectacle, University of Chicago Press, Chicago, 1988.

[12]   Commission of the European Communities, Evaluating Public Expenditure Programmes, European Commission, Brussels, 1997.

Table 1. Summary of the cases studied, and comparable cases

Cases / Dimensions	Case I	Case II	Comparisons with other cases with personal participation of the same consultant
Role of personal experience	Yes, the author was himself the consultant.	Yes, the author was himself the consultant.	(Yes)
Reduction of phenomena to essentials	Essential in analysing the case in this study, e.g.: • Questioning the efficient surface of the project • Revealing lack of commitment by people in the target country • Revealing problems in the implementation of the project	Essential in analysing the case in this study, e.g.: • Revealing crucial differences between the organisations that were targeted • Revealing problems in the implementation of the project	(This study does not focus on the other cases.)
Question of foreknowledge	Consultant was not provided with much material nor enabled to acquire it by himself.	Problems to access the target organisations were not well known beforehand, and ex ante information on those organisations was scant.	Consultant was almost always provided with solid background material and ample opportunities to supplement it.
Extreme situations, crisis, and absurdity	Extreme situations, crises and absurdity revealed that: • The local co-consultant had timing problems • The beneficiaries' commitment was low • Some of the project measures involved duplication • The project was to an extent outdated once it was implemented	Extreme situations, crises and absurdity revealed that: • The target organisations were very different, and the last two could not be approached at all • The organisations most needing improvement were the hardest to approach • There were too many consultants swarming around, and target people were burdened by many interviews and many training sessions	*Extreme situations, crises and absurdity had revealed that:* • Low commitment of recipients suggests that a project may not be really needed as such • Cross-checking of information is essential • Lack of inter-donor co-operation is a common Achilles' heel in development efforts • Projects are often outdated before implemented
Revealed role of dead "objectifications"	The project cycle applied was in part unsuitable. In particular, it was inflexible. Moreover, it presupposed many more stakeholders than could be managed well.	A complicated project structure with long implementation chains and solitary work periods of individual consultants impaired performance.	Although it is politically necessary for an individual consultant to pay lip service to lofty principles, it is also necessary to see the "real world".
Lessons learned	There are projects that are symbolic rather than substantive. An individual consultant must ask him- or herself, if it is possible to drop a project that is outdated.	There are strong assets in team consulting and sharing experiences between individual consultants. Often one learns more from negative than positive experiences.	The lessons that can be learned change as an individual consultant's experience accumulates. Beside learning, there is a constant need to unlearn.

East-West Co-operation in Public Sector Reform
F. van den Berg et al. (Eds.)
IOS Press, 2002

107

Ten Years of Cross-Cultural Co-operation: Lessons, Feelings, Findings

Arcady Prigozhin*

1. Introduction

This book is a good opportunity to assess Eastern (mostly Russian) and Western (mostly Dutch) co-operation. Not in general, but in a specific area of professional activity: development consultancy in management and organisation. A long period of planning and achievement, hope and disillusionment, and substantial advances in the face of remarkable obstacles. I'll describe it from the Russian side and from my personal view. Certainly, I believe both East and West took a common path which proved not to be easy. But the path should prove instructive.

Either on purpose or spontaneously the School of Management Consultants (SMC) of the Academy of National Economy under the Government of the Russian Federation has become a remarkable platform of West- East relations. It is perhaps one of the biggest fora of consultants from all over the world. That's why events and lessons here may be relevant in the context of future East-West relations.

To understand these relations we have to penetrate into the feelings of those who created and took part in them. I am one of them and that is why the picture I'm describing is rather subjective.

The East-West problem has been among the biggest curses on the Russian state and its society for centuries. It displays itself in almost every field – from political to cultural, socio-psychological to legal, and across business and the economy. The SMC is a forum where many of these fields come together.

Established by the Association of Management and Organisation Development Consultants (AMODC), the school has graduates who return for conferences, seminars and master- classes. They create partnerships, form ad hoc groups for common projects or just exchange ideas. They have become accustomed to meeting people of interest in the school, from either East or West, and this has helped them learn new methods.

At the SMC, students have met many experts from the Netherlands, Britain, South Africa, Canada, Israel and the USA. We have recruited groups of graduates and teachers for study tours in the Netherlands, Britain and Canada. We have organised conferences with participants from the West. It is extremely important to mention that several Western consultants have found clients in Russia. SMC has helped them in widening their professional practice in Russia. During SMC classes they have analysed their experience in

* Arcady Prigozhin, Professor, Director of the School of Management Consultants, President of the Association of Management and Organisation Development Consultants (Russia).

Russia in comparison with their domestic practice.

The SMC as an international meeting point came about most notably from a combined Russian and Dutch effort, all because of a crucial role played by a small Dutch consultancy firm. One spring day in 1991, while I was taking part in a conference in Budapest, a Dutch colleague of mine paid great attention to my attempts to explain to an international audience the problems of Soviet organisations. Within a few months I received a letter from him with a proposal to maintain contact. He visited our school in August 1991 accompanied by three colleagues. We started a workshop which was suddenly interrupted by the coup against Mikhail Gorbachev. The tension of the moment was a first common experience: watching together the tanks on television. Co-operation continued afterwards. I initiated a project entitled "Bridge between two cultures". It was supported, after some changes, by our Dutch colleagues and submitted to TACIS. Our very promising "Bridge" project had begun.

2. A micro Marshall plan for two schools

The idea of the "Bridge" project was to assist two new Russian professional schools: the School for Management Consultants in Moscow (SMC) and the School for Conflict Resolution in Kaluga (SCR). They received scholarships, equipment, trainers and study tours.

This micro "Marshall Plan" for both schools has worked out in different ways and led to opposite results. SCR disappeared when it ran out of foreign support. The main reason was a lack of demand for conflict resolution consultancy and mediation in Russia – despite an evident need. Russians are used to and still have a great interest in knowledge and research in this field. Russian entrepreneurs, heads of state and municipal organisations are ready to listen to psychologists and sociologists about how conflicts progress and how to avoid them. But they are not ready to pay consultants to help manage conflicts in their daily practice. The paradox is that one of the nations with the greatest number of conflicts has no demand for conflict resolution. It sounds enigmatic and I suppose the root of this situation is that the majority of Russian leaders fails to accept behavioural technology - as if there is a theoretical interest in negotiation but a habit of ignoring it in practice. Conflict resolution methodology has not suited our domestic management culture until now. That is why the micro "Marshall Plan" failed in the case of the SCR.

Success with the same model in the case of the SMC marks a movement to a maturing demand stimulated by an increasing need from society. Management gradually developed to recognise the value of consultancy. It is a natural- artificial process, a purposeful impact on inevitable tendencies, that has come about exactly at the right time. Therefore using the micro "M-P" model is only rational if it coincides with the actual social requirements.

3. Stages of development of East- West co-operation in the SMC

3.1 Stage I. Appeals (1989-1991)

First one must appreciate that on the Russian side the absolute majority of those acting in the first stage were Western-oriented scientists and teachers, some of them members of the Communist Party (as I was, for example). They participated in attempts to reform the Soviet system. We had visited the West officially and could see its advantages and problems. We had learned enough not to exaggerate Western achievements - unlike the majority of our compatriots.

The main attitude at this stage was: backward USSR (Russia) should borrow managerial skills from the West. Some of us sent messages requesting acceleration of our country's managerial development. I worked out the first version of the "Bridge" project at that period and disseminated it among Western consultants.

So at that time an attitude of "borrowing" was dominant. We tried to form a new professional community of management and organisation development (OD) consultants. Only a few of us adopted this goal as a personal mission and spent a lot of time on this unprofitable activity.

These were the years of Perestroika. Soviet-Russian citizens were paid great attention, and many Westerners were eager to listen to us. That's why at that time the role of an applicant was not so difficult and attitudes toward us were understanding. Again and again we asked for skills and experience. We wanted to open our country to Western management consultancy and to the education of Russian management consultants. We needed a School for Management Consultants.

It is important to be aware of our self-consciousness during that period. From time to time in the 1970s and 1980s I had opportunities to participate in conferences abroad. I suffered very much from the humiliating position of the Soviet delegation (strong control, lack of private money, shame for the actions of our government etc.) But simultaneously I felt the respect of my foreign colleagues. Respect for me as a representative of a superpower. Even enlightened persons respect power. But I shared their fear of uncontrolled power.

Stage II. Direct help (1991-1994)

A group of Dutch consultants spent much time and money on the foundation of the "Bridge" project as it was submitted to TACIS in Brussels. TACIS appreciated our plan very much and we hoped for a considerable sum of money. We were shocked when the TACIS official who had worked with our Dutch-Russian group was substituted and the newcomer had different priorities. I was puzzled not only by the rejection but also by the similarity with Soviet bureaucracy with regard to decisions being reversed. It became clear to us that Western organisations were not so perfect as we had thought. Our Dutch friends were also embarrassed but they convinced their Ministry of Education and Science of the value of our initiative. The "Bridge" became smaller, but it survived.

It was a period in which foreign professionals were idolised in the former USSR. The image of our SMC increased with the participation of Western trainers. Our main attitude at this stage was to learn: What were they? How did they work? Everything was interesting. We learned things in general, not in detail which came later.

During that time we very much appreciated our collaboration with an educational institute named SIOO. Like the SMC, it delivered courses to consultants. In our discussions with SIOO trainers we discovered common problems: such as how management consultants in the Netherlands made students accustomed to dealing with uncertainty and how to teach students to use that uncertainty as an professional opportunity instead of a threat towards themselves.

Thanks to our Dutch colleagues we had opportunities to visit many consultancy firms and even their clients. We studied a lot and were often pleasantly surprised. Good will and money helped us to start our own school. Half or a third of each group of students during this period had a Dutch scholarship. We will never forget that. I am always reminded of this with every new group of students at SMC.

Stage III. New contacts (1993-1995)

In the third period two other institutes suggested programmes for our students. But they were different from the experiences with our initial backers. The new contacts were commercial and needed to be completely financed. And we spotted the difference immediately. Now our main issue was to convince lecturers that we were not professionally naive. Each of them started by explaining simple matters that we had studied many years before. We tried to ask them to be more methodological and empirical but in vain. They saw us as professional nationals to whom they could deliver their standard programme. It was the difference between real interest and commercial services. Nevertheless thanks to these contacts, we could see the great diversity in consultancy.

Stage IV. Saturation (1995-1999)

Abundance of information led us to a more selective approach in our international contacts. Even in previous stages we gradually shifted our preferences to methodology instead of material help. This new attitude was to learn more about empirical methods of consultancy. We often put forward this question, unfortunately without much success. No western colleague refused but instead they tried to describe their methods of organisational diagnostic, group work, conflict resolution etc. But their proposals did not appear to be appropriate or practical. I will return to this point later.

A second change in this stage was the reputation of foreign consultants in Russia. The initial admiration was replaced by disappointment especially from managers. Now local consultants became preferable. The same happened in the school. During these years a new generation of consultants appeared. This generation was not only far more numerous but also much smarter and more successful. These students preferred domestic teachers to foreigners. They looked for methods that had been tried and tested in the "Russian snow".

A third tendency was that our Dutch friends became tired. There were many reasons: from the very beginning, both sides (especially the Dutch) stressed mutuality: we were partners. But on the Russian side we felt they saw themselves more as noble missionaries than as our real equals. The Dutch saw their work as a kind of charity that wasn't as profitable as normal consultancy. A lot of unpaid logistical activities were required of them (to meet, to arrange accommodation, to report to subsidisers etc.)

In reality, the "partnership" model worked out as a "parent-and-child" relationship which in the end became exhausting. Other problems emerged: not everybody was grateful for the support. Some students on scholarships did not complete their studies, others failed to gain a diploma. There were also misunderstandings, and I shall provide two examples in which I was personally involved.

In the beginning, our Dutch colleagues had control of the funding for the "Bridge" project themselves. But one day they suggested that I prepare a new budget. Because of our mutual status I assumed the money was intended only for Russian side and I structured the budget purely according to the SMC's needs. In fact, the money had to be distributed among both parties. The Dutch side was appalled by my plans which they thought were less than honest and too selfish.

On another occasion, I sent only a brief report about the SMC, not wishing to burden my Dutch partners with our problems. I would provide the full details at a later date. Imagine my shock when I was met with strong accusations of foul play. I hesitate to think of all the grievances that I failed to notice. The result was that the majority of our Dutch colleagues became fed up with the SMC and with me. Perhaps this saturation stage was a natural cut-off point for relationships based on good-will.

Stage V. Epilogue (1998-now)

As I said, contact was broken off by our Dutch colleagues. Nowadays our only contacts are with certain individuals who in general have broader interests in Russia. For them, a relationship with the school provides a useful source of information and influence, as well as an involvement in the development of Russia's consulting community. We began to invite them for definite tasks and we have particularly appreciated their role in our conferences and workshops.

4. How professional differences came to affect co-operation

Let me return to my observation during the saturation period. We had gotten into difficulty over the extent of our co-operation. I will analyse this in greater detail, because I have the feeling that this was more complicated than either misunderstanding or ill-will.

4.1 Difficulties in analysing the differences between two cultures

In comparing the two cultures, I found the following three outlooks unsatisfactory:
- a better versus a worse culture;
- a higher versus a lower culture;
- an advanced versus a backward culture.

Driven by patriotism and striving for scientific objectivity I tried to construct a scale with less moral impact. However I only partly succeeded. The huge difference between the two economies and the two management styles constantly pushed one towards one of the pyramids. Had it been a case of merely comparing the art and science of everyday life, then the "one versus another" pyramid would have been perfectly suitable. But because the economic backwardness of Russia (during the crisis) had to be included in the equation, it raised another question. The backwardness and the Soviet perversion had to be distinguished from real, specifically Russian features, i.e. the features of our national business culture. This had to be compared to the specific features of the Dutch business culture. Why was it important? After all, some disadvantages of the Russian culture would be overcome as Russia returned to Europe, but some peculiarities would remain.

Cultural differences within a country can be stronger than the differences between countries. The distinction between people is sometimes greater than the distinction between nations. Contemporary Russian society is so diverse and changes so rapidly that even now Russia's big firms are more diverse in relation to one another than to Western enterprises.

The main problem in comparison is in verifying perceptions, expressions, and opinions based on personal and limited experiences, which come with strong emotional involvement. Many of these are subjective and lead to prejudices and myths. The accumulation of information cannot avoid such limits and conditions. It is important that my remarks are treated in this context.

4.2 Are there categorical differences in management cultures?

Differences between two managerial cultures manifest themselves either in degree (i.e. one culture has greater characteristics than another) or in essence (i.e. what is typical for one culture might be totally irrelevant in another). First some of my observations on essential differences.

a) Let us look at the case of interim managers. If in the Netherlands a manager or a head of a department is ill, does not handle his job well or leaves the organisation, a firm can hire temporary management. If an enterprise is forced to seek radical change and innovation it can also hire temporarily a professional who specializes in implementing changes. They provide the innovation process with the relevant technology and arrange the process according to their knowledge and experience.

These services are unknown in Russia. So Russian managers have to be able to deal with the problems themselves.

b) Another difference is in the role and place of written orders and commands. Usually in a Russian machine-building plant, up to a thousand orders are issued, signed by the "first person". In chemical enterprises there are between 600 and 800 orders. In Dutch enterprises the figures is more like twenty.

The main reason for this difference stems from the fact that the Western management system is built on an organisational structure, i.e. a system of departments, rules and relations, which enable an organisation to function automatically (horizontal management culture). The role of a manager is first of all to develop, improve and renew the structure with a minimum of interference in the work of his employees.

In Russian enterprises and organisations, however, a centralised leadership is adopted: it is built on directions, assignments and instructions. The majority of them are in written form. The importance of organisational order in Russia is not high, staff instructions and department regulations are drawn up roughly and often they do not coincide with the actual duties of employees. Therefore in the situation where a Western worker, an engineer or a civil servant, is inclined to refer to procedures, a Russian turns to his boss. This is the manifestation of the vertical management culture.

c) In Dutch organisations many problem-solving programmes run simultaneously. The programmes are worked out and implemented by a mixed group of professionals from departments. This is an example of a temporary type of horizontal structure.

d) In Western management there is the tradition of solving problems in a direct confrontation between manager and subordinates or between employees of the same level. Their mutual responsibility is sufficient to implement oral assignments and agreements. In this respect, the horizontal management culture is a conventional system of agreements which have been developed during years of unforced co-operation, co-ordination of interests and actions.

In the post-Soviet reality the hypertrophy of one-man management still prevails and the aspiration of top executives is to interfere at almost every lower management level. On the other hand, it often happens in Russia that middle-level managers ask the top executive to sign orders, even though these fall within their competence, thus handing over responsibility to their boss; and the top executive usually agrees to sign these orders. In other words, a vertical culture is not only sustained top-down but bottom-up as well. This explains the abundance of orders in our management practice.

e) Orders differ also in their function. In our culture they represent not only the main means of management, but also the method of transmitting information and intentions to staff. In the West the role of orders is minor; a system of information that flows independently of orders has been developed.

f) In Russia, the deputy manager is usually the technical manager or the general engineer. In the West this position is often fulfilled by the commercial manager. This reflects a prevailing orientation towards production or towards clients and profits.

4.3 Consequences of differences in management culture on co-operation

In table 1 of this article I summarize further differences between the two working fields of Russian and Dutch OD-consultants.

Table 1. Differences in management-style of the clients of consultants

Dutch	Russian
• small is beautiful	• big is beautiful
• evolution from the hope for explicit knowledge to the art of management, intuition, vision and trust	• knowledge as the measurement of an organisation as a social machine
• preference of motivation above compulsion	• preference of compulsion to execute work above motivation
• initiative	• executiveness
• controllability as a common goal	• controllability as a high level of management
• management is orientated towards the use and activity of people ("strategic; human values in an enterprise"); "a useful person in a useful place"; "monthly communication days"; • "tailors approach"; functions and working place are not standard; individual approach is required; annual training, exchange of employees	• management is more orientated towards tasks and goals. An employee is first of all an executor of the executives' requirements. In the social sphere, management takes the form of guardian.
• easily accept their incompetence	• pretend to look competent when they are not
• make promises cautiously, high degree of responsibility	• make promises easily, and are not ashamed of not keeping them
• an oral agreement is as binding as a written one	• an oral agreement is not important, • a written agreement is highly valued
• pay more attention to detail	• pay more attention to the whole, neglect the detail
• negotiate slowly, step by step	• negotiate fast (thoroughness of a counterpart is considered absence of interest, unwillingness to sign contract) • sign a contractsign • sign the contract)
• execution of an assignment by a Western employee can be checked by its final result	• execution of an assignment by a Russian employee (in the CIS) requires continuous control

For this article it is important to stress that, although we are talking about the same profession (management consultants) the content of the work can differ. These differences can limit the possibilities and the values of cooperation. Here are two examples of these limitations.

• It's well known that Western business schools teach management skills. No doubt this is important. But I have seen many cases in which enlightened Russian managers return to their native firms and their colleagues perceive them as strangers; their initiatives are oppressed, their new skills amortised. Their new-found skills do not fit in with a vertical management culture.

• There was once a prevailing attitude that Western trainers should be involved directly in workshops and seminars, lecturing for Russian managers and consultants. But times have now changed and now the majority of foreign professionals appear weaker than home-grown ones. Now we have enough specialists catering for real demand and responding to it successfully. Many times have I witnessed the desperate attempts of Russian participants to convince a Western workshop-organiser to replace his/her compatriot with a reputable local lecturer. But mostly in vain.

More and more Western managers and consultants fail in jobs that can be better filled by their Russian partners. I have heard a variety of explanations: Western money should be paid mostly to Western citizens. The purpose of Western funds is to export the influence of Western culture. The best Western specialists are too busy or too costly to be involved in such modest projects. It is just Western arrogance, etc. Whatever the truth, co-operation without attention to the content of the activities can result in a loss of money and time and a negative reaction.

In table 2, I summarize the difference in work.

Table 2. Differences in management consultancy work

Dutch	*Russian*
• consultants are hired often and on different occasions	• consultants are hired incidentally and on an ad hoc basis
• the client takes responsibility for the implementation of consultants' suggestions	• the consultant takes responsibility for the implementation
• during the consulting period it is customary for consultants and client organisations' employees to work together in groups	• top managers and other employees of client organisations hardly realise the necessity of working together with consultants in groups
• consultants usually work for middle-level management	• consultants usually work for the top manager
• the consulting process is widespread	• expert consulting is widespread
• special attention is paid to consultant's communication skills, confidence, collaboration with his client	• less attention is paid to the psychology of the consultant-client relationship

5. Modest lessons

In conclusion, I will formulate a few modest lessons I have learned about co-operation in the SMC.

5.1   *Only when a initiative of co-operation is tuned in with processes in society can the results be sustained (see case SCR versus SMC). If there is a need but not a demand, a project will fail.*

5.2   *Different phases in development in society can require different attitudes and skills from the partner (see my analysis of phases)*

5.3   *The results of co-operation are strongly influenced by the content of the work of both partners. (see my examples about management styles)*

Note: I would like to thank the following people for their contributions to the SMC. First of all, all the partners of AO, Adviseurs voor Organisatiewerk, Driebergen, The Netherlands (Ernst Marx, Max Rubinstein, Jan Hendriks, Frits van den Berg, Frans Verhaaren). And the following "international" co-operators: John Simons (USA), Rita Aloni (Israel), Marianna Kranenburg (SIOO, The Netherlands), Martin Bostock (UK).

East-West Co-operation in Public Sector Reform
F. van den Berg et al. (Eds.)
IOS Press, 2002

115

The Issue of Sustainability in a Dutch-Russian Project

Frits van den Berg*

1. The project

This chapter describes a Dutch-Russian project in the second part of the 1990s. I concentrate on two aspects of the project: a description of the network of the stakeholders involved and the influence of this network on the sustainability of the results. The chapter is written from the point of view of my position as project-manager for the Dutch participants.

The formal goal of the project was to strengthen the position of a new profession in Russia. This goal was to be reached by co-operation of one of the Russian associations of these professionals with a Western association in the same field of work. The question, however, arose as to whether the goals were to be reached more by assistance than by co-operation. The associations in East and West were not at the same levels with regard to meanings of experience and financial position. In Western Europe the profession and the associations of professionals are mature; in Eastern Europe the profession and its associations were just emerging.

The terms of reference were written by the Russian association (the beneficiary). The main deliverables were:

- a description of the actual position of the profession in Russia for negotiations with the government.
- three different training programmes for about 150 Russian professionals
- a best practice guide in Russian, to be distributed by the association
- a business plan for the association.

Sustainability was not mentioned in the terms of reference.

In accordance with a publication of USAID[1] I should like to distinguish the impact and the sustainability of a project: "To have impact, a project or programme must influence policy and achieve change. Some accomplishments, such as passage of new legislation, are only intermediate impacts, a means to an end, since true impact takes place only when the end result of the new legislation has become observable. To be sustainable, a project or programme renews and supports itself independently of external funding by donors. Sustainability applies to products, ideas and institutions. If a product or idea is used by commercial ventures, training institutes and professional associations, then the idea behind it is sustainable whether or not the institution that originally promoted the idea continues to exist. Two ways that donors can achieve impact and ensure sustainability are by promoting sustainable institutions and funding dissemination activities."

* Dr. Frits van den Berg, AO, Adviseurs voor Organisatiewerk (Netherlands)
[1] See B. Walter (1999): Maximizing Program Impact and Sustainability: Lessons learned in Europe and Eurasia; Publication of USAID.

There was an international tender for the assignment, which was won by the Dutch association (the consultant). In the consultant's own proposal two aspects were added to the list of activities:

• a visit of the staff of the beneficiary to The Netherlands for preparation of the training courses;

• train-the-trainers courses for regular Russian teachers, in order to continue the training programmes under the responsibility of the beneficiary subsequent to completion of the project itself.

2. The network of stakeholders around the project

In contrast to other such projects, the donor or sponsor was not directly involved in the situation. It worked through a local Russian supervising Institute. The project network was thus:

Figure 1.

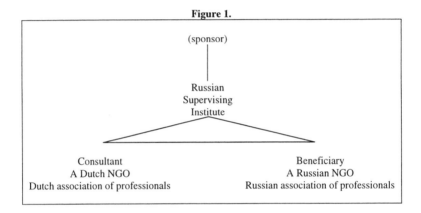

In the rest of this article I use the words Sponsor, Institute, Consultant and Beneficiary to refer to these four positions. In order to understand the processes of co-operation and pseudo co-operation during the project it is necessary to describe each of the positions in more detail:

• For the *Sponsor*, the project was one of many they had in Russia. It was a relatively small project, designed not to demand too much attention from the overloaded co-workers of the sponsor's office. During the project the sponsor was invisible to the consultant and beneficiary. The relationship between Sponsor and *Institute* was an experiment. The Institute wanted to show that they were able to supervise this type of project. Because the Institute got a percentage of the project-budget to cover the costs of supervision, they were not ideally motivated to show their added value by negotiating with the Consultant about the volume of work or the project-budget. The Institute did not communicate this financial arrangement with the Consultant until long after the project was undertaken. The Consultant, however, was surprised that during the contract negotiations, there were only formal remarks about the price ("can it be 2% less?"). The Institute tried to show their added value by interfering in the project, for which they possibly lacked the knowledge, but for which they had no time.

The Institute appointed a contact-person, who was personally interested in the project, but, who was also overloaded with other activities. As happens in Russian organisations, the higher levels in the Institute could overrule any decision of this contact-person. This was done by instructions, not only to their own staff, but also to all individuals involved in the project. This is not an uncommon situation in a hierarchical - management culture (see the chapter of Prof. Prigozhin in this book), but it was a continual frustration for the project-manager, who knew of this phenomena but had no means to counter its effect.

The managers of the institute could not understand the degree of flexibility needed in such a project. After an agreement on the planning was reached, no changes to reschedule the work of the members of the consulting team from one day to another was possible. The tension between Consultant and Institute on this issue was present during the entire project.

• *The Beneficiary* was a complex system in itself. Central persons in the project were two staff-members of the association. Behind or above them was the board of the association. Staff and board-members had their own goals, because they were related to private companies and thus wanted to get something out of the project for these companies or had their own ambitions. One of the consequences was that some of those involved lost interest in the project, because they saw no revenue for themselves.

In the Russian situation several competing associations exist. The project aimed at strengthening the profession by co-operating with only one of these associations. So resources of other associations (competencies, facilities, contacts) were not always available. It was only the Consultant's former contacts with key persons in other associations that sometimes allowed a broader approach.

The real beneficiaries of the training programmes and the best practice guide were of course, Russian professionals. Their requirements only became clear at the beginning of the courses. The terms of reference and the Consultant's proposal were based more on needs as defined by the Beneficiary than on the requirements of the professionals themselves.

One of the tasks of the Beneficiary was to identify authors for the best practice guide (The Consultant was responsible for the overall quality of the guide). The authors of the best practice guide were mainly Russian experts. They came into contact with the project at a late stage in its progress. Most of them were not committed to the project goals at all and had their own interests (payment for writing a chapter, promoting their own name, etc.). The atmosphere was not conducive to co-operating on the production of a good product, let alone an idea of teamwork to optimise the quality of the guide.

• In a formal sense the *Consultant* was a Dutch association of organisations of professionals. It was the Sponsor's requirement that only a national association could tender. However the staff of this association did not have enough capacity to handle the project or even provide project management and invited all member firms to participate in the project. The result was a consortium of five interested members. But at least three decisions influenced the quality of the team:

- only a national association could tender, although perhaps other parties could present a stronger team;

- The Consultant could not select the participating member firms on the basis of knowledge or experience. Each member firm had to be accepted on the basis of "their right to participate as a membership paying body".

- The firms involved were autonomous for the purposes of appointing their participating staff. Eventually this was not a bad team, but was it the optimal team? The fee for this project was about 50% of that which would normally be earned in The Netherlands. A vague notion of charity towards Russian colleagues thus began to develop.

We describe the structure of the team as follows.

• The project manager had five years of experiences in Russia and had contacts with several of the Russian associations. He knew the staff members of the Beneficiary and had an opinion about what might be needed in Russia. He represented the favourite of the Beneficiary in the tendering procedure. His personal goal was a long-term contact with the Beneficiary. He involved two of his colleagues in the assessment of the actual situation. Their main interest at that moment was "to do a proper job".

• The second participant of the consortium was an organisation with a long history in Russia and with Russian-speaking professionals. On the one hand, the type of project was one that they were used to. On the other hand, they needed this assignment to strengthen their position as a specialised department within their Dutch firm, which, at the time was discussing that very topic (today the East European section of that firm no longer exists).

• The third participant was a specialist known worldwide on the subject of one of the training programmes. He had a personal interest to work in a new environment (market). The support of his home organisation, however, was not strong. One of his goals was to investigate daily Russian life during the course of the project.

• The fourth participant was a firm looking for international experiences. During the project they found out that it was difficult for them to motivate their people to go abroad for several missions in a short period. They were able to find a retired colleague who could take over the work and who worked successfully on the project.

• The fifth participant worked hard to have the project on his list of references. During the project, his firm gave him a new position and his motivation disappeared. A part of his work was taken over by the project manager.

• There was neither budget to have a long-term expert in Russia nor could the project manager be constantly present. The project-manager had an office manager on a free-lance basis within Russia to assist in project logistics. She was involved in daily contacts, translation, interpretation and planning. However the Institute considered her as an assistant and not as a representative of the project team.

Although most of the consortium members had personal goals, they also had sufficient "professional pride" (with the exception of the fifth participant) to strive for good project results.

So the detailed network of the project was as indicated in figure 2.

It is impossible to have an overview of all inter-linking contacts and goals. A traceable influence, however, of personal goals and coalitions on the project's results can be detected. I refer further to this in the detailed description of the project's progress.

3. The results of the project

Nearly all deliverables were produced:

• A description of the actual situation was prepared.

• The training programmes were delivered for the required number of participants and with great success. The course materials were translated into Russian.

• The best practice guide was published, although there were unexpected problems with the distribution (e.g. the Russian law on distribution of publications was not taken into account).

• A business plan for the Beneficiary was produced. The quality of the plan, however, was poor.

Two strong points in the relation-network stimulated the production of the deliverables:

• professional pride and professional interests of the member of the consortium and the participants in the training programme

Figure 2. Detailed network of the project

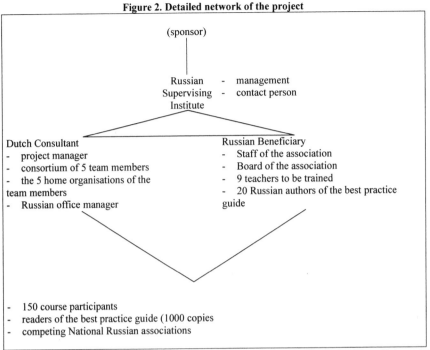

• existing relations between the project manager and the staff of the Beneficiary. This made it possible to discuss their personal goals and to find a way to accept them, without noticeably detracting from the overall goal.

4. Sustainability under pressure

After analysing what was attained and what not, the main problem discussed was the sustainability of the results. As mentioned, for sustainability I refer to the USAID criteria: to be sustainable, a project or programme renews and supports itself independently of external funding by donors. Continuation of the training programmes, updating the description of the situation, distribution of the best practice guide, use of the business plan by the Beneficiary were all problematic. Considering the project 5 years later, I see two fundamental problems and four project-bound aspects. Fundamental are:

4.1. On the one hand, a request for assistance has often been honoured because a beneficiary must cope within a difficult period of transition. On the other hand, sustainability presupposes a certain level of continuity and stability. In this case, as in more cases, this condition was not fulfilled; e.g. just after the project, the Beneficiary was transformed into an organisation with a completely different mission. In such an unstable situation, a business plan with a scope of 3-5 years is not considered relevant. Even the discussions about the contents of the business plan were strongly influenced by feelings of uncertainty.

The same mechanism can be found in the case of updating the description of the actual situation. Changes took place so rapidly that the work should have been repeated every year. Without financial support, there was no great interest from the Russian side to do this.

4.2. The second fundamental problem was that projects were often imbedded in a setting of welfare for the Beneficiary. The project was, first of all a source of material and then of immaterial income. The follow-up supposed a commercial attitude of staff and Board. Preparing for such a switch was not a standard part of a project. Because of this, the Beneficiary was not prepared to "sell" the training programmes and the business plan after the project.

At a practical level we observed that sustainability was negatively influenced by the pretended co-operation of the groups identified in the elaborated network.

a) As noted above, one of the consortium members had, as an individual goal, "the project on his CV". This goal was dominant for him and was put above the common goals. At the same time, the parties that should have had most interest in the business plan (staff and Board of the beneficiary), were shifting their attention to the development of their own professional practices. Although the Institute and the project manager were still concentrating on the common goal (producing a good business plan), the relation between these two stakeholders was not good enough to develop a common strategy. This was partly due to earlier irritations between them.

b) The position of the regular Russian teachers was complex. The project manager and the staff of the Beneficiary identified most of them. In the contract, it was specified that the Institute had to approve them. This was worked out by the Institute in the form of an "oral examination" of potential candidates. The Institute, however, was not able to plan these examinations in time. Names of candidates were lost. More than 50% of the candidates were refused for unclear reasons. During the project, the management of the Institute claimed the right to give instructions (e.g. about the time for train-the-trainers activities) to some of the Russian teachers. The Russian teachers were mostly in contact with one of the Dutch consortium-members. Sometimes it worked out well and individuals received additional training. In other cases, the Russian teachers "disappeared", especially after it became clear that the Beneficiary had made no plans to continue with the courses.

c) In most projects, a Consultant has contacts with the Sponsor. In this case, the Institute was a go-between. This influenced the co-operation in, at least, two ways.

    c1)   The Consultant studied the general conditions of the Sponsor carefully, especially during the tendering phase. The Institute had less knowledge of the conditions and mixed them up with some of their own "house-rules". This resulted in differences in expectations of the goals of meetings, reports, outcomes, etc.

    c2)   The Institute and the Beneficiary had contacts, because of other common activities. Naturally, during these contacts, the project was also discussed: the results of these meetings were not communicated to the project manager (who was mostly not present) or the office manager (who had insufficient status).

d) Exclusiveness of courses for members of the Beneficiary was not allowed by the Sponsor's regulations. So members of competing associations could also profit from the courses. These competitors had no interest in contributing to the continuation of a preferred position for this one competitor.

5. Conclusions and recommendations

5.1 With today's experience in East-West co-operation, deliverables such as study programmes and a best practice guide of good quality can be produced as a result of good co-operation between a Consultant and a Beneficiary. Although one still might wonder if the effort is co-operation or assistance.

To understand the dynamics of a project and bring forth sustainability, it is necessary to analyze in detail the network involved.

Personal goals and pseudo co-operation can be subordinated to common goals by parties that know each other because they have already passed the first two levels of the Jenei-LeLoup model in the relationship. In this way sustainability might be included in the set of common goals.

5.2 If sustainability is not in the core of the project from the very beginning, a "half-way" evaluation of the situation is needed.

5.3 Consultant, Sponsor and Beneficiary should adapt a common strategy for sustainability including defining a transfer of a welfare-oriented setting to a commercial setting.

East-West Co-operation in Public Sector Reform
F. van den Berg et al. (Eds.)
IOS Press, 2002

123

An Experience in East-West Co-operation: The Methodius Project in St. Petersburg

Katlijn Malfliet*

This contribution reflects on a concrete experience with the "Methodius" project in St.Petersburg, a training programme to support the independence of the judiciary and practising lawyers in Russia. It also tries to develop some thoughts on the paradigms on which co-operation in training between Western Europe and Russia implicitly or explicitly rest. Although the Methodius concept tried to avoid Western hegemonic mentality, the project was nevertheless confronted with the decisive role of internal factors in transition.

Such an experience makes one modest: our influence is restricted, the limits of our knowledge are impressive. The article ends with some concrete recommendations for co-operation between Russia and the West.

1. Introduction

The approach of this contribution starts from rather limited ambitions. We intend to provide the reader with a report of our experience on a training programme to support the independence of the judiciary and practising lawyers in Russia (St.Petersburg). Since the end of 1991 professional lawyers from St.Petersburg and Flanders have met each other on a regular basis with the particular aim to discuss their professional problems as practising lawyers, in adapting their activities and organisation to the new conditions after the collapse of the communist regime.

These meetings took place in the framework of the Methodius project, co-ordinated by the Institute of European Policy at the Department of Political Sciences of the Catholic University of Leuven (K.U.Leuven). In its first two years (1992-94), the project was financed by the Flemish government (i.e. the government of the Flemish community within the Belgian State). However, although Flemish in its origin, the project soon took on more international and European features. Restructuring and liberalisation of the legal profession, in this period of globalisation, also imply opening up to the international world and to Europe. In this framework co-operation with Flemish lawyers based in Brussels was considered particularly useful, as the Brussels bar is now being restructured to meet the challenges of elaborating a "common legal space" in the framework of the European Union. In September 1995 the Methodius project became a Flemish-European project in the framework of the TACIS-Democracy programme. The Council of the Bars and Law Societies of the European Community joined the Methodius project as a European partner. The project ended in 1999. Bilateral contacts between professional groups continue to this day.

Our aim is to reflect on our concrete experience with the Methodius project in

* Katlijn Malfliet, Professor, Research Director Central and Eastern Europe, Institute for European Policy, K.U. Leuven (Belgium).

St.Petersburg and to develop some thoughts on the paradigms on which co-operation in training between Western Europe and Russia implicitly or explicitly rests. What is the basic philosophy for such a European co-operation? What are the pitfalls and opportunities? With whom and how to work? What are the hopes, encouraging both sides to co-operate with each other?

The general objective of the Methodius project was to support the development of an independent judiciary and the legal profession in Russia by offering assistance to state institutions, responsible for providing legal training programmes (the Ministry of Justice, the research and training institute of the Prokuratura, the Law Faculty at St. Petersburg State University).

The Methodius concept is named after one of the patron saints of Europe. Cyril and Methodius (Thessalonica, respectively 827 and 825 AD.) received the title "the apostles of the Slavs" for christianising the Danubian Slavs and for influencing the religious and cultural development of all Slavic people. There is much irony in this reference to historical experiences with missionary activity in the Slavic world, as it will soon emerge that our project approach tried to avoid all missionary intentions. Besides this hidden joke, Methodius mainly refers to the methodological approach of the programme whose basic paradigm was that, if the West is to plant its concept of democracy and the Rule of Law in Russia, it must base its actions on a realistic appraisal of the historical and cultural forces at work. In addition to this paradigm of *cultural relativism*, the programme relied on a *network-concept of social and professional relations.* The programme tried to organise its activity with the full support of the local community and its leaders by creating a network among legal practitioners, academicians and legal experts, both in East and West. Members of the legal profession (advocates, notaries, judges, procurators, legal advisors in ministries and enterprises) in St.Petersburg and in the European Union were stimulated to exchange experiences and know-how on deontology, organisational structures and the specific transition problems of their legal professions, as well as their role in a democratic society. The idea was to organise and develop a network of professional and personal relations, both in St.Petersburg and in Flanders on which co-operation with long-term perspectives could rely. It was equally our conviction that a too optimistic and unrealistic approach on the part of the "new missionaries" could be harmful for long-term co-operation between East and West. This is why, in a third paradigm underlying the Methodius co-operation, the Methodius concept rejects the idea of unilateral help or extrapolation of democratic acquirements from the West and stresses the importance of *mutual and interrelated interest in co-operation,* with respect for each other's cultural tradition and language.

Moreover we were mainly guided by short-term amelioration tasks, rather than by long-term transformation options. Exchange of experiences and network building were more important to us than any consideration about changing attitudes and transforming society. In this sense we did not behave as missionaries, but rather as potential partners for future co-operation. Getting to know each other's approaches, capacities, and interests was considered as the first step towards mutual trust and long-term co-operation.

Within this carefully balanced framework several activities took place in the period from 1992 to 1997 in Belgium and Russia: conferences, round tables, internships, seminars, visits to courts and other working places for practising lawyers. We tried to proceed as carefully as possible. Quite some time and energy was spent in introducing our specific approach. The Methodius concept on legal exchange and training was indeed conceived as a "hallmark", a quality mark guaranteeing an in-depth and European approach, based on the creation of networks both in East and West, each partner being able to express him/herself in his/her own language, establishing a link between science and practitioners. Through this multifarious approach the Methodius concept, based on mutual interest for each other's identity, was conceived as trying to avoid an alienating effect in East-West co-operation. The idea was to "franchise" this concept to other places in Russia and to other post-communist states within the Commonwealth of Independent States. This was done successfully in a one-year programme with Jekaterinburg, Kazan', and Uzbekistan[1].

2. The concept

The official aim of co-operation programmes between Western partners and their counterparts in post-communist Central and Eastern Europe is usually described as promoting democracy and market principles in the post-communist states. This aim is currently much criticised from both the East and the West European side. One of the major problems is that, relating to this type of co-operation, absolutely no consensus exists on the desirability of the type of assistance, the goals to be pursued, the mix of Western altruism versus self-interest, the extent to which aid and conditionality should be based on sympathy for various class, gender, national and religious interests within the country of destination[2]. This confusion leaves too much room for extreme pragmatism and abuse in East-West programmes. The Belorussian Philosopher I.IA. Leviash expresses it as follows: "The politicised and selective character of the so-called 'Western aid' can be derived from the fact that states in Central Europe receive ten times the aid that is transferred to the CIS. Our states are not an aim as such, when the West transfers means of conversion. The aid is in the interests of security in the West. All this is far away from eternal values and shows the pragmatic character of Western interests"[3].

On the other hand, the collapse of communism forced all post-Leninist nations to face the task of building a new society based on a new constellation of values. For this, they looked towards the West, principally because of its economic prosperity. Institutionalising democracy and the Rule of Law was considered by them as an instrument to develop new economic and technological contacts with the West. Democracy and the Rule of Law were not considered as targets per se. On the other hand Western Europe (the Council of Europe and the European Union) in its structural foreign policy vested its hope for European integration and security in an extension of Western values of democracy and market principles. Contrary to the United States, the European Union was inspired by a perhaps unrealistic optimism about creating a pan-European structure based on values of democracy and market principles.

The problem of providing assistance to transition countries, and in particular Russia, is even more delicate where the Rule of Law is concerned. One of the first questions our Russian colleagues asked, when starting the programme, was: "How can we translate 'Rule of Law', this concept is unknown to us". The Rule of Law is indeed a common law concept which was unknown to Russian legal theory and the profession. Perhaps Russian legal theory was closer to the German concept of Rechtsstaat, born to counter the term Polizeistaat. As a concept, the idea of the Rechtsstaat reached its peak thanks to the eighteenth century German *Begriffsjurisprudenz*. Afterwards, the idea gave way to the most diverging interpretations. Civil law and common law endowed the notion with the most

---

[1] Malfliet, K., De Maeyer, E., Legal Perspectives. The Legal Profession and Human Rights in Uzbekistan. Vzgliad iuristov. Professiia iurista i prava cheloveka v Uzbekistane. Garant, Leuven, 1999, 325p.
[2] Breslauer G., Aid to Russia: What Difference Can Western Policy Make? In: Lapidus, G. (ed.), The New Russia. Troubled Transformation. Westview Press, Boulder, 1995, pp. 223-244.
[3] Leviash, I.IA., Srednaia Evropa: struktura i vektor istoricheskogo vybora (Central Europe: Structure and Vector of a Historical Choice). In: Vostochnaia Evropa: politicheskii i sotsiokulturnyi vybor (Eastern Europe: Political and Sociocultural Choice). Editions of Minsk State University, Minsk, 1994, p. 40.

varied of meanings. Within the common law concept, all translations that include the term "state" (Rechtsstaat, Etat de Droit, Pravovoe Gosudarstvo) are inappropriate to translate the term Rule of Law in that they misinterpret the essence of the idea of the Rule of Law. The decisive element and premise of the Rule of Law is indeed not the state but rather an autonomous, extra-state law: case law or Juristenrecht. Both concepts (Rule of Law and Rechtsstaat) aim at the same goal: the subordination of political power to the observance of legal rules intended to safeguard the freedom of citizens. But the difference between the two approaches should not be underestimated: in the case of the Rechtsstaat, the state subordinates itself to its own law, while the Rule of Law assumes that the political power that governs the state is subordinated to a law that it has not directly produced. The role and place of the state are indeed crucial in defining the exact meaning of *Pravovoe Gosudarstvo* in the current Russian legal culture. As we shall see below, in the focus of the Russian debate on collective identity for the legal profession, the tension lies between liberalisation of the profession and state intervention. In any case, although we perceived a lot of goodwill and interest, the general reaction was undoubtedly that, with the Rule of Law or Rechtsstaat, a fremdkörper would be introduced into Russian society[4].

This made us remember the problem of legal transplants, and the debate in comparative legal theory between Alan Watson and Otto Freund Kahn. In 1974 Alan Watson published his famous study "Legal Transplants" in which he argued that the history of a legal system was to a great extent the history of borrowing from other systems, and that such legal transplants have been common since earliest recorded history. A successful transplant, like that of a human organ, would "grow in its new body, and become part of that body just as the rule or institution would have continued to develop in its parent system"[5]. In that same year Otto Kahn-Freund warned that rules and institutions are not always transplantable, and that transplants which use "a pattern of law outside the environment of the organ" risk rejection[6]. The borrowing of the concept of the Rule of Law or Rechtsstaat provides an excellent opportunity to test these theories.

Here we have to remember, however, that Russia during the Tsarist period (in 1864 under the reign of Alexander II) already went through the experience of importing legal institutions and procedures primarily from France and Germany. This experience, although promising at the outset, was not a success and was slowly watered down[7].

Indeed one observes that, since the start of the Methodius project, the general perspectives for the introduction of a law-based state in Russia have become more pessimistic. This tendency is not typical of St. Petersburg or of the Russian Federation. Looking in general at post-communist transition in Central and Eastern Europe, one notices that progress has been made in the field of democratic transition and institutionalisation in general, but that the same cannot be said about the law-governed state. The judiciary is not well prepared for transition, is still badly paid and cannot cope with the increasing workload. The independence of the judiciary vis-à-vis executive and local power is not always protected efficiently[8].

Moreover, the socio-political environment in Russia does not favour institutional changes that bring Russia closer to a Western concept of the Rule of Law. The elites in the legal profession seem to have conflicting interpretations of what the Rule of Law really

---

[4] Ajani, G., The Rise and Fall of the Law-based State in the Experience of Russian Legal Scholarschip. In: Barry, D., Toward the Rule of Law in Russia? Sharpe, New York, 1992, pp. 64-87.
[5] Reid Elspeth, The Law of Trusts in Russia. *Review of Central and East European Law* 24 (1998) 43.
[6] Kahn-Freund, O., Uses and Misuses of Comparative Law. *Modern Law Review* 17 (1974) 27.
[7] Barry, D., Toward the Rule of Law in Russia? Sharpe, New York, 1992, Introduction, pp. 3-20.
[8] EU warnings to accession candidates in the framework of screening processes, as passim reported in *Uniting Europe. The European Integration Bulletin for Central and Eastern Europe and the NIS,* 2001.

means. Moreover, this debate between elites does not reach the masses, who are not interested in what the Rule of Law should be. The new institutions are not able to fulfil expectations in the new situation, because there is no collective identification with the Rule of Law. In general one can conclude that it was too easily taken for granted that the goal of any European democratisation project would be the creation of a Rechtsstaat and that our assistance was to be framed in a general concept of a European Common Foreign Policy, based on the assumption that the introduction of the Rechtsstaat was an important aspect of democratisation and consequently of European security and peace building. From the very start we understood the agenda of the project as something different than "Coming to the Rule of Law". The Rule of Law obscured more complex tasks and relations, related to a multifaceted and complex transition. The question is not whether Russia can go from Socialist Legality to the Rule of Law, but whether practising lawyers can regain independence and confidence as a profession, whether they can break loose from the grip of organised crime, authoritarian tendencies and the influence of the Ministry of Justice.

3. Challenges and positive experiences

The professional groups involved

The Methodius project was successful in creating a solid network of practising lawyers who were all concerned with the implementation of the *Pravovoe Gosudarstvo*, traditionally interpreted as the counterpart of the notion of Rule of Law and Rechtsstaat (Law-Based State) in Russia. Although the group was particularly aware of the difficulties attached to this concept in a Russian context, practising lawyers also felt responsible for grasping the opportunity to introduce a more 'civilised' legal culture in Russia. Leadership in St.Petersburg was generally supportive: we obtained explicit support from the mayor of St.Petersburg, A. Sobchak, and the governor of St.Petersburg Oblast', Iakovlev. During the first years of the project, our Russian partner consisted in an ad hoc group of high-level representatives of the professional groups involved: advocates (the presidents of the bar associations of St.Petersburg and of Leningrad oblast'), judges (the president of St.Petersburg City Court), Prokuratura (the Transport Procurator of Leningrad oblast'), notaries (the president of the Notarial Chamber of St.-Petersburg) and university professors (the Dean and some professors of the Law Faculty).

However, when the Flemish project turned into a European project in the framework of the Tacis-Democracy programme, a new requirement was not easy to fulfil: our Russian partner had to be a non-governmental organisation, with legal personality. The only non-governmental organisation, endowed with legal personality and representing practising lawyers in St.Petersburg was the former communist Association of Lawyers of St.Petersburg. This association clearly lost most of its legitimacy after the collapse of communism, but it was willing to co-operate within the project requirements. The professional groups involved reluctantly accepted the mediation of this meaningless organisation. This illustrated that working with NGOs in post-Leninist Russia was not straight-forward.

The basic reason for requiring an NGO partner, namely the fact that NGOs represent civil society, becomes absolutely irrelevant and even counterproductive when these NGOs are former communist organisations or have been set up by the state. Such "quangos" (quasi-NGOs) are, if not a real hindrance, at least an unnecessary intermediate level for co-operation. In our project we found the Association of Lawyers to be a superfluous, but not an impeding partner in our co-operation. Besides the Association of Lawyers, the Union of

St.Petersburg Lawyers, deprived of legal personality, proved to be a much more reliable, albeit unofficial, partner.

In Flanders the Bars of Brussels, Antwerp and Ghent showed their preparedness to participate in this difficult but challenging dialogue. The Belgian Public Ministry and the judiciary (the Justice of the Peace, the Brussels Commercial Court and the highest courts, the Cassation Court and the Constitutional Court) were willing to co-operate. The Minister of Justice and his administration became involved as well. Also the local Justice of the Peace in Flanders participated voluntarily in the project.

From the Russian side, members of the judiciary (the St.Petersburg City Court and Arbitration Court), the Procuracy, the lawyers working within the St.Petersburg and Leningrad Oblast' Bar Associations, the Union of Lawyers, the notaries, and the jurisconsults (corporate lawyers) tried to define problems related to the liberalisation of their profession within a new legal environment.

All groups of practising lawyers, involved in the Methodius project, lived through a period of tremendous change. The "Blueprint for reform of the administration of justice in the Russian Republic" was published simultaneously with the start of the Methodius project in St.Petersburg. The "Concept of Judicial Reform", prepared by an authors' collective of the legislative Committee of the Supreme Soviet of the Russian Republic, was adopted almost unanimously by the Supreme Soviet on October 21 1991[9]. This concept of judicial reform based its reform proposals in great part on the ideas of the 1864 reforms, as an answer to the glasnost-based critique of Soviet criminal justice.

(1) First of all the *judges* underwent a period of revaluation of their profession, but equally of enhanced expectations in an environment of changing legislation and complete reversal of the assumptions underpinning their role in society. Separation of power between executive and judicial branches was a vital aim of the reforms, and in consequence the establishment of an independent professional judiciary. During the communist regime, the courts were an integral component of the administrative command system, described by the Concept of Judicial Reform as: "organs of repression applying ritualistic juridical reasoning to prearranged sentences"[10].

The reforms proposed by the Concept of Judicial Reform were innovative and have been enacted into law quite quickly. Reforms related to the strengthening of the independence of the judiciary, the requirement of judicial authorisation for decisions previously within the competence of the Procuracy and criminal investigators relating to disregard of citizens' constitutional rights through search, seizure, or detention; the right to counsel from the time of arrest, the introduction of adversary procedure in criminal cases; the statutory enactment of a presumption of innocence; a privilege against self-incrimination, an exclusionary rule for illegally seized evidence and finally, the right to trial by jury[11].

The law "On the Status of Judges in the Russian Federation" of 26 June 1992 made an attempt to upgrade the judicial profession, by establishing social and legal protective measures[12]. Judges, it was declared, should henceforth be appointed for life (which implies non-removability until retirement age). The Law "On Liability for Contempt of Court and the Law on Judicial Organisation" increased the general perception that truly independent

---

[9] Kontseptsiia sudebnoi reformy v Rossiiskoi Federatsii (Concept of Judicial Reform in the Russian Federation). *Vedomosti RSFSR,* issue N° 44, Item 1435 (1991).

[10] Concept of Judicial Reform, at 8.

[11] The so-called «Jury Law» of June 7, 1993, implies a whole series of amendments to the Russian Constitution, the Criminal Code, the Code of Criminal Procedure and the Code of Administrative Infractions of the RSFSR: *Vedomosti RF,* Issue n°33, Item 1313, 2238-2264.

[12] Zakon RSFSR O Statuse Sudei v Rossiiskoi Federatsii (Law on the Status of Judges in the Russian Federation). June 26 1992, *Vedomosti RF,* Issue n°30, Item 1792 (1992).

courts were crucial to the creation of genuine legal and political change[13]. At the lowest level of the juridical pyramid plans were initiated to install Justices of the Peace (*myrovye sud'y*). Referring to the 1864 judicial reforms, the idea of trial by jury was re-introduced. An experiment with sworn assessors (*prisiazhnye zasedateli*) was started up, including a limited number of subjects of the Russian Federation. A commercial court (*arbitrazhnyi sud*) replaced arbitration procedures. These commercial courts had an early start, because they continued with some judges from the communist arbitration authorities. However, in the commercial courts we met with a group of well-educated and relatively young judges, enthusiastic and clearly taking the lead in the process of judicial organisation. As an institution, the commercial court formed a sharp contrast with the general situation in the Russian judiciary. In general the Russian courts of general jurisdiction were under-financed by the Russian Federal government while at the same time their workload had increased enormously[14].

(2) The Russian *bar* had been an elite institution, allowing its members to enjoy, by Soviet standards, a rather lucrative profession with an enviable amount of professional independence, which made it one of the most preferred careers of graduate law students[15]. By keeping its numbers low and monopolising the provision of legal aid, the bar managed to protect its corporate interests. The 1939 USSR Statute on the Bar abolished private practice and introduced the law consultation offices (Iuriskonsul'tatsii) as the basic organisational structure which the Russian bar retains today[16]. These law consultation offices were united in each region or territory of the country into *kollegii* of advocates, supervised and directed by the USSR Minister of Justice. When the process of reforming the Bar began during perestroika the country had approximately 27 000 advocates, fewer per capita than in pre-revolutionary Russia.

Judicial reforms opened up a plethora of new functions, some of which were wrongly in the hands of the procuracy. However, a remarkable paradox originated from these reforms: the bar's desire to protect its monopoly of legal aid made it reluctant to espouse certain aspects of reform. The advocates did not do away with their organisational structures in City and Oblast' bars (*Kollegii Advokatov*). However, the liberalisation of their profession put them at serious risk. This liberalisation affected the position of recognised advocates, as it became possible to engage in legal counselling work without becoming a member of the Bar. Soviet advocates indeed never enjoyed a representation monopoly to appear in court in civil and criminal cases. They feared a new separation of their profession into an elite group of sworn attorneys (*prisiazhnye poverennye*) and a less prestigious caste of private attorneys (*chastnye poverennye*) allowed to practice in specific courts in order to alleviate shortages in rural areas.

The shortage of advocates, created by the bar's monopoly, which had kept the number of advocates artificially low, became a problem when the right to counsel from the moment of arrest was acknowledged by the "Fundamentals of Legislation of the USSR and Union Republics on Court Organisation" in 1989. Paradoxically, the bar opposed the passage and implementation of this important right for the accused, claiming that they did not have enough personnel to fill the courts' needs and were not compensated for this representation. To meet this shortage and to break the monopoly of the bar, the Ministry of Justice

---

[13] Schroeder, F.C., Die Bestellung der Richter in Russland. *Recht in Ost und West* 6 (1995), pp. 165-168.
[14] Murphy, P., The Russian Courts of General Jurisdiction: In Crisis, Undergoing Reform, or Both? *The Parker School Journal of East European Law* 4 (1998), 210.
[15] Huskey, E., Between Citizen and State: the Soviet Bar (Advokatura) under Gorbachev. *Columbia Journal of Transnational Law* 1995, 110.
[16] Polozhenie ob advokature SSSR (Decree on the Bar of the USSR). *Sobranie Polozhenii SSSR,* issue n°49, n°394 (1939).

permitted the formation of legal co-operatives, in which persons with a legal education could provide legal services without being accepted into the *Kollegium* of advocates. To defend their interests the *Kollegia* of advocates united to form the Union of Advocates of the USSR in 1989. The Ministry of Justice reacted by organising in 1989 the Union of Lawyers of the USSR, which included other lawyers and part of the Bar as well. After the collapse of the USSR, Russian lawyers from the Union of Advocates formed the Russian Union of Advocates and those in the Union of Lawyers formed the Russian Association of Advocates. These two organisations finally combined in late 1994 to form the Federal Union of Advocates of Russia[17]. But St.Petersburg continued to use the distinction between the Union and the Association.

This evolution again reminds us of the experience after the 1864 reforms. Private attorneys were introduced by the Tsarist government in 1874 as a counterweight to the politically conscious sworn bar. This bifurcation of the bar recalls the distinction in the English legal profession between barristers and solicitors, and continues to dominate the debate on the future of the Russian bar. Further, the bar aimed at freeing itself from domination by the Ministry of Justice and from restrictive fee schedules that had resulted in the bulk of its income coming from illegal, under-the-table payments from clients, a payment system that left them open to criminal prosecution. The move to adversarial criminal procedure introduced a regime that required work and put one's reputation on the line but, as yet, paid little.

(3) During the communist regime the *procuracy* was part of an immense hierarchy extending to every corner of the Soviet Union. The *Prokuratura*, as the watchdog of the communist Party was near the top of the pyramid of power in exercising supreme oversight (*vysshii nadzor*) over the legality of acts of Soviet political, judicial, and administrative organs[18]. The procurator was spared the task of prosecuting criminal cases. The police investigated criminal complaints under technical procuratorial supervision and the trial consisted in the judge reading the investigative dossier alone in his chamber and then acting as both prosecutor and defence. The "Concept for Judicial Reform" proposed to eliminate all oversight functions of the Procuracy, except supervision of criminal prosecution, to subordinate procurators to the Minister of Justice and to attach them to the courts in which they would prosecute criminal cases. The Procuracy had to become a prosecuting agency along the centralised European model. What remained was a role the Procuracy did not desire: that of prosecutor, the responsibility of enforcing criminal laws and participating in adversarial criminal proceedings. The Procuracy opposed these reforms that would undermine its archaic role (dating from its first instalment in 1722 during the reign of Peter the Great) of general oversight over the application of the laws by both governmental and non-governmental organisations and that would necessitate its assuming the role of prosecutor in criminal cases.

The Law on the Procuracy of the Russian Federation of 17 November 1995 perpetuated the traditional procurational system[19]. While maintaining procuratorial oversight functions, it does not allude to oversight of the execution of presidential decrees, as did the original draft. During the Soviet period, the encompassing role of the *Prokuratura* in supervising the observance of law was sometimes viewed as the "fourth branch of the law". It is clear that the *Prokuratura* will remain an important institution in the new environment. The definition of the role of the *Prokuratura* will remain very important in the search for a

---

[17] Thaman, S., Reform of the Procuracy and Bar in Russia. *Parker School Journal of East European Law* 3 (1996), pp. 22-23.

[18] Ibidem, 1.

[19] Federal'nyi zakon o prokurature RF (Federal Law on the Prokuratura). November 20, 1995, *Sobranie Zakonodatel'stva RF*, n°47, Art. 472 (1995).

collective identity related to the *Pravovoe Gosudarstvo.*

(4) Finally, the *Notaries,* as in most continental countries, constitute a separate legal profession. During the Soviet regime, notaries were appointed by the state, mainly to perform acts for which a specific written document was required (certification of documents, registration of sales of dwellings and motor cars). The notary was more a clerk: in remote areas where no notarial office was available, certain notarial functions could be exercised by the local Council (Soviet). Soon after the collapse of the communist regime the notarial function became liberalised. In March 1993 a Notary Law, based on the Latin model, was introduced in Russia. Notaries could choose between remaining state officials or organising themselves as private offices. Private notarial offices soon became gold mines for those who were in the position to take advantage of inside information in a chaotic period of transition. State regulation and a moral code for the profession became necessary after a complete imbalance, created by the liberalisation of the function.

Project development

The initial steps within the project development were taken with enormous enthusiasm from both sides. The Western partners were willing to help and eager to experience the historic challenge of transition to the Rule of Law/ Rechtsstaat in Russia. For the Russian partners, the project came at the right moment because the Concept of Judicial Reform had just been published.

First, some general conferences were organised respectively in St.Petersburg and in Leuven, involving all professional groups and summing up the major challenges within the new legal environment. This collaboration was on the level of exchange of contacts and information. As general meetings, they provided a *locus* to explore the problems involved, transfer information and get acquainted with one another and with each other's needs and interests. Afterwards, we went to a second stage of systematic exchange of knowledge and experience. We decided to organise bilateral seminars involving separate groups of judges, advocates, procurators and notaries. Professional discussions, visits and exploration of professional collaboration resulted. In 1998–99 four seminars were organised in St.Petersburg. Young interns came to Flanders and co-operated with practising lawyers in Brussels and Antwerp. Finally, a round table in Leuven closed the project. The results were published in a bilingual book on the legal profession in contemporary Russia[20] Simultaneously, a programme of joint action was set up, helping the library of St.Petersburg State University, organising internships, formalising professional exchange relationships (a framework agreement between the Bars of St.-Petersburg and Brussels).

In our opinion, the bilateral meetings were quite effective because they gave the participants a chance to touch on concrete problems and to explore opportunities for co-operation in the future.

(1) The St.-Petersburg *judges* visited the Belgian Justice of the Peace, commercial courts and higher courts. They were impressed by the robes of the judges and the beautiful buildings in which Belgian judges were settled. But also court organisation and specific court procedures were explained in detail. Belgian judges were confronted in St.-Petersburg with the enormous difference between an enthusiastic group of commercial court judges and a group of city court judges, shocked and almost paralysed by chaotic transformation. For a two-day seminar in St.Petersburg City Court, the judges of St.Petersburg proposed a concrete topic: "Regulations on investment funds and legal protection for individual

---

[20] Malfliet K., De Maeyer, E., Shishkina, V., Professiia Iurista v segodniashchéi Rossii: vzgliad s Zapada i Vostoka. The Legal Profession in Contemporary Russia: Experiences from East and West, Garant, Leuven, 1996, 300p.

investors". Various judges from the Leningrad Region along with professors and students from the law faculty of St.Petersburg State University were in attendance. The European Union expert was an honorary judge of the Brussels Court of Commerce. These seminars were productive and useful with a lively exchange of ideas. The topic chosen had to address the issue of the unclear division of competence between city court and commercial court as quite a few legal problems had arisen in this new field of law.

(2) The *advocates* were under serious pressure. The St.Petersburg Bar Association and the Bar Association of the Leningrad region both tried to survive the turmoil of transition. They complained that it was extremely difficult to claim protection for human rights (for example in court procedures), when people feared for their lives and their survival. For the *advocates* it was important to create an independent bar, free from the tutelage of the Ministry of Justice. Their aim was to create a bar association on corporate principles. In this framework an ethical code of behaviour for *advocates* was seen by them as of primordial importance. In the framework of the Methodius project the Code of Conduct for European Bar Associations was translated into Russian. But also the changing role of advocates became the subject of discussions. Now that advocates have to earn their living in a free environment, the question is: Will they be able to help the poor? That is why a legal regulation for free legal aid, supported and financed by the state became necessary. In this perspective the state has to intervene when the free market services become incompatible with elementary guarantees of social justice. On the requirement of the Leningrad Oblast' Minister of Justice, the Belgian legislation on free legal aid was translated into Russian in order to prepare local legislation for the Leningrad Oblast'.

(3) The *Procuracy* manifested itself as the best organised and most prestigious group in the framework of our co-operation. The target group were students at the School of Higher Education of the Prosecutor-General's Office in St.Petersburg and the prosecutors of the Leningrad region themselves. The European Union expert was the Belgian national magistrate André Vandoren. In spite of the political complications (the murder of Deputy Galina Starovoitova some days prior to the seminar and the organisation of local elections in St.Petersburg under tight security measures on 6 December 1998), Belgian and Russian counterparts at the state level were able to discuss mutual co-operation. Both partners had to take into account different approaches, for example on the relationship between the procuracy and the bar. In the West we think of the Procuracy and the Bar as parties with almost diametrically opposed interests, but this characterisation did not apply either during Soviet times, or after the political reforms. During their visits to Belgium, members of the *Prokuratura* were shocked by the way advocates and procurators behaved to one another in a rather antagonistic way. "Shouldn't advocates and procurators co-operate in order to protect legality and detect truth?", they asked. This group, however, was driven by a well-defined mutual interest. It is no secret that a significant amount of drug trafficking continues unabated between St.Petersburg and Antwerp. It is therefore not surpassing that the Belgian authorities desire a closer working relationship with the Russian authorities. As transnational crime became a problem and the Russian mafia settled in Belgium (Antwerp and Brussels), the Belgian Public Ministry was quite interested in good contacts with the St.Petersburg Procurators. It was important for them to understand the organisation and working of the Russian *Prokuratura* in order to have effective transnational co-operation. Thanks to this concrete mutual interest, the co-operation of this group was the most effective.

(4) The *notaries* were interested in the Latin notary system. In their workshops, however, they chose to discuss a more concrete subject: the marital contract and the position of women in post-communist Russia. The notaries acting as European union experts were more than once shocked when hearing that the marital contract, newly

introduced in Russia, was being used as a legal instrument for different purposes, which often led to confusion among the notaries themselves as to what could be contractually stipulated. The marital contract was unknown during the communist period and was even rejected as bourgeois. It was interesting to hear how future partners tried to include non-patrimonial clauses in their contract, such as the promise to have a certain number of children, or to ban smoking.

4. Problems encountered

Although the Methodius concept tried to avoid a Western hegemonic mentality, we nevertheless were confronted with the decisive role of internal transition factors .

We met with various problems of transition from the Rule of the Party to the Rule of Law. Some of them were unexpected, some clearly temporary, others, however, risk undermining trust in the Rule of Law as such.

(1) While our project was ongoing, times changed and the profile of the *transition altered*. At the beginning of our project (and systemic transformation in the Russian Federation), we all shared the rather naive hope that the totalitarian system of real socialism could soon be replaced by a new institutional framework, based on a democratic constitution. However, we learned to take a more realistic and patient approach. When we first visited the St.Petersburg City Court, the restoration of this beautiful old building (once the headquarters of the pre-Revolutionary security services) had just started. Enthusiastically the President of the Court, Mr Poludniakov showed us the plans for the reorganisation and decoration of the building. When we came back, five years later, nothing had changed: there was no budget for the planned restoration. Perhaps this experience is symbolic of the whole transition in the field of the judiciary. Valuable initiatives for guaranteeing the independence of judges, installing courts and sworn assessors, were not carried out for lack of a budget.

(2) Judges, moreover, were not educated in the new tradition: their civil law approach made them feel comfortable when they could find a solution for a specific case in a rather deductive way: from the general rule to a particular decision. Judges expected greater regulation from the legislator. Instead of a sudden liberalisation, they asked for more guidelines, new controlling institutions, social adjustments, increased financing from the state budget and a clear division of competences between the courts. There were for example nearly insoluble problems regarding the division of competences between the civil courts and the new-style commercial courts. Often the construction of the legal person was paralysing judges in their attempts to protect the citizen against the consequences of the extreme liberalisation of the economy. The courts were overburdened with claims that were new to the judges. Often the judges were confronted with the problem of how to formulate a judicial decision in the absence of a legal regulation on which they could rely for their decision. In other words: the problem was so encompassing that it was impossible to find an adequate solution.

(3) A third problem was related to the *network*. St.Petersburg is the local level and the old guard has managed to retain its hold over the new institutions of governance. Monopolistic tendencies consolidated their grip and were not broken in the slightest.

It seemed rather important to pay attention to the varieties of relationships on which the co-operation was based. As western partners we have major problems in dealing with that kind of cliental network structures. Once the choice of network is made, one runs the risk of becoming a prisoner in it. It was for example impossible to open the profession to younger people or to a larger group in public administration. We were accepted and indeed trusted by an elite network, that did not want to give up its privileges of travelling abroad. One of the most surprising conclusions of the assessment of the Methodius project was the appreciation of our Russian partners because we had brought them together in a structured interprofessional framework for exchange of information and experiences in Russia. More important than listening to western experience and studying translated documents was the opportunity given to St.Petersburg judges, advocates, procurators and notaries to meet freely, talk and travel together. One of the major positive results of this co-operation was completely unexpected: the reduction of the transaction costs of post-Soviet interprofessional co-operation between practising lawyers at the local level. It seemed that we, through the Methodius project had fostered that co-operation. The Russian network still exists, while contacts with West European partners diminished as the financing came to an end. Even this phenomenon has its domestic origins. Since the beginning of the Putin period, Russia has tended to look inwards.. The general conviction was that Russia has to follow its own path towards legal reform and that this choice cannot simply be copied from the West European models , although contacts with Western Europe should not be broken.

(4) We encountered serious problems of *duplication.* Simultaneously with our Methodius project, an American project called "Bringing the Rule of Law to Russia", sponsored by the American Bar Association, was in progress in St.-Petersburg. This was a major problem, first of all because the American partner worked with a much higher budget. Secondly, the American approach was much more pragmatic: the idea being to introduce compatible legislation in the commercial law field in order to be able to intensify trade with the new Russia. What the Americans were pushing too much, was perhaps not sufficiently present in our West European framework: what was our co-operation aiming at? What were our co-operation targets? Which particular interests were involved? The Russian partner was left in some confusion by so many signs of interest in co-operation. But after some years, they were forced to conclude that many of these contacts had been superficial.

(5) Institutional contacts are the best ones. But mutual co-operation and institutionalised partnerships, which guarantee ongoing and continuing relations, not dependent on particular persons at either end, need governmental funding. They cannot be self-sustaining in terms of organisation and funding at both ends.

The judges were handicapped on both sides, East and West, because of their lack of financing and institutional organisation. Although we were well received by the St.Petersburg City Court and the Arbitration Court, there was no stable basis for further contacts.

We clearly saw the difference with the Bar, the Prokuratura and the Notary. They were well organised (the *Prokuratura* in a strictly hierarchical way) and much easier to deal with. In this sense, we plead for strong institutional contacts, based on mutual interests. The benefits for western partners should be well defined and, although not being structured primarily so that aid benefits western economic interests, it should go further than a cultural shock of "clarifying the role of domestic institutions and processes versus external environmental factors in determining outcomes" and "expanding the sensitivity of western partners to cultural values and historical factors in policy making and bureaucratic reform"[21].

(6) Finally, time tables posed a problem. The project programmes and the budgets covering one civil year created a rigid time constraint. Too much had to be organised in too short an interval. There was no time for reflection and research. People became exhausted. The fast-track is to be avoided: realistic goals for the region mean that we have to spread

---

[21] Jenei, G., and Leloup, L., East-West Co-operation in Public Administration. An Agenda for the Second Stage. Paper presented at the EGPA Annual Conference Cape Sounion. Greece, September 1999, 8.

these initiatives over long periods of time. A one-year initial period for research and exploration should not be considered a luxury.

5. Conclusion

Our aim with the Methodius concept was to establish networks for practising lawyers in both Flanders and St.Petersburg, so that a long-term basis would be created for co-operation and exchange of information. The advocates and the procurators were the most active in using these contacts afterwards. The advocates invited each other to the opening sessions of the judicial year and helped each other in some particular cases. The Public Ministry sees opportunities for co-operation with its Russian partners in the field of transnational criminal investigation. The training aspect and transfer of information stopped however with the end of the financing.

We returned from this experience with quite some modesty: our influence is restricted, the limits of our knowledge are evident. We have realised that "understanding" is the first important requirement: such a project must be based on an appreciation of adifficult and complex situation. However, it was deemed positive in that we started from a complex structure of professional groups in East and West, the programme was designed to provide multiple benefits and a wide range of subjects were covered. But we were soon forced to step back and restrain ourselves.

Indeed "selective engagement", a term suggested by Ernst Haas in the early 1980s as a prescription for moderating but maintaining US containment policy towards the USSR can be our guiding concept: no overcommitment but determination to get involved[22]. This implies searching for low-cost solutions that might have a large impact. The most important challenge is to preserve the gains achieved.

What has succeeded is the exchange of information, procuracy for advocates, and institutional co-operation for notaries. What has largely failed are internships and institutional co-operation between judges. Internships failed for different reasons: they were not in the mainstream of the project. They were considered more as a project spin-off. As a consequence they were not organised in a systematic way. For internships we asked explicitly for young and bright candidates. We did not realise the extent to which our Russian partner network considered this request to be a threat. This sociological explanation is probably the main reason why professional contacts succeeded and internships did not. The corporate nature of the Russian network (of middle-aged lawyers) did not make room for such newcomers. The selection was made by the St.Petersburg network without much system or preparation. The main motive seemed to consist of offering a privilege to one of the network's friends. For the Western partners, it was rather difficult to integrate the proposed internships into their normal activity. Language was the most important hindrance: most interns from St.Petersburg spoke English, while in Belgium Dutch and French are the languages most used in legal affairs. What we did not include, and what could have been very useful, was to organise internships for some selected Russian-speaking Western lawyers in St.Petersburg. In this way, by including them in the activity of the city court, the commercial court or the bar and the procuracy, we would have educated specialists, prepared to advise on European-Russian legal affairs. In other words, although the Methodius project started from the idea of mutual interest, we were not selfish enough when it came to organising internships and other exchanges.

---

[22] Haas, E., On Hedging Our Bets: Selective Engagement with the Soviet Union. In: Wildavsky, A. (ed.), Beyond Containment: Alternative American Policies Toward the Soviet Union, San Francisco, ICS, 1983, 93-124.

Institutional co-operation between judges failed because of the huge virtual distance in the situation of Russian and Belgian judges, because both sides lacked institutional organisation (although Judge Poludniakov of St.Petersburg City Court played a very positive role in gathering judges together and furthering co-operation), and because of lack of budget on both sides. While the bar, the procuracy and the notaries disposed of enough budgetary and financial space to welcome the West-European partners, the judges were increasingly forced to acknowledge their miserable budgetary situation.

As to transferability of knowledge and practices in a particular situation in a particular country, some doubts remain. There must be a process of mapping out the groundwork, of thinking through interrelationships and interdependencies, of trial and error, of moderating risks by avoiding overcommitment. There was, for example, almost no interest in having access to western literature on the Rule of Law, the historical source of information being the 1864 judicial reforms in Tsarist Russia. The advocates revived the memory of some excellent and morally outstanding personalities, such as A.F. Koni (1844-1927), a practising lawyer and writer, esteemed for his respect for justice, democracy and for his focus on civil and moral values in the defence of people before the courts.

It is important to take time, to prepare fall-back positions should events spin out of control. In order to come to sustained, institutionalised programmes we need some well-trained specialised mediators from both sides to carry out extensive co-operation serving, mutual interests and this should become more systematic. More ambitious goals are likely to fail and would perhaps create backlashes, both in St.Petersburg and in the West. As for the sources of programme support, we can conclude that the Flemish support was more direct, less bureaucratic and allowed more freedom to develop the programme. Once the Flemish programme went European we had a feeling of alienation, as if we were losing our grip on the efficient organisation of the programme.

Let us try to summarise our findings by qualifying a good East-West co-operation (in particular with Russia) as:

(1)*Well-prepared co-operation:* as the culture of Russia is so different from our own, we need some preparatory study before getting into a co-operation programme. One year of intensive research and conceptualisation of the project is, in our view, a minimum before starting co-operation. In this period of preparation, the sponsor should be asked more explicitly about his aim and the underlying philosophy of co-operation. This concept could also be discussed between the sponsor and the project manager.

(2)*Incremental co-operation*: the time schedule should not be too restricted. Partners need time to get to know each other, the network needs to adapt to the situation of co-operation, partners should define their interests and evolve from one stage of co-operation (information exchange) to another (institutional co-operation). At each successive step partners should agree on further plans, expectations and mutual interests.

(3)*Realistic co-operation*: one has to accept that cliental networks in a Russian context are unavoidable. It is useless to start from individualistic premises. On the other hand a realistic approach assumes that self-interest in co-operation should be mutual. It is important to explicitly define the interests at stake in order to become more goal-oriented. It should be understood that the interests do not need to be defined as economic interests: they can aim at scientific co-operation (joint publication of a book or an article), at the systematic organisation of exchanges or at establishing long-term institutional contacts.

(4)*Institutional co-operation* is necessary, even if institutions change their profile during periods of transition. Partner institutes can, in this way, adapt to each other, specialise in some of the topics requested and attract professional people. Professionalism and specialisation are essential when relying on intermediaries who know the language and the culture of the partner.

(5)*Government sponsored co-operation*: it is impossible to leave this kind of co-operation to the private sector, because public interests are involved. The sponsoring government can be regional (such as the Flemish or Leningrad *Oblast'* government), national (the Belgian or Russian government), supranational (the European Union or, why not, the Commonwealth of Independent States) or international (World Bank, IMF). In any case, the sponsoring should continue for several years, unless it is ended earlier for specific reasons, and be defined by the sponsor and/or the contract manager.

(6)*Result-oriented co-operation*: as a general result long-term relations of trust and co-operation between partners should be established. In contrast, the results should not be defined too specifically and should allow for considerable flexibility. It is important to establish networks that can rely on each other, whenever the opportunity or the need arises. All the rest follows from this. Control of project implementation should bear this in mind as a general criterion.

Our conclusion is that institutionalising programmes created through collaboration is most likely to serve the needs of Russian and Western partners. But for that, you need specialised actors and promoters from both sides. The only way to overcome this problem is to organise well-defined internships on both sides, to establish long-term contacts between "selected mediators" from both parties (and accepted by the partners). Institutionalising successful programmes with governmental support would be advisable for the next decade. More emphasis should be placed on problem areas such as transparency in decision-making and anti-corruption efforts, and on remaining constantly attentive to new problems and needs in more mature phases of transformation.

East-West Co-operation in Public Sector Reform
F. van den Berg et al. (Eds.)
IOS Press, 2002

139

East –West Co-operation: The Case of Public Administration and Management Education at the Faculty of Economics, Matej Bel University, Slovakia

Juraj Nemec*

Introduction

Extensive and comprehensive socio-economic change processes from an authoritarian to a democratic society, from a centrally planned to a market based economy, have not left university education systems in transition countries, untouched. Obviously, country transformations had to be accompanied by changes in educational institutions, to enable them to deliver what was required following the events of 1989.

It would be extremely difficult, if not impossible, to "recreate" university level education without outside support and help. Not only the transfer of knowledge and experience, but also the very important financial aid, are the main tools provided by the West to the East to support comprehensive changes focused on the preparation and daily running of the education system, to make it equivalent to systems in the western academic world.

The experience and future expectations from East-West co-operation in the Faculty of Economics, Matej Bel University in Banska Bystrica (previously the Faculty of Economics of Services and Tourism of the University of Economics, Bratislava), with special emphasis on the creation and further development of the public administration and management programme, are evaluated in this text. Three time periods are included in the description, analysis and synthesis provided in the paper, i.e. the first stage of co-operation, the recent situation and future perspectives.

Starting Point for East-West Co-operation

Prior to 1989, university education in Slovakia (Czechoslovakia at that time), was not of a poor quality, but in the field of economic disciplines, the Marx-Lenin theory was presented as the only valid method to run the national economy. The contents of studies and the management of institutions were very influenced by the leading Communist Party. Co-operation and exchange with foreign institutions were limited almost entirely to the "Socialist World" and contact with Western bodies was rare. It was argued that this was not required because of the different approaches on how to understand the economic and social basis of society.

* Juraj Nemec, Professor, School of Economics (Visiting Professor at the School of Economics Prague, Faculty of Management Jindrichuv Hradec, Czech Republic), University of Mateja Bela, (Slovakia).

After the "Velvet Revolution" in 1989 a very difficult task faced all academic education institutions: the necessity for a comprehensive change in content, but also to some extent, in the system of university education. This was much more difficult in the field of socio-economics than in technical sciences. Starting conditions were really difficult, characterised by the following problems:

- the almost absolute lack of "non-Marxist" literature
- the limited language skills of many teachers
- the impossibility to produce a large academic staff "turnover"
- the important financial limitations
- the technical communication barriers etc.

However, in spite of these barriers, there was important potential on the local side. The Faculty of Economics of Services and Tourism in Banska Bystrica was one of the first three schools in the former Czechoslovakia to deliver, from the late eighties, an academic degree in public administration and management. The basis of this educational course was not a typically legal one, as in other similar schools in the region, but based very much on management and economic disciplines. The main actors behind this unique approach were a group of highly professional academics, not really linked to political structures, but much more focused on a real quality-based university education and trying to revise important dogmas, such as public service non-productivity. Some of them were linked to the current regime's opposition (Kontra, Streckova). Many members of staff were willing and successful in undertaking massive, rapid changes.

In this respect, after 1989 the management of the faculty decided to continue this branch (as one field of studies) and to react to the need to prepare "new" public managers and administrators capable of performing in the public sector of a changing country. Large-scale curricula changes became necessary.

First Period of Co-operation – New curricula and transfer of knowledge

The first steps in the process of creating a modern public administration and management education within the faculty were obvious —to change the curricula and provide new teaching literature and materials for teachers and students. The early stages of this process were really difficult and during the academic year 1990/91, mainly old curricula, with to some extent, amended contents were used. Under these circumstances, any form of foreign support was greatly appreciated. This support began in 1991. More programmes to facilitate such help became available e.g. TEMPUS, bilateral and multilateral co-operation financed from Western resources, USAID and many others.

Curricula Creation

The responsibility of preparing, organising and managing public administration and public management studies in the faculty was delegated to the Department of Public Economics (KVE) and the Institute for Local and Regional Development (ROMAR). Both found their main foreign partners in the UK – the School of Social Sciences at the University of Bath for KVE and the Institute for Local Government at the University of Birmingham for IROMAR. The support provided by both, and other less important partners, quickly led to the creation of new, modern curricula that respected Western standards of public administration and management education. The contents of studies and also, as a next step, the contents of all respective courses changed, but this was only the first, less complicated stage.

Teaching Literature and Materials

A change in curricula and syllabuses was not sufficient to achieve a basis for quality of education. New study literature and teaching materials were needed. In the early phase, existing Western books began to be used, but this brought its own problems. The first problem was procuring them and for this, foreign aid was important. The second, but much more complicated issue, was to use them in standard teaching – a problem that could not be solved by Western partners. On the teachers' side, especially during the first stage, very few internal faculty members with good foreign language skills were able to adapt quickly to the new texts and use them as a matter of routine. On the students' side, it was even more complicated – Western partners were unable to provide enough copies for all students and very few students were able to use foreign language literature. Two processes to improve the situation occurred – the delivery of lectures by foreign guests and the creation of brand new study texts, transferring (or often in this phase, only translating) existing western knowledge. In 1992, new Slovak study texts and textbooks appeared with increasing frequency. Two (later three) main forms of foreign help arrived – the delivery of literature and study tours. With foreign funding more Slovak teachers increasingly had the opportunity to stay in Western universities and institutions for longer periods (one month and longer), bringing back not only know-how, but also most importantly, book titles. The libraries in the faculty grew thanks to the receipt of more and more foreign and newly written Slovak books, textbooks and study texts.

Processes became more simplified from the mid-nineties when, thanks to foreign help (at that time mainly the TEMPUS programme), Internet became available both to faculty staff and students. This came soon after our Western partners had adopted this extremely important tool which they were using as a matter of routine. The possibility of unlimited and free contacts with all partners in the world, hastened the process of improving all aspects of faculty and study branch performance.

Evaluation of the First Period of Co-operation

The first period of co-operation, focusing on the creation of new curricula and basic necessary preconditions for teaching was relatively short in the case of the Faculty of Economics – i.e. from 1991–1996. As usual this had both positive and negative effects.

Reasons for Co-operation

The reasons for co-operating were very simple and straightforward on the faculty's side. The local staff was willing to change and to achieve, as soon as possible, new standards - knowing very well that this would be impossible without massive foreign support. With this, any possibility to co-operate, even under unequal conditions - more as a rule than the exception - was welcomed. People were ready to travel, in spite of unfavourable conditions (travel by bus or car for long distances, very limited per diem from Western partners, for example, 50 NGL for one week, etc.), and welcomed any foreign expert, providing him/her with all available comfort.

For the foreign partners, reasons were much more diverse. In some cases, just a willingness to help was a motivation. In most cases, an important issue was other tangible and non-tangible benefits on the "supplier's" side. The most important problems were encountered with programmes involving larger amounts of resources and by this, providing effective opportunities to subsidise the "supplier's" budget via the help given. As a rule, the money was managed by Western institutions and frequently was used more to benefit than to help (for example, during one programme, the English texts for Slovak participants were translated into the Slovak language by Western people, employees of a Western partner. The quality was poor which meant they could not be used. This way, the money was kept in the "supplier's home"). However, in spite of this, at this time, any possibility to access the West was welcomed by the Faculty.

Organisational Issues

During the first phase of co-operation, the Faculty had limited, if any, impact on planning and organising the system of foreign support. In reality, the partners chose the Faculty and its role was passive. Documentation for projects, schedules, budgets and most of the other details were prepared by Western partners and the Faculty's impact on project management was very limited.

This situation, in spite of looking very negative, was not in reality. It might be possible to argue that with this the Faculty had no possibility to select its partners, but it did not have enough information and experience to choose the best partner (finally main partners did do a "good job"). Limited impact on the design of programmes was to some extent, also acceptable. There was no capacity (manpower, skills) within the Faculty to develop top quality projects. In some cases, when foreign partners were willing to deliver, and not just earn money, this situation to some extent represented a "win-win" strategy.

Transferability of knowledge

This issue was probably the most complicated one. It is now generally accepted (Coombes, Verheijen, 1997) that non-adopted Western models are of very limited, if any, use to CEE transitional countries.

During the first stage of co-operation, there was no capacity to adapt Western knowledge to local conditions either on the side of Western partners, or on the side of the Faculty. This problem was marginal in basic economic disciplines such as Economics, where it was possible to use Samuelson's textbook in English, or in the very early-translated version. However, many problems were quickly recognised in management and organisational economy courses, where general concepts proved not to be valid in relation to the specific conditions of transition. With this, students received comprehensive knowledge about management in the West, but they were not able to use most of the theories in practice after graduation.

The problem of transferability became increasingly evident especially in the later years of this first period of co-operation. However, at this stage there was no solution to the problem (Western experts were not able to fully understand the local environment and local experts were not prepared "to take over" at this stage).

Evaluation of Results

In spite of the many weaknesses connected with East – West co-operation during the first phase, as previously mentioned, in general the results from this stage were mostly positive. Thanks to comprehensive foreign material and intellectual support and to the efforts of faculty staff the basic standards of public administration and management education, close to that delivered in the West, were met. With this, the processes of preparation and implementation of basic standards of academic education in the field of public administration and public management were in principle, completed quickly (the Faculty of

Economics belongs to the group of the first CEE institutions to have achieved this level), by the mid 1990s.

What were the reasons for this success? The results may seem surprising, especially when we take into account that many foreign aid programmes and advice from this period, especially at national level, failed (e.g. providing advice as how to achieve health care reform).

There were three main reasons, which positively influenced the success of co-operation. First, co-operation was at an institutional and not a national level. At this level, the establishment of "trust" relationships is expected and recipients of assistance are direct beneficiaries. The second was curricula creation; if we are strictly speaking about curricula and teaching methods, there are not that many differences between East and West (differences appear in syllabuses and teaching materials at a later stage of co-operation). Third (interconnected to the first), the recipients of assistance – the Faculty staff – were willing and had the capacity to co-operate, learn and develop. They were ready to accept inequality and inconvenience in exchange for the opportunity to grow from a professional point of view. Fourth, the Faculty was lucky. Most, if not all "suppliers", were willing to deliver.

Recent Developments in East-West Co-operation: from acceptance to real mutual co-operation

Like a child, the Faculty had to spend the first years of its "new" existence with much support – in this case not from its parents and relatives, but from Western partners. As mentioned, after approximately five years the Faculty entered an "adolescent" phase with changing needs and approaches. The curricula and basic study materials were of good quality and became the first priority on the agenda. What was the role of foreign help at this stage?

As with adolescents who still need a lot of help – maybe even more than before – the same can be said for this period of East-West co-operation. However, such help, to be acceptable, had to be adapted from its previous formats to adjust to a changing situation within the Faculty (and also within society). The Faculty of Economics was, to a large extent, lucky in this phase too. Most of its partners recognised the changing needs for co-operation and reacted in an appropriate way, thereby helping the Faculty to grow from adolescent to maturity as the final step in this phase.

Many important processes evolved during this period, more or less linked to the quality and scale of international co-operation. During this time, co-operation was developed, not only East-West, but also East-East. Since the East-East evolution is not our main focus, we will not develop this issue much further. It is however, necessary to stress its importance (this co-operation was necessary to obtain as much information as possible on specific impacts of Western models in transition countries) and the fact that this kind of co-operation was much larger in scale and was supported by Western funds (for example, NISPAcee as the main international contributor was, in its early stages, almost exclusively dependent on financing from the West). The most important development trends during the second period of East-West co-operation within the Faculty are described in the following text.

"Higher Forms" of Co-operation

Compared to the first stage in the late nineties, the patterns of co-operation noticeably changed. The "one-way" flow of know-how from West to East was replaced by "two-way" channels and the more or less systematic exchange of knowledge and information was replaced by mutual co-operation and institutional partnerships with main foreign partners, based on the equal role of each party. The number of co-operative activities grew and came about in many different forms, with "old" but also many new partners (the University of Scranton in the USA probably being the most important). The most important forms of such co-operation in terms of the Faculty were:

• preparation of joint conferences, such as the Health Management Symposium

• joint research, presented in important local and international journals and during many international conferences

• establishment of joint scientific journals such as the Journal of Health Management and Public Health

• joint advising of the Slovak government on many aspects of public sector reform

• exchange of visiting professors etc.

As mentioned, compared to the first stage, the Faculty became increasingly and more an equal partner in many partnerships, in spite of the fact that the dominant financial inputs came from the West. Co-operation agreements, plans and schedules were, in many cases, prepared together, based on long-term negotiations and respecting the needs of the Faculty. Compared to the first phase, unequal or non-effective forms of co-operation fell by the wayside.

These positive features do not mean that everything changed from one day to the next but the Faculty was always accepted in principle, as an equal partner, at least in relation to intellectual capacity and inputs. The less positive experiences in this direction were connected, for example, to co-operation via the Phare programme, especially in the area of advising the Slovak government as to the expertise of the Faculty staff. This type of Phare activity was, as a rule, with few exceptions, managed by Western firms. Many so-called "experts" came via this channel, frequently with a very inept advisory capacity concerning Slovak conditions; they caused complications and slowed down the progress. The Western firm received all the glory for any success but where there were problems, it was the Slovak partner who was at fault. Because of this, the Faculty significantly reduced its participation in the Phare programme and in principle, stopped all institutional participation.

Approaching "Western" Standards of Quality of Education

As mentioned, at the end of the first period of co-operation, the curricula was developed, comparable to Western standards and guaranteed a basic quality of education of public administration and management in Banska Bystrica. However, this was only the first step and many efforts were required to further progress in this field. Increased mobility (see annexes) and improving Internet facilities became the main tools to ensure the continuous quality of improvements in education. The goal for this period was straightforward – to achieve a full Western-standards quality level, at least in most aspects of delivery.

Because of existing high quality curricula, the focus changed to other aspects of education, mainly the implementation of more active forms of student participation and to the development of a more comprehensive range of local literature (see next section).

The developments went relatively quickly. In 1998, the first branch in the faculty – economics of tourism – passed the international (EFAH) accreditation. In 2000, the public administration and management programme became a member of the European Association of Public Administration Accreditation, as a first step in obtaining approval towards achieving the general European Standard. In 2000, the Faculty received its international ISO quality standards certificate.

Development of Adopted Study Literature

Compared to the beginning, which was characterised by the translation and/or very limited use of existing basic Western literature, the situation changed dramatically. Improving the skills of teachers allowed not only translations, but also the adoption and creation of study literature. This meant that textbooks and other teaching aids reflecting local conditions in Central and Eastern Europe, which in most developed "Visegrad" countries are still very different to those used in the West, were created.

Through this, the need for specific local literature, taking local conditions into account has been met. Creation of local literature by local authors does not mean "the end" of co-operation in this respect. Foreign help was still necessary in other areas. Much literature, written by local authors, was prepared in co-operation with Western colleagues, for example, providing general background, or helping to prepare case studies and was co-financed with the West. The delivery of updated Western books and journals continued, having the same or maybe greater importance, thus allowing students with improved language skills to use both local and foreign resources.

Mobility

As described, the mobility of staff and students remained one of the most important issues of co-operation, which was still supported by Western resources. The numbers involved soon reached a "sub-optimum" figure and have more or less stabilised today. What is changing is the quality at both teacher and student level.

Most important are the developments in student exchange. Through increased participation in the Socrates programme (and other similar bilateral or multilateral programmes), a growing number of Slovak students have enrolled in outside public administration and management programmes, receiving credits from Western universities. This trend is an important tool and a catalyst for many improvements in the quality of education at the Faculty. Two important points should be stressed. First, students taking credits abroad bring much back with them – some of them obtaining assistant appointments after graduation, or becoming doctoral students of the Faculty, offering interesting courses in foreign languages. Today, more than 25% of all courses are available in English, German or French. Because of these factors, the Faculty supports a student's mobility as much as possible and in 2001, full ECTS principles were adopted for all "full" programmes at the faculty.

Evaluation of recent developments – where are we now?

It is not the author's intention to raise this issue but it is clear that two five-year periods have existed. The first encompassed the preparation of basic standards of public administration and management education at the Faculty. During the second period, comparative European standards were introduced.

The period 1996-2001 was short when compared with the scale of important achievements obtained within these five years. Both high quality local human resources and comprehensive international co-operation underpin this success.

Today, in many respects, education in public administration and management have reached international standards and many members of staff are known in their own country and in many other countries (including those in the West). Students and graduates are at a similar level as their Western counterparts.

As mentioned, one of the most important factors behind this is the continuous quality of international co-operation. Many teething troubles which were characteristic of the first stage, disappeared. This was also thanks to the fact that the Faculty began to select partners with whom they could co-operate on a greater scale. Benefits from this co-operation began to be equally spread – both in tangible and non-tangible forms. Intellectual benefits are now more or less of equal weight on both sides, giving incentives to Westerners to co-operate although money is limited. Most important, co-operation programmes and partnerships are planned long-term with relative equality on all sides, reflecting the needs of the parties involved.

More positive features connected to the current stage of co-operation could be mentioned, but in doing this, the picture would become too optimistic. The situation is not a perfect one. We mentioned previously the example of the Phare advisory programmes, in which there was no opportunity for the Faculty to select its partner. In such cases, two choices are available – either to accept the risks connected with the eventual quality of the unknown partner, or to decide from the beginning, not to participate. Both are unsatisfactory, but the possibility of working from the beginning with an ex-ante selected Western partner is still more a question of theory rather than a real possibility.

Many Western institutions and especially firms, which are willing to begin new co-operation activities, underestimate the intellectual capacity of the Faculty. A recent offer from a Western company in the Phare programme is a typical example:

• In 2001 we heard a French expert describe the current Slovak problems in the area of public procurement as a necessary precondition to begin the training of local people by our staff.

• The original fee for Faculty experts was 60 Euro/day, including travel and other costs which is much less than the basic pay for teaching part-time studies at the Faculty.

Thanks to developments achieved, there is the possibility of selecting partners in most cases and to greatly influence the content and formal arrangements of co-operation plans, but in many areas, especially where EU structures and bureaucracy are concerned, this is far from perfect. New public management outcome based approaches, partnerships and other progressive ideas come from the West, but in many instances these are not values we can perceive in real East-West co-operation today.

Perspectives – Foreign support is still required, but how it is received will change

There is no doubt that the scale of East-West co-operation within the Faculty and also as a general principle, will grow, both in the short and long-term perspective. However, many qualitative aspects of such co-operation will still change.

Short-term Problem: finance

In spite of the fact that the Faculty achieved many European standards, from a short-term viewpoint we are still not ready for the West to withdraw its resources, especially financial.

We can present some practical figures to support this. In Slovakia, universities in 2001 remained state-owned budgetary organisations, with separate income and expenditure budgets (this means all income generated by the school is transferred to the state budget). Being linked to the limited resources of the state budget is the main reason for increasing financial problems at all universities in Slovakia. With a limited budget, there are no resources to finance foreign activities and salaries are very low, compared to those in the West.

During the 1990s and also in 2000 and 2001, the total yearly faculty budget for all international activities was close to 1,000 US dollars. The internal budgetary resources available to buy foreign literature for the entire public administration and management programme did not exceed 500 US dollars/year. The average monthly salary of a university professor is slightly more than 2,000 US dollars. On the other hand, the total value/cost for the foreign mobility of our teachers amounted to more than 100,000 US dollars in 2000.

These figures clearly show that the Faculty, unable to influence this unprecedented financial situation, still must rely heavily on outside resources. It is too early to withdraw from foreign donors, especially if further progress is our target. However, the processes of obtaining such funds should change.

The system of block grants could be replaced by activity grants. With this, much more equal, fair and transparent competition could be incorporated into the process of allocating resources, of increasing efficiency and effectiveness of all support and simultaneously providing pressures to increase the quality of the Faculty.

This becomes a somewhat curious situation. Western support has helped the Faculty to achieve high international standards, allowing it not only to be a partner, but also in some cases to be a competitor. Not everyone is able to accept that this is the most positive result of foreign aid and foreign co-operation, but those who are clever should. For my part, as a professor, the best result I could achieve would to have my students become better than their professor; this also pushes me to work harder.

However, cases of competition replacing co-operation should not arise too frequently. The possibility of working together and joining forces, especially for programmes in developing countries such as Albania, Middle Asia former NIS republics, is a much better solution.

Long-term Perspective: West-West co-operation?

According to the most optimistic scenario, Slovakia may become a member of the EU in 2003 or 2004. This is neither a very long-term perspective (even if we look more realistically at dates of possible adhesion) nor an obligation. In spite of not being of the same quality, most quality targets must be achieved – the most important being the full mobility of students and staff and comparable programmes.

Because of accession processes, increasingly less direct and exclusively specialised funds are allocated to Slovak institutions in the region today. After becoming an EU member, the only way will be competition for funds on an equal basis with other institutions. It is also to be expected that the role of the Faculty will dramatically change – from "recipient" to "supplier". To some extent today, but especially after becoming "one of those from the West", Faculty are and will be expected to participate in less developed parts of the world, for example Central Asia. The Faculty and its staff are becoming more greatly involved in these activities today. No doubt, this will mean important funding possibilities. On the other hand, it will bring new experiences and, to some extent, the opportunity to give what we were given. Having specific knowledge on the transition from "socialism" to a market-based democratic society, the inputs of CEE experts will be increasingly required to support progress in the less developed parts of the "post-socialist" region.

Conclusions and recommendations

Many types of foreign assistance have been seen during the last ten years in the development of public administration and public management studies at the Faculty of Economics of Matej Bel University in Banska Bystrica. However, the need for various forms of assistance changed as the institution developed.

In the first stage of co-operation (1991-1996), foreign support was the main catalyst for a quick change of curricula and syllabuses and for the creation of a necessary base of local and foreign literature accessible to both students and teachers. During this phase the support was often chaotic, the influence of the Faculty on its structure and contents was limited, but in principle, progress was made – we can call this period the "acceptance period".

The basic standards, close to those in the West were achieved relatively quickly, thanks also to Internet, which became available not much later that in foreign universities. The phase of continuous upgrading of the quality of education to reach Western standards had begun, ending in principle, by the end of the century. In spite of some important achievements, foreign assistance and international co-operation was more than necessary during this period.

The main feature of this period was increased international co-operation, but based on new principles. As the Faculty had achieved basic standards and local capacities had been upgraded, the Faculty could then select the most appropriate partners to reach its goals. The principle of acceptance was replaced by the principle of selection (limited selection), focusing on co-operation based on more or less equal partnerships with foreign partners, especially concerning intellectual impacts and the right to influence and create the contents of the co-operation. In spite of this, everything was not perfect during this period; for example there were difficulties connected to the Phare advisory programmes. We might call this period the "partnerships" period.

In our opinion, the scale and range of international co-operation will grow in the future, both at the Faculty (organisational) level and at the national level. This co-operation will have, in the short –term, two important dimensions:

• intellectual and management capacity equality (foreign partners will have to accept that the Faculty is "on the same" level and may be more knowledgeable about local specific experiences),

• financial background inequality (until the general environment changes – a new progressive university education law will be passed – the Faculty will not be able to allocate sufficient resources for international co-operation and foreign resources will still remain the basis for co-operation).

The success of future co-operation will be increasingly more dependent on the approaches of the respective foreign partner/candidate for partnerships. The former "child" is now a "young, but relatively inexperienced person", looking for his/her best partners, proud of what he/she has achieved in a relatively short period of ten years, but still financially dependent. The relatively high level of quality achieved means that the Faculty and similarly other high quality university institutions (at least in ·Visegrad countries) will become more selective when deciding upon foreign co-operation. These are the issues that potential Western partners will have to learn and respect; they must not to blame themselves during initial contacts especially when willing to find a real partner.

The longer-term perspective of East–West co-operation in CEE countries that have a genuine chance of becoming a member of the EU by the middle of the decade (and hopefully sooner for Slovakia) means a change towards new formats and approaches to West–West co-operation. Two main dimensions of co-operation might be expected:

different partnerships serving the mutual benefits of partners and partnerships; and/or co-operation agreements focusing on delivering advisory activities in less developed countries. To a great extent the Faculty's role today as "recipient" will slowly be replaced by the role of mutual partner and "supplier". This is what we are hoping and working for.

Experience from this case might also be used to provide some general recommendations for any Eastern university willing to enter into, or extend its relations to the West. Basic issues to be considered might be as follows:

1. The first step should be the assessment of the current stage of the development of the school and the definition of needs for, and expectations from, co-operation.
2. The selection of the Western partner should be made carefully (if possible); expected goals from that co-operation should be respected. The possibility of selecting the partner should increase as the school becomes more developed.
3. The benefits from co-operation should be distributed to both (all) partners as equally as possible, but the expectations of the Western partner (especially when providing resources) must still be respected as the main factor.
4. Resources coming from the West are, in most cases, not charity but usually serve to fulfil, more or less, the donor's goals.
5. The number of co-operation agreements should not be limited, but it is more effective to have a few "main" partners, willing to co-operate, especially on the basis of non-financial benefits.
6. When entering any kind of consortium partnership or bidding for tenders, such as in Phare, USAID or any other kind of programme, it is advisable to be very careful and define clearly all aspects of co-operation before the bid is submitted.
7. Schools in less developed CEE countries may now look not only for Western partners, but also may benefit very much from co-operation with more developed partners from the East.

Bibliography

Coombes, D. – Verheijen, T. (ed.): Public Management Reform: Comparative Experiences from East and West. European Commission, 1997

Jenei, G. – LeLoup, L.T.: East West Co-operation in Public Administration. An Agenda for the Second Step. EGPA conference, 1999

Verheijen, T. – Connaughton, B.: Higher Education Programmes in Public Administration: Ready for the Challenge of Europeanisation? University of Limerick, 1999

Verheijen, T. – Nemec, J.: Building Higher Education Programmes in Public Administration in CEE Countries. NISPAcee/EPAN 2000

Annexes

Table 1 Mobility of internal Faculty staff 1992-2000

Year	Total number of study trips	PA and PM staff
1992	25	3
1993	37	3
1994	56	11
1995	84	not available
1996	89	not available
1997	109	n.a.
1998	114	31
1999	106	20
2000	127	32

Table 2 Foreign guests at the Faculty 1992-2000

Year	Total number of foreign guests	PA and PM guests
1992	7	1
1993	20	1
1994	47	8
1995	58	not available
1996	59	15
1997	57	not available
1998	84	15
1999	44	8
2000	39	8

Table 3 Mobility of students (organised via Faculty) 1992-2000

Year	Number of students
1993	15
1994	26
1995	55
1996	43
1997	63
1998	60
1999	51
2000	50

East-West Co-operation in Public Sector Reform
F. van den Berg et al. (Eds.)
IOS Press, 2002

151

East-West Co-operation Models: An Analysis of the "Babes-Bolyai" University Public Administration Programme

Călin Hințea, Dan Șandor*

The purpose/focus of this article[1] is to evaluate the impact that international co-operation programmes have had on the development of the Public Administration (PA) Programme of "Babes-Bolyai" University (BBU), Cluj-Napoca, Romania. The development of the PA Department of BBU can be seen as a very interesting educational experiment, from the point of view of East-West collaboration in PA higher education. It is an example of the decisive impact of co-operation in developing and maintaining this organisation at a high level of efficiency and effectiveness while, at the same time, providing assistance in the adaptation to the new needs of Romanian society.

The following evaluation considers several elements including the context of the programme's development, its targets, the means to reach these targets, and indicators of success. In the last section, we will attempt to draw some conclusions about the impact of international co-operation.

1. General framework

After the 1989 revolution, Romania had to deal with many new and complex economic challenges, from the scarcity of funds and budgetary transfers to technology; the impact of the information society linked to changing citizens' perceptions and growing expectations, to those related to the desire for European integration. There is no public administration that can avoid the influences from its own environment (Rainey, 1997:79); and this is certainly true for Public Administration in Romania.

All these unexpected challenges did put Romanian public administration in a serious dilemma, related to its own way of functioning and its capacity to answer to new requirements. Countries in transition have ways to try to reach similar targets related to the modernisation of administration. Reinventing government (Osborne, Gaebler, 1993), or the New Public Management, are terms which have defined the discussion about new types of administrative structures, characterized by a specific culture oriented towards obtaining results in a less centralized public sector.

Romanian public administration was confronted with a double dilemma. First about the

---

* Călin Hințea is a Assistant Professor at the Faculty of Political and Administrative Sciences, Babes   Bolyai University, Romania and Sorin Dan Șandor is a Assistant Professor at the Faculty of Political and Administrative Sciences, Babes Bolyai University, Romania.
[1] We would like to express our gratitude to Professor David Ringsmuth for reviewing this paper and for all his useful suggestions.

existence of its own very complex and conservative cultural, governmental and administrative environment and, second, about the need for rapid adaptation to international requirements of Euro-Atlantic integration. Romanian public administration is still in the phase of improving its efficiency through the establishment of a Weberian-type bureaucracy. There are still problems in Romania that "ancient" history in western countries: the stability of the public servant/service; the citizen (as a "subject" of Public Administration) who understands the role that public administration should have in a democratic society. From this perspective, the leap towards a "post-bureaucratic" administration seems to be a slow and a difficult one. Professionalism in administration is still to be achieved.

One of the problems with which public administration reform has to deal is personnel. The quality of human resources is crucial. In many cases, modernisation of public administration was strongly encouraged by the appearance of a new generation of public servants who were "results-oriented", not procedures/process–oriented, and who were trained/educated differently. The importance of these two characteristics is highly visible in the case of the Romanian public administration, which has to deal with an enormous number of bureaucratic procedures, highly legalistic and rigid structures; it must acquire managerial skills and knowledge. The task of meeting these obstacles and challenges has fallen to universities, which are supposed to create a new generation of public servants.

The Romanian educational system is still far from fulfilling these needs. The former minister of education, Andrei Marga, (Korka, 2000:2) criticized very harshly the system, and exposed its lack of modernity. Substantive reform began in 1997, but there is still much to be accomplished

2. Romanian higher education in public administration

Public Administration education in Romania only really started after 1989. Now, more than twenty PA programmes exist. They include programmes in public and private universities, offering 4-year undergraduate programmes, 3-year undergraduate college programmes, and an 18-month Master's programme (Hintea, Ringsmuth, 1999).

In 1995, as the result of a meeting of representatives of Public Administration schools and the Ministry of Education, a framework for the Public Administration curriculum for the whole country was developed. Initially, this plan contained "law" or law-oriented courses to an overwhelming degree. This caused individual universities to propose modifications to it and to modify it significantly. Their association in particular academic faculties heavily influences all these programmes. In fact, PA programmes are located in Law, Economics or Political Science faculties, a fact that has been decisive in the way they understand and teach public administration.

In May 1999, at the initiative of The Ministry of Education, and at the request of several universities, a meeting concerning curricula in Public Administration took place. The result was a major and important change. The idea of a single plan/formula/curricula that consists mainly of law was abandoned. The representatives of the various PA programmes agreed upon several important issues:

• The need for reform, emphasizing an interdisciplinary approach and compatibility of PA programmes with the modern and European values and standards;

• The curricula of PA schools would respect four disciplines: administrative sciences, law, economics and social and political sciences;

• Based on these four disciplines each programme would build its own curricula and syllabuses in keeping with its own internal requirements and those of the job market;

- The need to adapt training programmes to the market and reform demands.

In addition, the idea of transferable credits was adopted. Participants agreed that it would be beneficial and would allow a more integrated educational system in the field of PA. Although the accomplishment of all these decisions has not been easy to accomplish, it is clear that these changes represent an essential transformation of the way in which PA higher education is now perceived in Romanian universities and constitutes the basis for future changes.

Recently, the efforts of Romanian universities to create a professional community of those involved in higher education in the field of Public Administration have intensified. Various ideas to form a national and multi-national community interested in and capable of discussing problems related to the development of Public Administration education and capable of sharing insights and implementing decisions about its future were developed. This type of approach is in its infancy in Romania, and the lack of communication between the actors in the field is still the general rule.

It is interesting to note the fact that pressure for integration also constitutes an important factor in favour of those PA programmes that promote a modern interdisciplinary model.

At Babes-Bolyai University the study of Public Administration started in 1995 when a BA programme was initiated under the administration of the Political Science Department. In 1996, the PA Department was established. The Department of Public Administration and Human Resources Management is part of the Faculty of Political and Administrative Sciences and contains programmes of study ranging from a Master's programme and a BA programme in Cluj, to college-level programmes in Cluj, Sfantu Gheorghe (in Romanian and Hungarian), Satu Mare (in Romanian, Hungarian and German) and Bistrita. The BBU PA Department has as a major goal: to offer quality education linked to the needs of students, staff, public administration and satisfying European/international standards.

3. The objectives of the programme and the impact of international co-operation

Starting a new academic programme in Romania, especially in a new field, is a very interesting enterprise. It has many aspects that resemble the development of a business. The first step is that of assessing the need for that type of education and starting it with very scarce resources. At the very beginning we began without an adequate curricula, without a teaching staff, without teaching materials and books, without proper logistics. The only chance that such an endeavor would succeed was to have help from international sources. International grants are indeed very often decisive in building new programmes.

In the case of the BBU PA programme, a Tempus programme grant made it possible to start a PA programme as a minor in the Political Science programme in 1992. The initiative was short-lived, however, because the Romanian system of education did not recognize "minors" at that time. Nevertheless, this initiative was a source of experience for starting the PA programme. In 1995, some of the students who graduated from that programme later joined the PA department.

The Department of Public Administration, which began in 1996 - one year after the PA programme was launched, started with only one professor, one teaching assistant and one junior teaching assistant. The decision to establish such a structure was a consequence of the strong support from the Social Science Curriculum Development programme, which is described more fully below. From this small beginning, the department began, assumed, and achieved very ambitious objectives.

The main objective was the development of a public administration programme to produce well-prepared graduates capable of coping with the needs of a new public administration. The model that was followed was Western-oriented.

Specific targets were taken into account:
1. Building a curricula based on Western experience, with Western consulting, but also adapted to the Romanian situation;
2. Improving the management of the department;
3. Developing the teaching staff, both in terms of number and quality;
4. Providing access to knowledge in the field for teachers and students, through original and translated literature;
5. Developing teaching materials, publications;
6. Building a research capability;
7. Improving material resources;
8. Involvement in the community.

Co-operation with the West was seen as the key to reaching these targets. Some of the collaborative programmes in which the Public Administration programme was involved included:

SSCD: In April 1995, the USIA funded a project which was administered by the International Research & Exchanges Board and the American Council of Learned Societies: The Social Science Curriculum Development programme, **SSCD. SSCD started** a co-operation project to develop empirically based and multi-disciplinary social science curricula at the Institute of Sociology of Warsaw University, the Center for Public Affairs Studies at Budapest University of Economic Sciences, and the Faculty of Political Science, Public Administration and Journalism at Babes-Bolyai University in Cluj-Napoca, Romania. The primary objective of the SSCD project was to help universities in the region train the next generation of academics and policy makers to have a strong influence on democratic transitions. Support for curriculum development, faculty and student research, and the development and acquisition of relevant teaching materials and equipment were the focus of the project.

In addition, the SSCD wanted to connect the academic world to the surrounding community through student internship programmes, faculty/practitioner conferences, and select research efforts.

Tempus 1 – The first Tempus programme in which the Political Science Faculty was involved. The aim of this programme was to assist in the development of the political science education in Romania and also to create a minor in PA. At that time public administration was not yet an academic field. The impact was significant in developing political science curricula, equipment and a library and also in building a certain experience in international co-operation.

Tempus 2 – This Tempus programme was a further step in the development of international co-operation, and was directly aimed at supporting public administration higher education. It was created with partners from Tempus 1 and had as goals the improvement of the training and consulting capacities of Romanian partners: BBU, Bucharest University and Iasi University. As a result of this programme, and based on the support of foreign partners (Université Libre de Bruxelles, Université Paris XI Sceaux, Genoa University, Lapland University Rovaniemi), the Training Centre for Local Public Administration and the Centre for Analysis, Management and Public Policy were established.

Tempus 3 – The objective of this programme was to implement a European (French) Master's Program (DESS) in Public Administration at BBU, based on the support of the

French partner (Université Paris XII Val-de-Marne, Faculté d'Administration et Echanges). This was based on the model of the French University, courses taught by foreign professors, internships in Romania and France, etc., Romanian students, (public servants from local public administration), received a French university degree. The impact of this programme was significant in developing the capacities and experience of the BBU faculty and staff in co-ordinating graduate programmes in public administration.

Master's Programme in Public Services Management. Developed as a result of previous cooperation with State University of New York (SUNY) at Albany, and with NASPAA support, and an USIA grant, a Masters Programme in Public Administration was established. This programme has both Romanian and American professors, and it is targeted at public servants from local public administration in the Transylvania region.

Within this framework of co-operation, several means were designed to achieve the PA department targets:

• **Faculty development visits** were used to acquire new knowledge, to improve the teaching quality and new teaching methods, and to develop new courses. Important lessons were learned in improving the management of the department. Of particular assistance in this respect were the visits sponsored by SSCD at BUES Hungary and at SUNY Albany, NY, which aided in improving the curricula based on the experiences of host institutions. Tempus 1, SSCD, Tempus 2, Tempus 3 and USIA sponsored such visits.

• Using **visiting scholars** for teaching, consulting, training. Visiting professors were used not only to teach courses in the department but also to be involved in the development of the department, for which their experience was very useful. They were also involved in training activities and in common projects with Romanian scholars in research and publications. Their presence at BBU was also very important for the development of the philosophy of the department, for its organisational development, in particular, because members of the department were very young and lacked experience. In addition, their intellectual presence improved the image of the department, helping to establish co-operation in relation to PA programmes and also with officials from Romania and abroad.

• Grants for purchasing **Books/Journals/Equipment**. In this respect SSCD was very useful in providing basic and advanced text and journals, equipment such as computers, modems, copiers, fax machines, printers, computer software, overhead projectors and systems that allow computer projections. With this help, the faculty set up a good library and a computer network, which, at that time, was the best at the BBU. Further acquisitions, either from local resources or from Tempus and USIA programmes have maintained and expanded those facilities.

• **Translation** programmes were supported by SSCD to provide basic texts in Romanian. A NISPAcee programme supported translation of SIGMA/OECD publications in Romanian. This helped students to access materials included in bibliographies, which, until then were almost entirely in foreign languages.

• **Research** programmes were sponsored by SSCD, enabling both extensive research projects and small research efforts that helped young faculty and students obtain practical research skills. For the first time in Romania applied research was utilized in local and central administration. Until then research was not seen as having a part in a PA curricula, but the results of these projects and their dissemination showed that this was a necessary component of an academic programme. From this point of view international cooperation was extremely useful in providing models, techniques, literature and specialists.

• **Dissemination** of the knowledge gained was made by different means. The Transylvanian Public Administration Review, TPAR, was initiated in 1999. It was originally sponsored by SSCD and later by Tempus, and now is self-supporting. The

TPAR's major aim is to provide a forum for PA academics and professionals. International co-operation was helpful, not only in terms of financing, but also by the presence on the editorial board of several European and US scholars, and many articles were written by foreign specialists.

The first two International Conferences in Public Administration, held in Cluj (1999 and 2000), were also supported by SSCD who served in uniting the Romanian PA academic community and many professionals, especially improving communication and co-operation between them. Each conference has also seen a significant international presence, connecting the Romanian PA community with the international community.

- **Internships** for students started at the Faculty in 1993 as a student initiative. The aim was to make the students familiar with the real world and practices in the institutional environment and also to increase their opportunities for employment after graduation. The institutionalisation of internships was influenced by these common practices in Western PA programmes. SSCD provided substantial support in the first years for the internship programme. Now an internship is a mandatory part of the PA programme.

- **Student exchanges** have been very useful in obtaining new perspectives, mentality and knowledge. The SSCD was the first international co-operation project to offer such exchanges. Now the SOCRATES programme is the most instrumental in offering such opportunities.

- **Training programmes** for public servants started in 1999, based on a grant from the Open Society Foundation (OSF). Also, in 1999, a Tempus programme was initiated to support training programmes having as a major goal the institutionalisation of such programmes and establishing a training center. The success was quite astonishing. In the first year of the programme there were over 230 applications for the 60 places offered. In 2001, a Senior Management Programme for high-ranking officials was launched with the help of visiting scholars from the US and Europe. Again the number of applications was far larger than the number of trainees accepted. Now, due to previous accomplishments made with international support, the training programmes are done in co-operation with the Territorial Training Center for Local Public Servants, a government-established NGO, which is under the academic supervision of our department.

- **Consulting** was one of the ways in which the department wanted to be involved in the community. International programmes were decisive in starting such activity. Due to a Tempus programme, the Center for Analysis, Management and Public Policy was established as the consulting unit of the department, with a view to providing consulting services for local and central authorities. International cooperation led to the improvement of consulting skills and participation in international teams of consultants.

- **A different style of management**. Under the influence of Western models a more flexible style of management was adopted. While the traditional way of managing Romanian academic departments is a rigid one, based on academic ranks, in which there is little communication and collaboration, the department put a strong emphasis on flexibility, communication, result-oriented practices, and obtaining non-budgetary resources.

4. Measures of success

There are several measures we can use in assessing the success or failure of a programme. Such measures can be quantitative or qualitative, input- or output-oriented. In Romania, the National Council for Authorisation and Accreditation is using quantitative and input-oriented measures. For instance: the proportion of full-time teaching staff must be over 70%, the proportion of professors and assistant professors among the full-time teaching staff must be over 20%; the existence of academic facilities, such as classrooms, books. There is also concern for the curricula of the programme and for each course, but the means of control over teaching content are not very well regulated. Sometimes NCAA inspections request modifications in the curricula. As an example, some members of this commission, who are partisans of a particular curricula, insist upon arbitrary requirements for each domain of study, but these observations are not mandatory.

Another possibility is to use performance indicators. As an example, we will take the definition developed by Cave, Hanney, and Kogan (1991:24): "a performance indicator is an authoritative measure—usually in quantitative form—of an attribute of the activity of a higher education institution. The measure may be ordinal or cardinal, absolute or comparative. It thus includes both the mechanical applications of formulae (where the latter are imbued with value or interpretative judgements) and such informal and subjective procedures as peer evaluation or reputation rankings."

Performance indicators are replacing more traditional input-oriented measures, such as the number of students enrolled, with goal - or result - oriented estimates of outcomes or value-added, such as the quality and employability of graduates.

We think that a balanced approach must be taken, even though it may seem heterogeneous. There are several performance indicators such as reputation rankings or peer evaluation that can not be used in the case of the BBU PA programme.

There are some quantitative and input-oriented indicators that can help to assess the development of the PA Department.

1. The number of students in the programme has increased from 40 in 1995 to an estimated number of 520 in the 2001/2002 academic year;
2. The number of teaching staff had increased from 3 in 1996 to 17 in 2000. Also, junior faculty received significant promotions in academic degrees and rank. Currently, the greatest number of them are lecturers, which is very significant, considering that the majority are about thirty years of age.
3. The evolution of the number of candidates for admission in the PA programme is quite positive[2].

Number of applications/place for the 4-year PA programme

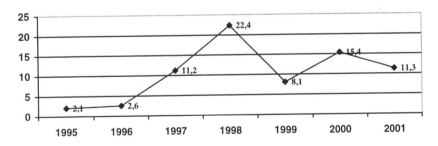

---

[2] This indicator is one related to many things beside the quality of the programme. A high number of candidates usually means that there is a great interest in the field of studies and that the university offering that programme has a good reputation. Some other factors, like the admission system, can be very influential. In 2000, when the PA programme of Bucharest University was launched, due to admission, based only on the baccalaureate degree, there were 57 candidates/place!

4. The number of public servants included in training programmes reached around 90 for the academic year 2000-2001. This is the largest figure in the three years since the launching of the programme. The number of applications continues to be far greater than the number of places available.

5. The material resources are constantly increasing. In September 2001, a new building will be available, providing an additional, 1500 square meters for the needs of the Faculty.

6. The number of institutional co-operation agreements and relationships has increased every year. The number of partners has increased with academic partners and Romanian public institutions, involving consulting and research.

7. There are a large number of teaching materials which have been developed by the members of the department. Romanian manuals, textbooks and case studies are available for many of the courses. Still there is much to be done. Also, the number of publications, books and articles, authored by the members of the department has increased.

8. The number of students involved in exchange programmes has increased in the last two years, due to the SOCRATES programme. The number is still relatively small, but a significant increase is expected to appear for the 2001-2002 academic year when two agreements between our department and Western universities will become operational.

There are also some qualitative indicators concerning the input:

1. Curricula development can be regarded from different points of view. One of them is the number of new courses. Since 1996, 23 new courses have been developed in the department. More than 4 new courses have been added each year, and all the others were revised and improved.

2. Modifications were made in the structure of the curricula. In 1996, the focus was on law courses (72%) while in 2001/2002 only 25% are on law. A greater importance is now on management and general administration courses, public administration structures and institutions, processes and public policy.

Curricula structure

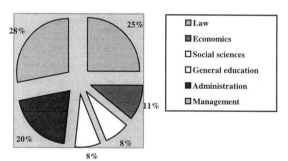

3. The quality of the teaching process is at the present moment assessed only by testing student satisfaction. The process is a regular one, includes all the students in the programme and is aimed both at the quality of courses and the qualities of the teaching staff, both in absolute value, which is considered to be good or very good in the majority of cases, and in ranking the quality and attractiveness of courses and teachers. While the overall good to very good evaluation may be influenced by the lack of criticism of the students, there are some signs that this evaluation is genuine, since they are enthusiastic recruiting agents for the programme.

In terms of performance indicators we have data only about the employability of graduates, but only after two generations/classes, which makes any judgment premature. Of the first graduates, in 1999, 95% were employed or continuing graduate studies within one year of graduation. While complete figures for the 2000 class are not yet available, preliminary figures indicate that approximately 74% are already employed or continuing their education. Can this be considered a valid indicator of success? This is of course debatable. It can be a measure of success due to several aspects: the medium level of employability in BBU is lower. (less than 60%) The level of unemployment in Romania is about 11%. There are serious budgetary restraints for new recruitment in public service; the majority of those who got a job are working in public administration.

What was the contribution of international co-operation in each of these indicators?

The impact is low in areas related to the particular specificity of Romania as in the case of the number of students or candidates/place that can be very important for a programme. In all other aspects they can be very influential.

Programmes having international support boost the number of applicants. Much of the material resources were obtained with western support. Many teaching materials were also supported from different kinds of co-operation. The curriculum was changed under the influence and with the help of foreign aid. The quality of the teaching process has much to do with the knowledge and techniques learned in faculty development visits, and to visiting scholars who usually had good evaluations from the students.

5. Conclusions

Indicators can not capture much of the impact that East-West co-operation can have on a programme. One of the facts not taken into account is the stage in which such co-operation occurs: before the very start, during the first years of a programme, or when a programme has been well established. The situation can be very different in each of these cases.

In the case of starting a new programme, availability of international support can be a very strong factor in such an enterprise. While a university may have very little to offer, the existence of Western universities that are willing to help and some donor organisations that will provide material support may be decisive in the decision to establish a new programme. In this case the influence of co-operation may be extremely important in all aspects of the programme, especially when Eastern and Western counterparts have similar aims.

If help comes after the programme has started, the problem will be to adjust the needs of those in the programme to the aims of the Western partners. The need for change may be viewed quite differently from each side.

In the case in which a programme is well established, international co-operation can be helpful only in improving things, especially at the qualitative level. There is already a routine to cope with, however aims may be very different.

The history of BBU PA Department shows how important international co-operation can be for the start and the development of a programme.

Starting new programme,such as the Master's, gives new dimensions to the entire programme. Each new initiative taken by the BBU PA Department has had international support, but that support was also useful for improving already-existing programmes: a faculty development visit in the framework of the American Master Programme will not be used solely for the purpose of that programme, as the knowledge, skills, techniques acquired can/will be useful during the entire programme, or for trying to develop further programmes.

Jenei & LeLoup (1999) made a classification of co-operation into five different categories or hierarchical stages: *Exchange of Contacts and Information, Systematic Exchange of Knowledge and Experience, Joint Action, Mutual Co-operation* and *Institutionalised Partnerships*. Trying to put our department's collaborative programmes into this framework can be a difficult enterprise. In many of these programmes there were several partners, and the PA programme was only one of them -or in the case of the Tempus 1 programme, only an experiment. The department has grown over the years, its needs and contributions changing at a fast pace.

From the point of view of our department, there is a certain and almost continuous increase in the quality of relationships with Western partners. Tempus 1 can be considered, with its scope being the political science department, as in the *Exchange of Contacts and Information* stage. The co-operation with some of the partners did grow, ending in the Tempus 2 programme at a *Joint Action* level. In establishing a training centre and with some partners co-operation went beyond the framework of the programme, very much like a *Mutual Co-operation*. Tempus 3 can also be seen as *Joint Action*, with the building of a French Master's programme. The SSCD programme, very influential in the development of our department, had many aspects of *Joint Action* and helped build some *Mutual Co-operation* relations with other institutions involved in the programme. The Master's programme in Public Services Management started as a *Mutual Co-operation* project with the ambition to become an *Institutionalised Partnership*.

What are the main things that an Eastern university wants from an East-West co-operation and how can they be used? Usually there are three main issues in each such co-operation: faculty development visits, visiting scholars and material resources. The way in which they are handled can bring success or failure.

Faculty development visits can become something very different from their intended goal. Due to low salaries in Romania, where a full-professor in a university has a monthly wage of less than $500 US dollars, such a visit can easily be conceived as a way to make some money, or a trip, with all expenses paid. Seldom do the international co-operation arrangements establish an adequate mechanism for the selection of participants in these visits. Such a procedure is very important in order to try to match the interests of the co-operating partners, and to ensure that the right person is sent to the right place. A real cost-benefit analysis should be made: what can be the benefits in sending person X to place Y? What knowledge, abilities, techniques will he or she acquire? How will these be useful for the programme? What courses will be developed? Another evaluation should be made to determine whether the purpose of the visits is to improve the management of the programme, curricula development or establishing and developing useful contacts and bilateral relations.

Visiting scholars can be very important, in a positive or in a negative way. There are some cases in which some of them did fail, sometimes because they were not good enough or because they did not try to understand the specificities of the country they were in and tried to apply mechanically the models they knew. Others did a fairly good job in teaching. Truly positive impacts will occur only if those who are involved try to engage in the problems of the host department, try to share some of their experiences relating to the problems of organizational development, mentality, curricula, in working with the staff and students in research, etc.

Material resources are always scarce. It will always be useful to have money for equipment, library, and publications. It is also very important to try to evaluate the way in which such resources are used, because sometimes they are poorly managed and utilized. Also it is very important if the organisation that uses those resources can sustain efforts after the external support ends.

International co-operation should also be evaluated from the point of view of what has been achieved in terms of informal collaboration. Did co-operation help in forming new links and networks? If, after co-operation ends, the Eastern partner is still isolated, then it was a failure. International co-operation can be very useful in terms of establishing new contacts and good personal relationships with Western universities or persons; a wider knowledge of your programme can then be established. Very often good personal relationships can be the start of a good co-operation initiative. Knowing the programme and knowing the people are essential for those who want to collaborate with an Eastern university. In our case the SSCD programme helped us to make connections with SUNY Albany and NASPAA which were developed in the Master's programme of co-operation.

At the base of a serious co-operation project, we must consider three main points:

- Common understanding of the objectives;
- Good personal relationships;
- Mutual openness benefits that a Western partner can draw from such a co-operation project (besides a better knowledge of problems in the East) are as great or greater than those received by the "recipient" institutions and individuals.

Another important thing in trying to evaluate the success of East-West co-operation has to do with the major aim: trying to help the East to change. In any process of change, the main thing is mentality. It is extremely important that the profile of the chosen partner be linked to a capacity to act as an actor of change. There must be a capacity to disseminate information, abilities, and to influence the environment.

The main element which should characterize a "success" of a East-West co-operation project concerns the creation of structures, mechanisms, abilities and mentalities able to be sustained, long after the formal institutional programme ends.

Bibliography

Cave M., Hanney, S. & Kogan, M., 1991, The Use of Performance Indicators in Higher Education: A Critical Analysis of Developing Practice, Second Edition. London: Jessica Kingsley Publishers;

Hintea, Calin and David C. Ringsmuth. 'Public Administration Education: Romania.' Verheijen, Tony and Juraj Nemec (eds.) 2000. Building Higher Education Programmes in Public Administration in CEE Countries. Bratislava : NISPAcee;

Jenei, Gyorgy & Lance T. Leloup (1999). East-West Co-operation in Public Administration. An Agenda for the Second Stage. Paper presented at the EGPA Conference, Cape Sounion, Greece.

Korka, Mihai, 2000, Strategy And Action In The Education Reform In Romania, Fourth Conference of the European Ministers of Education, Bucharest, Ministry of Education;

Osborne D., Gaebler T., 1993. Reinventing Government: How the Entrepreneurial Spirit is Transforming the Public Sector. London: Plume

Rainey, Hal G., Understanding and Managing Public Organizations, Jossey Bass Publishers, San Francisco, 1997

Șandor, Dan, Hințea, Calin, 1999, Profesionalizarea funcționarilor publici, Revista Transilvană de Administrație Publică, nr.2, 1999

East-West Co-operation in Public Sector Reform
F. *van den Berg et al. (Eds.)*
IOS Press, 2002

163

Conflicts and Motivation in Projects for Central Banks

Renger J. Afman*

1. Introduction

Background

After the restructuring of 1991 in the former Soviet countries, aimed at the realisation of a well functioning market economy, an intensive process of exchange and co-operation got under way between people and institutions in Western countries and those in transition countries. This resulted in a variety of contacts, projects and institutionalised collaboration on different levels and of many kinds. The projects and activities in question often differed in character from projects within Western countries, and the same is true for the ways people worked within those projects.

Purpose of this paper

The purpose of this paper is to give some insight into experiences of people from a Western background who worked on projects in (CEE) countries in transition to a market economy after the aforementioned restructuring. A number of relations and conflicts on the personal and organisational levels will be discussed from the point of view of the schematic outlines presented by Jenei/Le Loup and Van den Berg in 1996[1]. This could be of interest not only to those working (or intending to work) in such projects, and to those who are in charge of projects, but also to managers responsible for human resources.

The paper is intended to be an account based on personal experience. Findings are brought together and sometimes compared that came up in two types of projects:

• Technical assistance for central banks in countries in transition, provided by people from Western central banks;

• Projects carried out by private firms for industry and for a variety of institutions in countries in transition.

Characteristics of these types of projects are described in section 2. Sections 3 and 4 elaborate on conflicts and motivational issues on the individual and organisational level. Section 5 outlines some of the effects of the work experienced by consultants and people in

---

* Renger J. Afman is a certified management consultant and is a partner in AO Management Consultants (Driebergen, Netherlands). Since 1994 he has worked on organisational development and training in Central and Eastern Europe and Asia. He also co-ordinated the technical assistance by the Dutch central bank to CEE central banks for a few years.
[1] György Jenei and Lance T. LeLoup; Frits van den Berg; schematic outlines presented in the Study Group on Co-operation in Permanent Education, Training, Research and Consultancy between Eastern and Western Europe of the European Group of Public Administration, 1996.

recipient organisations. Section 6 concludes with some recommendations.

2. Types of projects

This section contains a description of the two main types of projects under study. These projects are in fact characterized not by the activities themselves, but by the organisational context. In 1996, Jenei/Le Loup and Van den Berg presented stages and levels of collaboration. Their schematic outline has been followed in the sections below to order the material. In this section the character of the assistance to central banks is described and a tentative classification of the assistance according to this outline is presented. The reader may like to use the outline to classify his or her own experience in any given collaborative setting.

Technical assistance provided by Western central banks

Western central banks (donor banks) provide so-called 'technical assistance' to central banks (recipient banks) in countries that are in transition to a market economy after the restructuring in the communist world in 1991. The assistance is known as 'technical' in the sense that it provides knowledge transfer and consultancy (while other assistance can be financial or political). The purpose of the assistance is to encourage institutions and people in the countries in transition to function according to the demands of a market economy, and to prevent aberrations due to a lack of knowledge and training. In the case of central banks, the aim is the development of the central bank as an institute; the development of individual staff members is instrumental to this. With this in view, international agreements were drawn up by the central banks of the G-10 countries. Forms in which assistance is provided are, for instance:

• Long-term assignments (six months to three years, residential);
• Short-term visits (one to four weeks), ad hoc, or repeated assistance in longitudinal development processes;
• Training programmes (one or two-week courses);
• Visits or secondments to Western central banks.

The missions lasting one or two weeks led by the IMF have a rather different character, namely, one of monitoring and issuing advice. The mission teams are comprised of people from various countries.

The assistance is paid for by international institutions such as the IMF and the World Bank, by country-based institutions such as USAID, the British Know-How Fund, the European Union (especially TACIS and PHARE programmes) and donor central banks themselves.

Table 1 shows a tentative classification of the assistance to central banks according to the schematic outline by Jenei/Le Loup and Van den Berg.

Projects by private firms

Private firms work on a broad range of projects, of which the beneficiaries are in governmental and private sectors in the receiving countries. This article has drawn on projects in the field of information and communication technology (ICT) and consultancy work in organisational and change processes.

Table 1.

Stages (Jenei/Le Loup)	Levels (Van den Berg)		
	International	*Organisations*	*Individuals*
1. Contacts	IMF: exchange of t.a policies BIS: information; informal meetings	Contacts by telephone/ fax, and in the context of meetings	Contacts in the context of meetings and other t.a.
2. Systematic exchange	BIS: meetings of co-ordinators; database on t.a. IMF: country co-ordinators Conferences of c.bs in the same IMF-constituency	Establishment of co-ordinators within c.bs. Bilateral exchange between c.bs.	Exchange by people working in the same field Spin-off to extra professional exchange and consultancy on a personal basis
3. Joint action	IMF Missions Training Programmes for CB Russia, CB Ukraine, financed by EU	T.a. assignments and contracts between two c.bs., sometimes financed by EU or others Bilateral t.a. in general Secondments Visits	People involved defining tasks, roles and consultancy relations
4. Mutual co-operation	*Generally until now the t.a. has not been reciprocal. But in the third millennium this could be the case in some of the projects. In some recipient countries people are now speaking of technical co-operation rather than technical assistance.*		
5. Institutionalised partnerships	IMF-constituencies Joint Vienna Institute (for training)		Resident advisers

➡ = strong relation/influence
t.a. = technical assistance
c.bs. = central banks.

ICT projects in Eastern Europe mostly concern telecommunication companies and industries related to them. These projects are financed by the receiving companies themselves (or Western parent companies) and/or governmental or EU funding programmes. In some cases this involves sending specialist personnel, in other cases the Western IT company has responsibility for a particular project.

The nature of the consultancy projects on organisational change is more specifically dependent on the persons concerned. In these projects it is essential to guarantee co-operation with counterparts in the East.

In all types of private projects co-operation with other western consultants and specialists is now quite common.

Projects for central banks and private projects compared

A comparison of projects between central banks and those carried out by private firms shows a number of differences. As regards central banks:

• Standing relations already exist between the institutions involved (where only changes in personnel are important, and sometimes crucially so);

- Funding is not usually a problem. Having the right people to give the assistance to may prove to be more difficult.
- In respect of private projects:
- Funding for private contracts is limited and always a point of concern, mainly for the contractor but also for the consultant. In those cases where the contractor is not the client, special complications may arise;
- Obtaining assignments (mostly through proposal and selection procedures) takes a lot of time and energy, although the advantage is that a good deal of thought has already gone into the project in advance.

Not surprisingly, it is the political context that influences both implicit and explicit wishes about the possibilities of change and development, not only with central banks, but also with private clients.

3. Motivation on the individual level and conflicts between individuals and organisations

Consultants: personal and professional motivation

In many cases, the 'what' and 'how' of specific assistance to central banks is not precisely defined, while the field in which it operates is very broad. This leaves a good deal of room for personal priorities and interests as motivating factors for the work, something which is equally the case for both parties, for those offering as well as those receiving assistance.

Private projects on the other hand are more often defined very precisely, but there the organisational and inter-organisational environment, in which the assignment has to be carried out, is often not very clear and interests are diverse. Private projects can be more complex than those in Western countries because of a greater variety in historical, cultural and economic contexts.

Since the organisational circumstances in the recipient organisation cannot be known very well in advance and since the consultants' managers do not know these either, an important task of self-monitoring falls to the consultants themselves. Weak control from above generally requires strongly motivated people who can take initiative and organize their work in rather unstructured circumstances. They should have relatively clearly defined ideas about what to do and how to act. These ideas may originate from their own individual professional norms and values, as well as from the norms of the western organisations in which they were educated.

Indeed, people involved successfully tend to show these professional abilities and strong motivation. But personal factors can also play a role. Moreover, purely professional motives may not always be strong enough to meet the difficulties of dealing with projects. Without close personal involvement the energy to do a good job will often fade away. Generally, personal motives strengthen one's professional role and energy. A personal involvement in the tasks to be fulfilled, or a strong desire to help certain people in the client system, can keep the consultant on track. But of course personal motives and beliefs may also present drawbacks:
- Consultants will come into contact with a different organisational culture. Their reaction may be to consider it 'dysfunctional'[2], and disappointment may set in;

---

[2] György Jenei and Lance T. LeLoup 'East-West Co-operation in Public Policy Programs: Lessons from Experience' (see first chapter of this book).

- During long assignments people can start to suffer from fatigue: problems can be intractable, personal resistance can prove strong, so the initial enthusiasm dwindles. Support by higher-level managers, in contacts with recipient institutes, could lighten the burden considerably.
- Again, in many cases the work abroad is not a particularly important element in the personnel management of the home institutions, so, with a view to their own careers, people feel they should not participate in this work for too long.
- Finally: the situation at home. Many professionals like to spend some time in countries abroad, but for their families this is generally not pleasant, and if it happens often or for long periods, it tends to be increasingly upsetting.

In the institutions involved, these are all points of concern. The usual solution is to replace those involved by fresh people. Indeed, it is better not to keep someone too long on the same assignment – probably better from a professional point of view as well!

The consultants within their own organisations

Consultants wishing to work abroad often face particular attitudes and circumstances in their home organisations that are not necessarily helpful to them. As regards technical assistance for central banks, some managers within the donors banks involved are not structurally motivated and are resistant to sending their good people to CEE countries. In private institutions, managers often prefer to give priority to Western clients. Here the core business of the home institutions lies not in the countries in transition but in Western economy and servicing Western clients. Then again, people are not assessed on their work abroad, but on their work within their own central bank or institute or for Western clients. For the same reasons the professional, emotional and managerial support by management or colleagues, assuming there is any such support, may be less forthcoming on a foreign assignment than at the home base. All this must be born in mind, while realizing that the work abroad is itself generally more difficult than work at home.

People within recipient organisations

Central bank organisations compared

With some exceptions Western central banks originated in the nineteenth century. They reached their present position in a smooth process of development of tasks and roles and all along they were able to develop their own internal culture. In Anglo-Saxon and Scandinavian countries, The Netherlands and Germany (that is, most of the former Protestant Christian countries), they have a strong culture of independence from the banking business as well as from government and parliament. They are relatively closed, technocratic organisations, which keep themselves far removed from political influence. The employees show strong loyalty to the organisation.

In contrast, the central banks in Eastern Europe originate from institutions led by the central government. These institutions provided money to industry, agriculture and other organisations. The restructuring of 1991 caused a discontinuity of tasks and a change in position of the institutions. One result of this is that the functioning of departments and directorates depends to a relatively great extent on the persons involved. Because there is no basic new organisational culture, members of the organisation are not guided in any specific direction. In addition, many of the people involved lack thorough professional (e.g. managerial) attitudes, because their training has not included any such attitudes.

In order to implement the new tasks and fill new roles, the central banks after 1991 sometimes succeeded in attracting many new managers, sometimes they did not. In the latter cases, a group of 'apparatchiks' from the old regime may strongly resist the current development. In a number of cases we see that the management of recipient banks areeager to obtain a lot of assistance, but that they have very personally coloured priorities. Where this is the situation, professional motives can easily be opposed to what the leaders want. Conflicts may arise from the following:

- The central banks suffer from strong parliamentary influence: parliaments may appoint, for instance, members to executive and supervisory boards, though they also do so because in the transitional situation many new laws must pass parliament. The president of the central bank is also often a member of parliament.
- Another conflict of loyalties can be found in the field of personal business or career interests. For many bright young people in particular, the central bank with all its training facilities, including opportunities in the field of assistance, means simply a step forward in their careers. Some people (both young and old) exploit central bank contacts and opportunities primarily for their own business purposes.

In many cases, however, thorough co-ordination does take place that can result in consistent and effective assistance activities. In these cases professional motives and organisational wishes tend to be consistent with each other.

Other organisations
The situation of central banks has been elaborated to demonstrate some of the effects of technical assistance as seen so far. In the private sector situations may resemble those at central banks more closely than we might expect. This is because the CEE private sector used to be closely connected to political power structures, which is something that tends to continue, especially if the same people are managing the sectors of industry, trade and banking who were doing this before the restructuring. Furthermore, the diversity in personal goals and interests can be seen not only in governmental and central bank organisations but also in private companies. The impression created is that the degree of organisational loyalty tends to be lower than we see in Western organisations – even allowing for variation in Western countries.

Consultants and partners in the recipient organisation
As mentioned already by Jenei and LeLoup[3], the transfer of knowledge and experience makes it necessary to have one or more active counterparts for the western expert. If these cannot be found, the consultant's work needs to be directed at getting them. The management in the recipient organisation has the task of fulfilling this need.

4. Conflicts between Arrangements on national and supranational level and motivational factors on the organisational and individual level

Currently, some assistance and consultancy are given according to international agreements. The work at ground level will be difficult, if the international programme has been arranged without any contribution from the institution which is to carry out the work: a framework has already been set. One example of this can be seen in the international training programmes for central banks. Tensions arise because the work of individuals is structured and monitored according to the international agreements – in which the

---

[3] ibid.

participating central banks are only slightly involved or not involved at all. The central banks can choose whether or not to take part in the programme, but cannot strongly influence the way in which it is structured. On the other hand, within the participation agreed upon (to present certain courses or workshops, for instance), the individual professionals can prepare their own programmes and mostly have the freedom to do so as they wish. In practice, however, this very freedom in many cases prevents the individuals involved from co-ordinating their work with colleagues from other central banks who are working in the same fields: co-ordination determined by international agreements is mostly concerned with form and not content.

As assistance and consultancy is given by many different institutions and in many different financial formats, co-ordination between all these institutions is difficult. In practice, only recipient parties are in a position to do this. Since most assistance to central banks used to be given at no cost to the receiving parties, they would generally accept much of it without stringent checks on consistency, etc. This situation, however, has changed in the late 1990's: CEE central banks are now more critical as their state of development and know-how is growing fast. So the quality of assistance (training and consultancy) has been monitored more carefully in recent years. The same tendency holds for consultancy work in private areas: the client is becoming more critical. And indeed, a growing independence among client organisations is healthy for the quality of project work and for the motivation of people involved on both sides.

5. Some results of assistance and consultancy

Results for the people in the recipient organisations

In terms of knowledge, abilities and attitudes (including norms and values) we can clearly state that the result for many people has been a broadening and deepening experience. People leaving an organisation take their experience with them to their new organisations. Development, however, is often fragmentary – so young people who have a good educational background pick up most.

In terms of norms and values the visits and secondments to Western countries have a significant influence, and there is fortunately much more East-West travel nowadays than there used to be. People with 'western' experience often excel thanks to views they have developed and the influence they can exert compared to their colleagues who have not benefited from this training and learning. But it has to be said that one cannot be sure whether these talents were there in the first place, leading the man or woman to take hold of this new experience, or if the experience itself created extra capabilities.

As to the effect on work and behaviour, the results of short training courses are not overwhelmingly positive. What has a far better effect is systematic technical assistance in the form of longitudinal consultancy that includes certain training elements. This holds true in Western countries, too, where generally getting a course ad hoc does not have any significant effect.

As a general proposition, we can say that basic theory and knowledge is now available within central banks and many other organisations. In several cases a lack of specialised knowledge and skills can be seen, especially, for instance, in the managerial field where a tradition still needs to be built up. However, working in conformity with 'new' knowledge and skills also presents difficulties. These are visibly due to lack of personnel with the appropriate skills and know-how (good people having left the organisations), political hindrances and the personal priorities of officers and employees. But another reason must be mentioned as well: much consultancy work (especially training activities) is focused on transferring knowledge about content and not enough on the process of learning itself. Knowledge is obviously necessary, but if there is no continuity in an organisation and if no climate of learning has been established, then all training and transfer will be fragmentary.

Yet an increasing number of organizations in CEE countries show high levels of expertise (for example, in the field of telecommunications). As to the front-runners in new central banking, increasingly their officers are now involved in assistance to other countries. This is important because they can share their own experiences as to the transition process.

In conclusion, we may say that technical assistance and consultancy to organisations in countries in transition often produce good results, thanks to strong personal involvement. Nevertheless, a great variance may be noted in the success rate of the assistance, due to drawbacks created by the historical, political and personal context of those specific organisations involved. This article has tried to point to some of the effects and drawbacks that have to be envisaged in developing, leading and realizing projects in this field and in supporting the people involved.

Results for the consultants

Although much consideration has been given in this article to difficulties and drawbacks, there is nonetheless good reason to pay due attention to the fine results which the work in the types of projects under review can have, and often has had, for the consultants concerned. Essentially they benefit from a great many new experiences and knowledge. Their experiences enable them to put their existing knowledge and ways of thinking into a broader context, which in turn leads to more reflection and new insights. Of course, there are other results too. One is the fact that many consultants derive great satisfaction from helping people to make essential steps forward – not least those who often encounter far greater difficulties and problems in their work and lives than are generally encountered in Western organisations.

6. Recommendations

This article has presented some personal experiences and observations in projects in CEE countries. Arising from this is a number of recommendations that should enable recipient organisations to derive maximum benefit from projects while minimizing drawbacks for consultants:

1. Strive for continuity in relations between both the recipient organisations and those offering assistance, and between individuals concerned.
2. As a consultant, work therefore with an eastern counterpart: among other things, this encourages firm establishment of working processes, sustainability and availability of support when difficulties arise.
3. Pay attention to explicit link-ups between aims on the organisational level in the recipient organisation and those on a personal level with the individuals involved.
4. Ensure consistent and mutually agreed definitions of programmes and interlinked assignments. This is an important task for the recipient organisation!
5. Divide up complex or lengthy projects into modules or phases: clearly achievable goals that can be taken step by step are necessary, for instance, to maintain the motivation of those involved.
6. Effectiveness and sustainability are dependent on consultants transferring knowledge

and also focusing on learning processes; both parties must pay due attention to this.

7.   Select consultants with the necessary personal characteristics, such as the ability to organise and when necessary adapt their own work, the ability to work with intercultural differences, intrinsic motivation, etc.

8.   Make sure that the consultants are prepared for possible drawbacks; they must have a good understanding of gradual, step-by-step development.

9.   Provide support for consultants both from within the assisting organisation as well as from the recipient organisation (managerial, professional, emotional support).

10. Be aware as a (personnel) manager in an assisting organisation that the work abroad is exceptionally useful to the consultants' work on the home front, providing them with a wealth of new insights.

A version of this paper, which elaborated specifically on the technical assistance for central banks, was presented in the Study Group on Co-operation in Permanent Education, Training, Research and Consultancy between Eastern and Western Europe at the 1998 Annual Conference of the European Group of Public Administration (Paris, September 1998).

East-West Co-operation in Public Sector Reform   173
F. van den Berg et al. (Eds.)
IOS Press, 2002

East-West Co-operation in
Public Administration:
Ethics, Lessons and Conclusions

Lance T. LeLoup and György Jenei*

1. Introduction

In the decade that has ended, many profound changes have taken place in Central and Eastern Europe (CEE) and the states of the former Soviet Union. Reform of the public sector during the transition to democracy and market economy has been extremely difficult. At the same time, many new challenges faced the United States and Western Europe at the end of the Cold War: how to assure a peaceful, stable transition and economic growth for both sides. East-West co-operation to reform education in public administration, public policy, and public management as well as public sector reform have been important aspects of this process. The case studies and reviews of programmes written by the contributors to this volume have shown many varied programmes with their share of successes and failures. In the new century and millennium, many changes are taking place and East-West co-operation is entering a new phase. The accession of CEE nations to the European Union is becoming the most dominant force in shaping the direction of public administration. At the same time, the United States has suspended some aid programmes and closed many offices. For example, USIA programmes, such as the Social Science Curriculum Development Grant (SSCD) that provided significant co-operation and exchanges between CEE and western nations, has been terminated. Some Tempus programmes are ending. On one hand, this can be seen as a measure of some success in the region. On the other hand, it represents a serious challenge to preserve the gains that have been realized.

What have we learned from the last decade of East-West co-operation to make more informed decisions about new directions in the next decade? What will happen if there continue to be significant cutbacks in Western aid? What kind of assistance will come from the EU? In this chapter, we attempt to summarize what has been learned about the East-West co-operation to date. What has succeeded and what has failed? More importantly, why? We begin our assessment by looking at the importance of ethical issues and what problems and issues have developed in that area. Next, we take an overview of the kinds of programmes that have operated since 1989. Then, we assess how the programmes fit the hierarchy of co-operation that was introduced in chapter one. Finally, we draw some conclusions about East-West co-operation and suggest some new directions that may need to be considered in the future.

* Lance T. LeLoup, Washington State University (United States) and György Jenei, Budapest University of Economic Sciences (Hungary).

2. East–West Cooperation and Ethical Issues

Ethics is an integral part in all stages of co-operation from the sporadic personal contacts to institutional partnerships. Different ethical issues emerge on the individual, organisational, national and international levels, and special relationships can be observed between the levels and the stages.

Different forms of co-operation on ethical issues emerged among West and East European countries in the 1990s. They fall into two categories. The first concern the relationship between different scholars, and the question as to whether they will be able to understand one another in the exchange of their experiences and different ethical codes. Differences in moral principles or value systems may make co-operation easier, or introduce obstacles that may have to be overcome. Particularly between the states of the former Soviet Union and the United States, a potential clash exists, notably between individualism and more collective values; and one side has had little experience with the other.

In the case of certain training programmes, participants returned to their workplace after finishing the programme and tried to implement what they had learned. However, acquired knowledge did not work, given their organisational, political and cultural environment. During the training programme the practitioners simulated games, but then they had to put into practice what they learned. Failures occurred. What were the reasons for these failures?

Behind the failures and unsuccessful attempts one can observe the difference between teaching public administration and working to improve public administration. One can teach public administration theories, methods and techniques --- and the students can understand them[3]. But these bodies of knowledge function in the special political, economic, social and institutional framework of the West. They embody traditional mechanisms, generally accepted values, norms, and attitudes and to some extent depend on the existence of a civil society. The framework and the value system however, cannot be exported. That is why the assimilated knowledge is not quickly implemented.

Second, ethical issues can involve differences in civil servants and civil services. The crucial point is whether, for ethical requirements of the day-to-day work in public administration, more autonomy, business-like managerialism, and blurring of boundaries between public and private have the same consequences in the East and West. For example, in the last decade efficiency and effectiveness have been of increasing importance in the public sector. But there is an emerging anxiety that broader responsibility may threaten or weaken the legal state (in German: the "Rechtsstaat"). There is also concern that this growing autonomy of bureaucrats and the expansion of business-like managerialism will damage the integrity of civil servants and the sound ethical basis of the public sector. This is more of a problem for Central and Eastern European countries, where the legal state and constitutionalism do not have strong historical traditions and political systems have been oppressive.

Public administration in Central and Eastern Europe had no Weberian period in which the very essence of bureaucratic activities was to execute on a legal basis the orders given by the legitimate power. The problem is whether the trend of new public management can be applied in Central Eastern Europe directly without this tradition. Some have suggested building public administration based on legalism and adopting at the same time a business-like managerialism in the public sector. Some argue that there is a value vacuum in CEE because the old values have disappeared or been weakened and the new values are not yet strong enough. In other cases one can see conflicts when old and new values impact events at the same time.

In the case of corruption for instance - especially in the East-European region - the civil servant must support his family using and often misusing opportunities provided by his position. On the other hand, people have developed a tax-evasion practice that can be characterised by the following slogan: "When you do not cheat the state you steal from your family." This in itself is an ethical statement, but not one that conforms with a Weberian notion of administration. In Eastern Europe the political system is influenced by clans. It is obvious that the day-to-day life and actions of the public administration has to follow the expectations of the clans. The consequence is that corruption is built into the system. This type of civil service can not function without corruption. Every service has its fee. Under this system, what is immoral is when civil servants require more than the traditional price of the service or when they fail to provide the promised services.

The mutual learning process depends in part on the compatibility of ethical standards and cultures in different societies. This is not simply an East-West related problem, as sometimes projects are transferred from one part of Eastern Europe to another part. The Muslim republics of Central Asia are also involved in co-operation and therefore involved in the mutual learning process as well. This raises the problem of whether these autocratic systems - in which the whole power of the former communist party is concentrated in the hands of the President - should be supported by the West? Many conclude yes out of fear of Islamic fundamentalism. The more general question is whether reforms are intended to work within the existing system or fundamentally change the system.

Ethical factors are important to East-West co-operation for other reasons as well. First there is a continuing push for more "direct" democracy in the region and social groups seek more opportunities for participation. The integrity of public servants has a growing importance. There is also an increasing complexity of public issues and people often feel that they have lost much of their ability to participate meaningfully in the public sector. And sometimes they blame public servants for a lack of integrity without understanding the ongoing processes.

In addition, large bureaucracies are being transformed, flattened. The information age increasingly substitutes ad hoc and temporary forms for permanent ones. The increasing autonomy of public agencies gives a growing importance to the ethical side of the personality of civil servants. However, their commitment to public values is crucial. Do they have a strong orientation towards serving the public or do they have hidden or expressed oppressive tendencies?

Media coverage of public administrators and their ethics is also a factor. Much information is false and bad information often generates better ratings than good information. Journalist, radio and TV talk shows often focus on successes and failures and miss what is really going on. Under these circumstances, there is a growing importance as to the transparency of the civil service. But in the long run, the crucial issue is whether the performance of the public sector is convincing, or not. For what people think of civil servants and how they evaluate their integrity, is decisive.

Recognizing the importance of ethical issues in analyzing and comparing East-West co-operation, we now turn to a summary of programmes, the level of co-operation they achieved, lessons, and recommendations for the future.

3. An Overview of Co-operation Programmes

To the credit of governments, foundations, universities, and citizens of many western nations, numerous individuals were anxious and willing to help with the historic challenge of transition in post-communist societies. However, like the market system itself, these efforts were not centrally co-ordinated among either the Western or the Eastern partners.

There has been tremendous variation in programme; a history of duplication in some cases and gaps in coverage in others.

Programmes can be categorized in several ways and these categories are important because they may reveal significant differences in terms of explaining relative success or failure. Perhaps the most obvious way is to categorize co-operation on the basis of the Western partner/source of funds. Co-operation programmes may be divided into the following sponsors or implementing organisations:

- *Western Governments and the European Union*: Many co-operation programmes in public administration and public policy were sponsored directly by the United States, European governments, or the EU. The United States Information Agency (USIA) sponsored many programmes among Central European countries and the former Soviet Union. Other foreign aid from the U.S. found its way into co-operation efforts in this field, and well established international co-operation programmes, such as the Fulbright programme, directed efforts toward Central and Eastern Europe. Most European nations had their own programmes to help the region, such as the United Kingdom's "Know-how" programme, and the German's "Konrad Adenauer" and "Friedrich Ebert" programmes and others. EU programmes have been particularly important in the region with Phare and Tempus programmes having a number of direct links to the modernisation of public administration and curriculum development. These programmes were also intended to improve co-operation between EU member states.
- *Private Entities, NGOs, Nonprofit Foundations, International and Professional Organisations.* A number of private foundations in the U.S. and Europe took an active role in developing programmes in Central and Eastern Europe. Some of the most prominent are the PEW Foundation, the Soros Foundation, and the Ford Foundation. A significant number of programmes in public policy and public administration were developed or assisted, ranging from the creation of the Central European University by Soros to PEW support for developing the first public policy book about Central and Eastern Europe written by CEE scholars. The Organisation for Economic Co-operation and Development (OECD) has also been a major actor, sponsoring Phare programmes and the Sigma programme to support and improve governance and management in CEE countries. Professional organisations were also important sponsors of co-operation, such as the lawyers involved with the Methodius project. The National Association of Schools of Public Affairs and Administration (NASPAA) in the U.S., the European Group for Public Administration (EGPA), and the Network of Schools and Programs in Public Affairs Central and Eastern Europe (NISAcee) have all been active participants in co-operative efforts.
- *Universities.* Particularly in the fields of public administration and public policy, universities in the United States and Western Europe have been important partners in co-operation at many different levels. In our cases, the Center for Public Affairs Studies (CPAS) of Budapest University of Economic Sciences (BUES) developed relationships with a number of scholars and universities, including Washington State University, University of Missouri - St. Louis, University of Wisconsin, State University of New York at Albany, Syracuse University, University of Texas, and in Europe, the Catholic University of Leuven in Belgium, Erasmus University in Rotterdam, and Aston University in the UK, to name but a few. Other programmes also have long lists of partners. Many of these co-operation programmes were made possible by government or foundation funds, but in many cases, universities made contributions out of their own resources in support of these efforts.

These three categories provide just an approximation of the various sources of programmes in the fields of public administration and public policy. They are neither exhaustive or exclusive since there are programmes that are based on several organisations. Also NGOs and non-profit organisations often administer government-funded programmes. As we have seen, co-operation in public administration has taken many forms.

- Developing new public policy and public management programmes at universities based on various models at western institutions.
- Making available and accessible to Eastern partners the Western public administration and policy literature, ranging from research methods to highly theoretical to highly applied approaches.
- Creating curricula and teaching materials to provide the content of programmes based on European and American models.
- Fostering collaborative research programmes, including joint conference papers, articles, edited volumes, and research grants.
- Organizing and sponsoring domestic and overseas internship programmes.
- Developing educational resources and technologies, particularly in libraries and including computers.
- Assistance in developing in-service training programmes, seminars, and courses for public sector employees.
- Faculty development activities including language skills, research methods, course development, and research activities.
- Faculty and student exchanges between Eastern and Western partners.
- Training courses for central bankers.
- Professional development for lawyers and other professionals.
- Exchange of policy analysis and proposals in housing, social programmes, and other areas.

Given the various sources of financial support and the many different kinds of co-operation, are there certain programme characteristics - or relationships between Eastern and Western partners - that determine relative program success? We now turn to a set of questions and criteria for measuring the impact of East-West co-operation.

4. Criteria for Determining the Results of Co-operation

The preceding chapters have provided many detailed insights from a great variety of cooperation-programme cases involving a host of participants and countries. Based on these studies, we believe that the following criteria are important in determining the results of East-West co-operation.

- Did the programmes have clearly articulated goals from the outset or were goals clarified as programmes moved up the hierarchy?
- To what extent were efforts made to specify either outputs or outcomes and were they required by sponsors or developed by partners?
- To what extent was sustainability and institutionalisation considered from the outset or did it become more of a concern as programmes moved up the hierarchy?
- What was the scope of the programme, ranging in scope from very narrow (one institution or department) to national?
- Does there appear to be any relationship between relative success and institutionalisation (moving up the hierarchy) and programme scope?

• Was the goal to change a certain process in society or was the goal to assist a certain beneficiary in the country?
• Measuring the effects of co-operation in public policy and public administration might be more specifically tailored towards educational programmes and results:
• Did the organisational status of co-operation partners change during the course of the partnership?
• What are results in terms of students or in-service employees served?
• What are other specific output measures in terms of education and training, curriculum development, or dissemination of information?

The criteria for assessing results may be different depending on which side one is looking at. CEE partners may ask the following questions:
• How has the status of public administration, public policy, and public management changed over the course of co-operation?
• Have there been any changes in the national policy for education and training in public administration and public policy?
• What levels (pre-service, middle management, top management) received the most emphasis and have results varied by level?
• How have responsibilities changed between partners during the course of the co-operation?
• What are the most obvious achievements, the most obvious failings, and the most difficult aspects of the programmes to measure objectively?

5. Programme Results and the Hierarchy of Collaborative Relationships

Chapter 1 showed the hierarchy of collaborative relationships that can exist between organisational units and individuals from the East and West. However, we note that *co-operation and collaboration can be effective at any level and need not necessarily become institutionalised.* In fact, for many programmes, there is no reason to continue or institutionalise a programme once a certain result has been achieved. In other cases, however, institutionalising programmes through collaboration most likely serves the needs of CEE nations as well as their western partners. Looking at the cases described in this volume, what kind of conclusions can be made about the hierarchy of co-operation?

Exchange of Contacts and Information: As expected, informal exchanges were often the first steps in moving to a more formal kind of co-operation. There are many examples. Collaboration often begins with meetings, contacts, and the mutual exchange of information. This can be useful since partners may not be well informed about the needs and interests of each other. The cases in this book all went beyond this initial level.

Systematic Exchange of Knowledge and Experience: Many examples of East-West co-operation get to this step and beyond. Partners become better acquainted and the relationship can expand to meaningful dialogues, visits, initial exchanges, and the exploration of collaboration. In other cases, when funding sources have been identified by a western partner, these early exchanges and visits can be crucial in determining which cities, ministries, or universities are engaged in more formal programmes of co-operation. The cases of co-operation in this volume all progressed past this point as well.

Joint Action: The third stage of collaborative relationships, marked by identifiable projects and activities, may be the most common form of co-operation. We have seen programmes for developing university curricula, training civil servants, assisting central bankers and personnel in the judicial system, as well as working on housing policy and exchanging expertise on running social programmes. The product can be a library, a teaching programme, a training course, visits by consultants, internships, formalizing exchange relationships, and developing research activities. It appears that this is the most prevalent level of co-operation. Many of the programmes we examined had finite time lines and encompassed specific goals and objectives.

Mutual Co-operation: This stage of co-operation was reached in a number of cases, but is fundamentally more difficult because of inequalities and imbalances in East-West relationships. It is characterized by collaboration that becomes more extensive and regular, and across a range of activities, not just a single project. However, a truly mutually co-operative relationship can exist only if there is a relative balance between partners based on agreed upon strategies meeting the needs and interests of both partners. This remains more difficult because of continued resource differences and the fact that needs change over time. Successful mutual co-operation may not be necessary if joint action programmes have achieved a specific set of results. Sustainability is a difficult challenge as several of the chapters have shown.

Institutionalised Partnerships: Finally, the highest levels of collaboration are institutionalised partnerships where the relationships are on-going and continuing, not dependent on particular individuals at either end. In our experience, they are the most rare and difficult to sustain. Perhaps the most important characteristic of these relationships is that they are self-sustaining in terms of funding and organisation on both ends. This is very difficult to achieve although it is still too early to tell in the cases of some programmes that could become institutionalised partnerships over time. In our view, the most important source of institutionalised relationships over the next decade will be the European Union, as was suggested by the Bouckaert article. All in all, most cases of East-West co-operation examined in this book have not become institutionalised. That is not a statement of failure, however, because many of the cases were tied to specific programmes for specific periods of time.

6. Challenges and New Directions in the Second Stage of Co-operation

The lessons learned from the previous decade are important for partners in making decisions during the second phase of co-operation at the beginning of the 21st century. In planning the next stage of co-operation, it is essential to draw effective lessons from the first stage. Based on our experience and those reported in the earlier chapters, it seems that certain new challenges will arise and new directions will be needed.

1. *More emphasis will be needed on institutionalising successful programmes.* This may involve finding ways to maintain financial support or to develop new sources of financial support. Another possibility, as suggested by Khapova is to use new technologies and the internet to better sustain and institutionalise programmes.
2. *More emphasis should be placed on making East-West partnerships more equal.* As progress is made, it should be possible to move to a model in which there is a greater balance among partners. This can include partnerships between organisations such as NISPAcee and EGPA. It can also involve acknowledgements by western partners that CEE partners may have caught up and reached parity requiring a new definition of the partnership in the future.
3. *Co-operation programmes must be tailored to particular needs and contexts – one size definitely does not fit all.* This point is made by a number of authors in looking at both university and public sector collaboration – it is essential to have a match of the situation and the required action to ensure relevance and validity.

4. *Cultural differences must be recognized and dealt with at all stages of programme development.* This conclusion was reached by numerous contributors to this volume. The most successful programmes were those in which partners on both sides made explicit efforts to understand and take into account cultural differences. This requires a certain flexibility in project planning and a recognition of different management and leadership styles. As Vartainen wrote, "the co-operation project is begun with the work that identifies ... the potential cultural problems in the project implementation. This concerns especially the main concepts used in the project work as well as the overall attitudes to the working ideology." In a similar manner, Prigozhin's useful table comparing differences in perceptions and the management style of clients suggests the same conclusion, specifically differences between management oriented towards people as opposed to management oriented towards goals and tasks.

5. *Successful co-operation must be well-prepared, incremental in terms of flexibility with a time schedule and realistic.* These conclusions by Malfliet concerning the Methodius project in Russia hold true for a number of the other cases.

6. *Successful co-operation must differentiate between personal goals of participants and organisational goals.* A number of authors differentiated between these two types of goals and showed that East-West co-operation projects ignore that distinction at their peril.

7. *As accession to the EU becomes more important to CEE countries, co-operative partnerships with the U.S. may need to move in different directions.* Since EU membership is becoming a dominant external determinant of many aspects of national politics, American partners may need to find ways in which they can fulfill different goals in working with CEE nations. For example, they may want to put less emphasis on civil service reforms and more on introducing new scholarships and approaches to public policy and public administration.

8. *More emphasis in co-operation programmes must be placed on problem areas and emerging policy issues such as transparency in decision making and anti-corruption efforts.* The experiences of the past decade have shown progress in many areas of public administrastion and public policy, while new issues have emerged. The issue of official corruption has become much more important, for example. Co-operation programmes in the second stage must be constantly attentive to new problems and needs in more mature phases of transformation.

Much has been achieved in the first stage of East-West co-operation that is now ending. At the same time, we have also learned lessons about co-operation from non-co-operation and failures. The efforts have largely been worthwhile, and many important changes for the good realized on both sides. As the new era of East-West co-operation unfolds, we believe it is important not only to better assess the effectiveness of programmes that have already been implemented, but to use the lessons and experiences for selecting new programme directions as we enter into the second phase.

About the Authors

Ari Salminen is Professor of Public Administration and Head of Department of Public Management, University of Vaasa, Finland. University of Vaasa, PO Box 700, FIN-65100 Vaasa, tel: +358 6 324 8419, fax: +358 6 324 8465, e-mail: ari.salminen@uwasa.fi

Arkady I. Prigozhin is Professor, President of Association of Management and Organization Development Consultants, Director of the School for Management Consultants of the Academy of National Economy under the Government of the Russian Federation (Moscow, Russia), 82 Vernadsky avenue, Moscow, 117571, Russia, tel/fax: +7(095) 433 25 26, e-mail: smc@ane.ru (office)

Călin Hințea is Assistant Professor at the Faculty of Political and Administrative Sciences, Babes-Bolyai University (Cluj Napoca, Romania). str. Universitatii nr.7-9, Facultatea de Stiinte Politice si Administrative, 3400 Cluj Napoca, jud. Cluj, Romania, tel: 4064431361, fax: +4064431361, e-mail: hintea@polito.ubbcluj.ro

Dr Geert Bouckaert is Professor of Public Management and Director of the Institute of Public Management at the Katholieke Universiteit Leuven in Belgium. Instituut voor de Overheid, Van Evenstraat 2a, B-3000 Leuven, Belgium, tel: 32-16-32 32 70, fax: 32-16-32 32 67, e-mail: geert.bouckaert@soc.kuleuven.ac.be

Frits van den Berg is a certified management consultant and a partner in AO Management Consultants (Driebergen, The Netherlands) AO Management Consultants, PO Box 112, NL, 3970 AC Driebergen, The Netherlands, tel: +31 343 512 544, fax: +31 343 514 717, e-mail: adviseurs@ao.nl

György Jenei is Professor and Head of Department of Public Policy and Management in the Budapest University of Economic Sciences and Public Administration (Hungary), BUESPA H-1093 Budapest Fővám tér 8, tel: +36 1 218 81 97, fax:+36 1 218 14 66, e-mail: gyorgy.jenei@public.bke.hu

Hugo Van Hassel is professor emeritus of the Public Management Institute, Katholieke Universiteit Leuven. He is former president of EGPA. Public Management Institute, E. Van Evenstraat 2A, B-3000 Leuven, Belgium, tel: +32 16 25 64 28, fax: +32 16 25 64 28, e-mail: hugovanhassel@freegates.be

Jacek Czaputowicz PhD is the Deputy Head of Civil Service in Poland and Vice-Chair of the Public Management Committee of OECD, Paris. Office of Civil Service, Poland 00-582 Warsaw, Al. J.Ch. Szucha 2/4, tel: +48 22 694 7387, fax: +48 22 694 7488, e.mail: jacek_czaputowicz@taranis.usc.gov.pl

Joaquim Ramos Silva is associate professor at the Institute of Economics and Business Administration, Technical University of Lisbon (ISEG/UTL) and researcher at Centre of Research on European and International Economics, Rua Miguel Lupi, 20; 1249-078 Lisbon, Portugal, tel: + 351 213 925 902 / + 351 213 953 156, fax: + 351 213 953 155, e-mail: jrsilva@iseg.utl.pt, webpage: www.iseg.utl.pt/~cedin/portugalbrasil

Juraj Nemec is professor of public economics and public management at the Faculty of Economics, Matej Bel University in Banska Bystrica, Slovakia, and visiting professor at the Faculty of Management, Prague School of Economics in Jindrichuv Hradec, the Czech Republic. Ekonomicka fakulta UMB, Tajovskeho 10, 97400 Banska Bystrica, Slovakia, tel: +421 48 4462313, 4152788, fax: +421 48 4152788, 4152793, e-mail: nemec@ef.umb.sk

Katlijn Malfliet is professor at the department of Political Sciences at the Catholic University Leuven (Belgium). She is also Research Director Central and Eastern Europe at the Institute for International and European Policy of the same department. Van Evenstraat 2B, 3000 Leuven, Belgium, tel: 32 16-32 31 43, fax: 32 16-32 31 44, e-mail: Katlijn.malfliet@soc.kuleuven.ac.be

Lance T. LeLoup, CO and Mary Johnson Distinguished Professor of Political Science, Washington State University, Pullman, WA 99164-4480, tel: 509-335-8929, fax: 509-335-7990, e-mail: leloup@wsu.edu

Markku Temmes is Professor of Public Administration and Research Director in the Department of Political Science in Helsinki University, Finland. Deparment of Political Science, PO Box 54 (Unioninkatu 37), FIN-00014, University of Helsinki, Finland, tel: +358 09 19124825, fax: +358 09 19124832, e-mail: markku.temmes@helsinki.fi

Pertti Ahonen is Professor of Public and Financial Management at the University of Tampere, Finland. In 1999-2001 he was Professor of Public Management and Policy at the European Institute of Public Administration, (EIPA) in Maastricht, the Netherlands. University of Tampere, Department of Administrative Science, 33104 University of Tampere, Finland, tel: +358 3 2156 256, fax: +358 3 2156 020, e-mail: hlpeah@uta.fi

Pirkko Vartiainen is acting as a professor at the University of Vaasa, Department of Public Management (Finland), University of Vaasa, Faculty of Social Sciences, Department of Public Administration, PO Box 700, 65101 Vaasa, Finland, tel: +358 6 324 8420, fax: +358 6 324 8465, e-mail: piva@uwasa.fi

Renger J. Afman is a certified management consultant and is a partner in AO Management Consultants (Driebergen, The Netherlands). Since 1994 he has worked on organisational development and training in Central and Eastern Europe and Asia. He also co-ordinated the technical assistance by the Dutch central bank to CEE central banks for a few years. AO Management Consultants, PO Box 112, NL, 3970 AC Driebergen, The Netherlands, tel: +31 343 512 544; fax: +31 343 514 717, e-mail: r.afman@ao.nl

Sorin Dan Şandor is Assistant Professor at the Faculty of Political and Administrative Sciences, Babes-Bolyai University (Cluj Napoca, Romania), str. Universitatii nr.7-9, Facultatea de Stiinte Politice si Administrative, 3400 Cluj Napoca, jud. Cluj, Romania, tel: +4064431361, fax: +4064431361, e-mail: sandor@polito.ubbcluj.ro

Svetlana N. Khapova is a prospective Ph.D. student at the Faculty of Public Administration and Public Policy, University of Twente, The Netherlands. Faculty of Public Administration and Public Policy, University of Twente, PO Box 217, 7500 AE Enschede, The Netherlands, tel: +31/534 894 554, e-mail: s.n.khapova@bsk.utwente.nl

Tony Bovaird is Professor of Strategy and Public Services Management at Bristol Business School (University of the West of England). Specialises in performance measurement, policy evaluation and strategic management of public services. Member of the team commissioned by government to evaluate the long-term impacts of Best Value and the UK local government reform programme from 2000-2005. University of Western England, Bristol Business School, Frenchay Campus, Coldharbour Lane, Bristol BS16 1QY, tel: 44/117-344 37 35, fax: 44/117-344 22 89, e-mail: tony.bovaird@uwe.ac.uk

Author Index